FRED ALLEN

BOOKS BY ROBERT TAYLOR

In Red Weather
Saranac
Fred Allen: His Life and Wit

FRED ALLEN
His Life and Wit

ROBERT TAYLOR

LITTLE, BROWN AND COMPANY
BOSTON · TORONTO · LONDON

Library of Congress Cataloging-in-Publication Data

Taylor, Robert, 1925–
    Fred Allen : his life and wit / by Robert Taylor.—1st ed.
        p.   cm.
    Includes index.
    ISBN 0-316-83388-6
    1. Allen, Fred, 1894–1956.   2. Entertainers—United States—
    Biography.   3. Comedians—United States—Biography.   I. Title.
    PN2287.A48T39   1989
    792.7'028'0924—dc19
    [B]   88-38141
                                                               CIP

10 9 8 7 6 5 4 3 2 1

MV-PA
Designed by Joyce C. Weston

*Published simultaneously in Canada
by Little, Brown & Company (Canada) Limited*

PRINTED IN THE UNITED STATES OF AMERICA

To Gillian and to Douglas

My boy, you must get a little memorandum-book; and every time I tell you a thing, put it down right away. There's only one way to be a pilot, and that is to get this entire river by heart. You have to know it just like ABC.

— Mark Twain,
Life on the Mississippi

Contents

HUMORIST IN PRINT

Photographs follow pages 116 and 244

Acknowledgments

The devotion of Portland Hoffa Allen and her late husband Joseph Rines to the memory of Fred Allen is responsible for the archive of Allen manuscripts, letters, documents, and recordings at the Boston Public Library. Were it not for their exemplary efforts, I would never have been able to complete this book. The primary sources for it derive from the Fred Allen Collection and from interviews over the past five years. I shall miss afternoons in Dr. Laura Monti's Rare Book Department, especially the assistance of Roberta Zonghi and Giuseppe Bisaccia. I am indebted also to Arthur Curley, the library's director, and Liam Kelly and Jane Manthorne, assistant directors, all of whom were invariably helpful and indeed became essential collaborators.

Other collections useful in the making of this biography have been the Lincoln Center Library of the Performing Arts, New York City; the Harvard University Theater Collection, Jean Newlin, curator; the Library of the Museum of Broadcasting, New York City; the Old Orchard Beach (Maine) Historical Society; the Biddeford (Maine) Public Library; the library of the Australian Consulate, New York City; the Massachusetts Historical Society, Boston; and the Boston University Mugar Library Rare Book Room, under the direction of Dr. Howard Gottlieb.

It was Elliot Norton, Boston theater critic, who suggested to me Fred Allen as a biographical subject. One of the pleasures of my subsequent research has been meeting Allen enthusiasts nationwide, from Larry Swindell of Fort Worth to my Colgate classmate Howard Enders, and, one lucky afternoon, Arnold and Lois Peyser, also working on the BPL's Allen papers in preparation for a one-man theater production. As always, I have depended on Charles Liftman, systems editor of the *Boston Globe;* and I am grateful for the understanding and patience of those professionals who have contributed to the final result — Ned Leavitt, agent-scholar and Red Sox fan; Michael Brandon, who read the text with a jeweler's eye; and Fredrica Friedman, editor par excellence. Instrumental, too, have been Arnold Auerbach, Sherwood E. Bain, James Bell, Steve Bergman, Edwin Briggs, Henry Brougham, J. Bryan III, Charles Claffey, Vivian Collum, Les Cotter, Prudence Crowther, Patrick Curran (former consul-general of the Republic of Ireland in Boston), Tina Daniell, Peter Davison, John Deedy, Mark Feeney, Jane Fennelly, Ann Ford, John and Ruth Galvin, Albert Hackett, Arthur Hepner, Ed Herlihy, Dorothy Hermann, Jerrold Hickey, Al Hirschfeld, John K. Hutchens, Shirley Jellerson, Hal Kantor, Herbert Kenny, Margaret Kieran, the late Monsignor Francis J. Lally, Karl Levett, Harry and Ellenita Lodge, Patrick McGilligan, Francis McNiff, Philip McNiff, Lawrence and Amy Bess Miller, Margo Miller, M. R. Montgomery, Hobe Morrison, William Mullen, Thomas Mulvoy, Mrs. Pat Rinaldi, George Ryan, Fred Shane, Mary-Leigh Smart, Jerome Talbert, Ross Terrill, Rick Tetzeli, Douglass Shand Tucci, James Tugend, Theodore and Vas Vrettos, Sylvester Weaver, Edward Weeks, and Herman Wouk.

A progression from Auerbach to Wouk invariably evokes life's symmetries and those distant evenings in the early fifties when I had the privilege of dining every night — in cafeterias — with the wittiest man in Boston, Edwin O'Connor. He often brought along a Fred Allen script, and Ed, then editing *Treadmill to Oblivion*, would read aloud sketches, "doing" (as T. S. Eliot and Dickens put it) the police in different voices. It never occurred to me that thirty years later I too would study what I then thought of as the sacred texts; nor could I foresee that I would also be fortunate enough to experience a symmetry of a different order — life with my wife, Brenda, in love and admiration.

ENCHANTMENTS AND ENCHANTERS

The great advantage of a Commerce education was that it wouldn't interfere with any plans you might have for the future.

— *Much Ado about Me*

1 | This Drudgery, This Sham, This Gold-mine

The Saint Patrick's Eve storm of 1956 did not develop suddenly or without notice, but the rapid flakes that began falling during the afternoon of Friday the sixteenth surprised New Yorkers eager for spring. Snow streamed on the wind like buckshot and settled into blowing drifts. Blizzard conditions prevailed, crowds milled in plane, rail, and bus terminals, and as darkness shrouded the chaos of the weekend rush hour, stranded commuters fiddled with the knobs of car radios and sought information about the weather. For a while radio seemed as necessary as it had seemed two decades before; and among a clamor of forecasters lasting well into the night, other and more familiar voices intruded. Dave Garroway's *Monitor* broadcast on the radio network of the National Broadcasting Company featured a conversation about vaudeville between John Royal, NBC executive and former Boston theatrical agent, and the comedian Fred Allen.

Of Allen, Broadway columnist O. O. McIntyre commented that "he sounded like a man with false teeth chewing on slate pencils." Though vivid, this was undoubtedly extravagant. An anonymous newspaper critic held a different opinion: "His voice is baritone and brisk with a dry-palate quality." Allen's voice, however, was an aural fingerprint. The phonetic whorls and grooves of its patterns revealed a well-defined New England origin, a clear-cut rather than twangy sound, and his delivery could have originated only in the taciturn hinterland north of Boston.

"Why do I talk through my nose?" he once said. "In New England, where I come from, the early settlers found winters so cold that when they tried to open their mouths, their tongues froze. Finally, they learned to talk through their nostrils. Otherwise, conversation during the winter months might have become extinct. So now you know why today Rudy Vallee [the crooner from the state of Maine] sings through his nose and I talk through mine."

Vaudeville kindled in Allen an affectionate glow. At sixty-one, he was completing his memoirs, and among the miscellaneous phases of entertainment he had known, the footloose vaudeville days of his youth remained brightest in memory. Had his snowbound listeners known, there was a poignant symmetry in the subject of the program, for they were hearing Fred Allen's last broadcast.

ONCE, AMERICA was filled by voices. They came into your living room through the radio, sounding as familiar as family or the neighbors. Everyone listened. In 1947, Harry S. Truman, the sixty-three-year-old president of the United States, completing his second year in office, awoke punctually at 5:30 each morning, and after a brisk two-mile constitutional through the empty streets of Washington, confronted the nation's business; in the evening, seven o'clock dinner over, he retired to a White House study with an armful of intelligence reports, news summaries, and other papers, relaxed in a chair, and turned on the radio.

The president followed the same routine observed by millions: a day's work, dinner, and a favorite program. Radio was a communal activity, like the movies, but was also intimate — part of the household furniture, in fact. It measured the hours with the accuracy of a clock, yet permitted a flexible play of the imagination. You knew its voices in a way that you would never know film stars, those models of behavior and projections of desire, for radio asked you to imagine its personalities. Franklin D. Roosevelt had been a radio president, and his resonant optimism had triumphed over the physical ignominies of paralysis and rallied the country; Winston Churchill through radio had persuaded the world of the impossibility of Britain's defeat; and the plain Missouri diction of Harry Truman himself created an indelible characterization. The sound of each voice — the breathless frenzy of Clem McCarthy at ringside or paddock, the Metropolitan Opera introduced by the burnished baritone of Milton Cross, the dark Shakespearean thunder of Orson Welles — emerged from the bureaucratic conditions of broadcasting but allowed leeway for private myth.

The official birth of network radio had occurred November 15, 1926, with the inaugural broadcast of the National Broadcasting Company over a hookup of twenty-four stations; the effective demise lay ahead, September 30, 1962, when the Columbia Broadcasting System canceled the last two dramatic shows; but in that spring of 1947, radio seemed imperishable. A new vocabulary, words like *plastic, stainless steel,* and *cellulose* in magazine advertisements, promised civilian plenty after the lean years of war. Hindus and Moslems rioted across India, the Truman Doctrine sought to cordon Turkey and Greece against Communist expansion, the House Un-American Activities Committee sifted testimony about domestic conspiracy, and, according to *Time* magazine, the man on the street believed global peace would reign "if Moscow could be stopped." It was a period of transition between prewar and postwar attitudes, but of course no one knew that: the future had already arrived. In the spring of 1947, the Northrup Company manufactured the sixty-five-mile-per-gallon, streamlined Salsbury, a vehicle "which combines the best features of an auto and a motor scooter." The ads showed a suburban husband leaving home astride the machine — the Salsbury had more of the motor scooter than the auto in its pedigree — and waving at his family. Like the Salsbury, America in early 1947 was a composite of the brand-new and the old-fashioned, and nowhere was this more evident than in radio.

Radio addressed people directly. Devised to sell merchandise and other products, it nevertheless subscribed to the power of the spoken word as faithfully as a nineteenth-century textbook with its stress on elocution, rhetoric, and lyceum oratory. There was always something slightly behind the times in radio, even though as a communications medium it postdated the movies and the metropolitan press. By its very nature radio evoked the traditions of the stump speech and pulpit so prominent in earlier America and applied those traditions to the new values of a corporate society.

Nowhere was this more evident than among radio's pioneer comedians. That very first NBC network broadcast had featured the old century and the new — Weber and Fields, the German-dialect team whose rowdy act came out of a format of broad caricature, and Will Rogers, the cowboy humorist, whose jokes approximated everyday conversation. Early radio comedians straddled two eras. Indeed, Eddie Cantor and Al Jolson, former stars of the *Ziegfeld Follies,* occasionally donned burned-cork makeup harking back to the heyday of the minstrel show. The first wave of radio comics brought widespread theatrical experience to the new medium; they had stampeded into broadcasting studios following the catastrophic 1929–30 Broadway season when 87 percent of the dramatic shows and 69 percent of the musicals failed.

A few suffered "mike fright": Joe Cook, forlorn without his props, detested talking into a mechanism rather than playing to an audience; Ed Wynn "dried up" on his radio debut in 1922 and couldn't continue a live studio broadcast of his Broadway hit *The Perfect Fool,* the first ever of a stage show. Wynn had never panicked before; he knew his role, but as he ventured on one joke after another and heard nothing, he began to perspire and tremble. Finally he turned to the announcer and said, "I can't do anything." A makeshift assembly of people who happened to be in the studio — phone operators, electricians, cleaning women, and others — was recruited on the spot. Once Wynn heard laughter, he settled down and completed the broadcast. Over a career spanning an appearance on the first vaudeville bill of the Palace Theatre, Hollywood character acting, and television, he contended that his nonsense was visual and refused to do a radio program without an audience. During his Texaco *Fire Chief* broadcasts, he changed costumes and makeup continuously, including a pair of oversized flap shoes that he had purchased in 1906 for $3.50 and maintained subsequently at a cost of $1,400. His network success diminished the luster of the live performances that meant so much to him as a performer and writer of comedy material. "I spent $750,000 publicizing myself as 'The Perfect Fool,' " he lamented, "and almost overnight it is forgotten and I am known only as 'The Fire Chief.' "

From under $2 million in 1920 to almost $843 million in 1929, sales of radio sets multiplied while vaudeville came to resemble an abandoned estate awaiting a sheriff's auction. A handful of headliners resisted the microphone on professional grounds, notably the four Marx Brothers. Why give away routines that they had painstakingly developed and that audiences would pay to see? Besides, radio could transmit only a partial notion of their performance. At length even the Marxes relented, and while radio could not accommodate Harpo's mute antics, Groucho and Chico were signed for a Monday-night gambol about lawyers, *Flywheel, Shyster and Flywheel,* sponsored by Esso gasoline.

Immigrants for the most part, or from immigrant backgrounds, radio comedians had the alertness of the newcomer to nuances of speech. They personified the cheeky rhythms of city life, the concisions of slang, the throb of change. A disproportionate number were Jewish, from the shtetls of eastern Europe, the world of Chagall and Kafka. (Alsace, which had produced Captain Alfred Dreyfus, could also claim the patriarch of the Marxes.) Denied avenues open to native-born Americans, ambitious Jewish talents achieved success in the freer atmosphere of the stage, and took advantage of cultural traditions sympathetic to performance. There was virtually a school of gifted Lower East Side personalities: Jolson, of course, and Cantor, Sophie Tucker, George Burns, Fanny Brice, George Jessel, and the master songwriter Irving Berlin. Knockabout immigrant experience was transformed into sentimental myth. And yet the most innovative Jewish comedian on radio, Jack Benny, practiced a different style. Season after season, he developed the possibilities of situation comedy, and the character he created, vain, miserly, and self-important, existed outside ethnicity. While he never left his Jewish identity in question, Benny did not look back; if Groucho and Chico Marx constituted the verbal hustle of immigrant humor, Jack Benny seemed inseparable from the character he portrayed, and his comic inspiration, the expressivity of the pause, had closer associations with poetry than prose.

Benny's precursors were the fathers of the American sitcom, Freeman Gosden and Charles J. Correll. On *Amos 'n' Andy* the white duo portrayed Harlem entrepreneurs who owned the Fresh Air Taxi Company, so called because the jalopy that was their sole asset lacked a windshield. From the start of the show on radio in 1928 to its departure from television in 1953, *Amos 'n' Andy* was dogged by racial controversy. Gosden and Correll always insisted they were poking fun at human nature, not deriding blacks. Although rooted in the American South — Correll was related to Jefferson Davis, while Gosden's father had been one of seventy-five daredevil Confederate cavalry raiders under General John Singleton Mosby who refused to surrender at Appomattox — there is no reason to believe them insincere. They were stock company actors who began using black patter on a Chicago station in 1925. But the team's Southern antecedents probably blinkered them to the program's retrograde attitudes (in still another irony connected with the show, its signature tune, "The Perfect Song," was the "Love Theme" from D. W. Griffith's *Birth of a Nation*).

Amos 'n' Andy was reactionary in its reliance on minstrel-show traditions, yet innovative in its concept as the first serial comedy with realistic characters or types. Depression-weary listeners could identify with Amos Jones and Andrew H. Brown, who, like themselves, found their cupboards bare; could recognize the traits of neighbors like Brother Crawford and Madame Queen; and could relish the orotundities of the trickster George Stevens, Andy's nemesis — "the Kingfish" of the fraternal order of the Mystic Knights of the Sea. Never has a U.S. entertainment phenomenon rivaled *Amos 'n' Andy,* which for a brief interval (1930–1932) commanded the total attention of the nation. "There are three things which I shall never forget about America," recalled George Bernard Shaw; "the Rocky Mountains, the Statue of Liberty and *Amos 'n' Andy*." From hobo jungles to the White House, the mundane world stopped for fifteen minutes at seven o'clock on weekday evenings; movie theaters piped in episodes between reels; department stores carried the dialogue for the convenience of late shoppers; factories staggered shifts; auto theft soared; plumbing fell silent; and one of the representative memories of the period involved walking along a street on a spring evening and hearing the same voices float from the open windows of house after house.

Amos 'n' Andy prompted radio's 1932 trend to "personality" performance. The program gradually lost 20 percent of its audience after its 1931 peak — a disastrous reversal for the National Broadcasting Company and the sponsor, Pepsodent toothpaste. All at once, distraught advertisers began searching for ways to regain evaporating listenership, and desperate remedies were proposed. "The program producers brought on the 'personality' performer," remarked Edgar A. Grunwald, looking back on 1932 from the eminence of *Variety*'s annual radio directory for 1937. The basic idea was to enlist talents who could bring ready-made audiences into radio.

Thus columnist Walter Winchell was engaged by Lucky Strike cigarettes; Kate Smith, who had stopped the De Sylva–Brown-and–Henderson musical *Flying High* with her rendition of "Red Hot Chicago," made guest appearances with Rudy Vallee before stepping out on her own; Maurice Chevalier, radiating Folies-Bergère charm for Chase-and-Sanborn coffee, took home five thousand Depression dollars a week; Bing Crosby, formerly of Paul Whiteman's Rhythm Boys, practiced his emollient crooning and whistling; and the Corn Products Company decided to take a chance on a comedian named Fred Allen.

Had the sponsor examined Allen's credentials, the company might have decided he did not fit the Corn Products mold. True, the comedian attracted an audience, but one rather different from the vast and indeterminate listenership that comprised an ad agency's demographics. Allen had just spent three years with Clifton Webb and Libby Holman in a pair of the most sophisticated revues ever seen on Broadway, *The Little Show* and *Three's a Crowd*. Webb's suavity, Holman's passionate torch songs, and Allen's bright comic monologues established a standard few revues would ever surpass. The sponsor proposed costuming Allen as a Keystone Kop who would belabor incoming patrons with a padded nightstick. In this, Corn Products merely followed fashion, for slapstick in the early thirties reflected the anarchy of social turmoil after the Crash. Zanies brayed and brandished the verbal equivalent of inflated pig bladders. Jack Pearl as "Baron Munchausen" spun preposterous tall stories, German-dialect yarns that were questioned by his straight man, Cliff Hall, who set up the catchphrase "Vas you dere, Sharlie?" Joe Penner, a burlesque clown, stocked a personal armory of catchphrases soon to reverberate over the swings and baseball diamonds of every schoolyard: "Wanna buy a duck?" "You nah-h-asty man!" and "Don't ever doooo that!" In the primeval days of radio, circa 1925, such universality did not exist. How could a Georgia sharecropper of the twenties decipher *The Village Grove Nut Club Show,* which broadcast from Greenwich Village and featured a comic called "Lehigh Vallee, distant brother of Rudy"? A scant seven years later, though, the medium's power to connect placed small towns and isolated farms within the frame of reference of big cities. By the Second World War, Bob Hope could mention the Brooklyn Dodgers or Dorothy Lamour and count on instant intercontinental recognition.

"I will be one of those Captain Andy fellows calling everybody 'folks,' " Allen complained. (*Show Boat,* the 1927 Kern-Hammerstein musical with homespun Cap'n Andy on the bridge, still exerted a lingering spell.) An actor between engagements, he needed the job; still, he would not be folksy without a fight. It took him four days to talk his way out of the Keystone Kop role, but in the end he received the green light for *The Linit Bath Club Revue,* a show that would prove as original and venturesome in radio comedy as Jack Benny's.

Who was Fred Allen? To his peers, he was a dazzling presence — "The Guy with Blitzwits," as the title of a 1940 *Saturday Evening Post* profile by J. Bryan III described him. No comedian in show business had a quicker mind or a comparable genius for the impromptu remark, and he not only performed but wrote the bulk of his prepared material. Except for a single trait — his mobile glance, the hallmark of the professional juggler he had once aspired to be in vaudeville — his appearance was unremarkable. Audiences did not guffaw at the mere sight of him as they did at theatrical clowns. Just under six feet and weighing 175 pounds, he had, in the phrase of columnist Sidney Skolsky, "the build of a good upper-rung light-heavyweight." High cheekbones lent Allen's features a faintly saturnine cast; he parted his sleekly combed hair in the middle, and the pouches that developed beneath his narrow blue eyes in later years — undoubtedly attendant on ill health — are absent from his formal photographs of the early thirties. Artist-writer Ludwig Bemelmans called Allen's face "the sharpest knife I have ever seen," while Bryan, contrasting the fiction of appearances with the actuality of Allen's charity, labeled his countenance "villainy's ledger . . . an alphabet of pouches, squints, and seams." These were reactions to his comic persona, the disillusioned cynic; in fact, if Allen was not a leading man, neither was he a grotesque, and in the 1938 film *Sally, Irene and Mary* (or "Sally, Irene and Lousy," as he privately dubbed it), he even became a plausible romantic light comedian. Arnold Auerbach, a young writing colleague on the Allen radio hour of the midthirties, first saw him, bow tie undone, shirt-sleeved, bespectacled, and chomping on a wad of Tuck's five-cent plug tobacco, as "a cantankerous small-town newspaper editor." Then, preparing to go outside into rainy weather, putting on rubbers and taking an umbrella, Allen created a different impression. "Under the correct gray topcoat and sober fedora, the newspaper editor had vanished. Now I saw a New England banker."

When Allen entered radio, he was thirty-eight years old and an entertainer half his life. He had perfected a vocal delivery suitable for any theatrical circumstance, and that delivery, with its alterations of tempo and tone, was the result of countless rehearsals. Skolsky observed other physical details, beyond the gunpowder burns on Allen's right hand, caused by a stage manager's miscalculation, and the comedian's chipped back teeth, the outcome of a vaudeville routine in which he threw a turnip into the air and attempted to catch it on the tines of a fork held in his mouth:

> He wears expensive clothes but they don't look it. One of his pockets is always crammed with notepaper. Easily the busiest man on Broadway. Rants about overwork, but can't stop. Starts work Saturday morning, and Sunday night, a

week later, he's still at it. His desk is high with mail, clip-
pings and notes. On an index card he lists things to do
for the day. Reads as much as a book critic does, and he
buys his own books. He eats in places like Joe's Delicatessen near Carnegie Hall, or Dave's Blue Room. He's a slow
eater and orders an Italian dinner once a week. He never
wears tails or a dinner coat. Smokes cigars, chews tobacco. Sleeps in a twin bed. Prefers a bath to a shower.
Insists on eight hours sleep. Company must know when
to leave. Sign in living room tells guests they can leave
at two because "I Need My Rest." He is not funny to
talk to.

Comedy was a serious matter, so Allen, unlike most comedians, was never "on" in private life. Literate and modest, he
claimed to have launched his career casually: "The only reason
I went into vaudeville was that even a third-rater could earn
three times as much as a stenographer or a clerk. I put more
books in my trunk than anything else; I carried around *The
Outline of History* for a year. Back home, while I was touring,
my girl friend married a Harvard student she met at a dance."
However casual his start, performance had become less a
career for him than a calling. During the twenty years leading
toward *The Linit Bath Club Revue,* he worked with concentrated diligence and purpose. His exacting apprenticeship recalls the rites of passage of one of his precursors. "When I was
a boy," wrote Mark Twain about a similar coming of age,
"there was but one permanent ambition among my comrades
in our village on the west bank of the Mississippi River. That
was, to be a steamboatman." Fred Allen later nurtured aspirations to become a writer or journalist, but as a schoolboy, he
decided he would be a comedian. He would learn his trade
absolutely. He would study the vast and restless river of comedy, train his memory to hoard a multitude of jokes and comic
situations, the soundings and crossing-marks of his craft, and
put it all down in a manageable form. On the lined pages of
an account book, he registered the results of his early bookings, along with instructions to himself:

Good entrance (speak up louder)
Applause (good)
Bows two (4–5 minutes juggling four balls)

As he negotiated sandbars, bends, and cross-rips, the currents of his personal experience merged with the rush and sweep of life bearing him onward. To be sure, he had stamina, a sense of purpose, a whirlwind wit, but stamina wasn't enough; he also had to handle stretches he couldn't fathom. "Here was a piece of river which was all down in my book, but I could make neither head nor tail of it: you understand, it was turned around," wrote Twain, learning to be a Mississippi pilot. "I had seen it when coming upstream, but I had never faced about to see how it looked when it was behind me. My heart broke again, for it was plain that I had got to learn this troublesome river *both ways*."

The professional poise Fred Allen brought to *The Linit Bath Club Revue,* the faultless pace and timing and sense of medium so unlike the stilted pioneer radio comedians, had been acquired in a harsh school. He had undergone periods of deprivation and loneliness in which he trudged between cheap lodgings, greasy-spoon restaurants, and dank dressing rooms. The corridors of Mrs. Montfort's, his first New York boardinghouse, were so long and dark he might have been "walking down a giraffe's throat," and the pillow on his bed could have been a teabag. Assuming that humor is sublimated or displaced hostility, as Freud defines it, Allen had plenty to feel hostile about. His father was an alcoholic and for years Allen too drank heavily, consuming, he told columnist John Crosby, a quart of whiskey a day — but only in the speakeasy era. "Fred did not get those bags under his eyes by chance; he earned them," said a close friend, the artist Al Hirschfeld. "And he was original even in his drinking days. I never saw him affected by alcohol. He'd sip from a highball glass while writing or talking and he always remained exactly the same. An odd thing, though — this suggests how unusual he was — during Prohibition he drank, but the day after Repeal, Fred stopped altogether. He didn't drink at all for nine or ten years and for the rest of his life he practiced moderation."

More complex than any of his colleagues, Allen had a streak of gallows humor. His jokes could rankle, brood on taboo themes — death and decay and deformity — the obverse of his shimmering drollery. Yet, in fact, he was as vulnerable to sentiment as a stage Irishman or a soap opera addict, and was acutely sensitive to the misfortunes of others. He himself had sustained emotional traumas; still, he spurned facile emotion. His loathing of the hackneyed was so ingrained that he sidestepped even the greeting "hello." In a rare departure into rhyme, he wrote:

> *Hush little bright line,*
> *Don't you cry,*
> *You'll be a cliché*
> *By and by.*

The quintessence of Allen's life was his religious faith, his marriage, and his work. A devout Catholic, he refused on principle to flaunt his multifarious charitable benefactions, but when he emerged from a stage door, he attracted flocks of panhandlers who swarmed about him like gulls around a mackerel trawler. Though he also gave generously to organized charity, he enjoyed this spontaneous largesse: its appeal for him did not lie in princely benevolence, but in recognizing faces, talking to people on a one-to-one basis, and responding to individual need. Allen in 1932 had been married five years to Portland Hoffa, a chorine in the line of *The Passing Show of 1922, George White's Scandals,* and related musical diversions. The couple, following the custom of other headliners (George Burns and Gracie Allen, Jesse Block and Eve Sully, Jack Benny and Mary Livingstone), had become a husband-and-wife vaudeville act. Such partnerships, Allen pointed out in his memoirs, "enabled the vaudevillian to ask for more money; the increase bought his wife's wardrobe and paid her fare and expenses." There were additional benefits. "Working in the act also occupied the wife's time on the road. A wife who was not in the act had to wait around in the hotel or in the dressing room until the husband finished his artistic chores. With a vaudeville act, Portland and I could be together, even if we couldn't find any work." Portland, brown-haired, slender, and pert, had fresh, open features and a nimble comic style and soon developed into an ingratiating comedienne; her breathless vocal projection retained a startled clarity that proved highly adaptable to radio.

The couple occupied an unostentatious apartment in New York's Warwick Hotel and spent summers in a rented beach cottage in the working-class resort of Old Orchard, Maine. But whether in New York or in Maine, Allen was compulsively working. Reared by Victorian elders, he found work a natural reflex, and the pocketful of scrap paper observed by Skolsky was the raw material of Allen's comic method, the source of ideas that might strike him as he walked along the street. He folded each sheet of paper into four thrifty squares, and when inspiration knocked he jotted down impressions in capital letters so tiny that to one kibitzer "it looked as if a microbe with ink on its feet had briefly rumbaed on the paper." The inspiration might be a quirky name (Eustace Gammon, Cymbal Simon), a graphic image ("Glasses ride his nose sidesaddle"), a piece of comic business ("Phrenologist reaches up and feels his own head and quits"), or a mini-scenario ("Hollywood sketch — Tarzan can't yell — Throat doctor examines — Agent pleads — Executive cuts salary — Tarzan yells"). Wherever he went, uptown or downtown, he fetched along a book, magazine, or newspaper to be perused at a drugstore lunch counter, on a park bench, waiting for a rehearsal, and he would mark relevant passages, tear out articles, and stuff them in his pockets along with the folded sheets. "As the day wore on my pockets seemed to be herringbone goiters," he recalled, "and I looked as though I was a walking wastebasket."

Allen had a fresh idea for a comedy radio program. Instead of relying upon stale vaudeville techniques, the show would adapt the narrative continuity of *Amos 'n' Andy* to the conditions of "personality" performance: a complete story every week, a comic situation featuring a different metropolitan background, a store or bank or office. The listener would laugh at the jokes and want to follow the fortunes of the characters involved, thus insuring the program's longevity.

The Linit Bath Club Revue was not expected to last more than a few months. To everyone's surprise, including Allen's, the show scored one of the hits of the 1932–33 radio season. Portland's scatterbrained dialogues with an imaginary Mama and Papa were a popular feature. Almost from program to program, a developing sense of the potential of radio gave the scripts creative excitement. Allen was accustomed to playing to audiences in a theater, and at first the broadcasts had some of the stiffness of Broadway routines carried over into a different medium; but as he gained experience, the scripts approached his ideal — theater of the imagination in a domestic setting. Notwithstanding his years spent amusing live audiences, he felt that live audiences in the broadcasting studio detracted from the program's power to affect individual listeners. By the start of the thirties, however, it was too late to bypass the studio audience with its servile applause and arranged mirth, so Allen, evolving a new kind of comedy, made the best of the situation.

"It has always seemed to me," he later told interviewer John K. Hutchens, "that this alleged entertainment should be geared down to the tempo of life in the home. If a visitor banged into your living room and carried on his conversation yelling and hawking his points, in the manner and at a tempo employed by most radio comedians, you would hasten his departure."

Over the ensuing seventeen years, the success of Allen's approach confirmed his belief in the existence of an intelligent mass audience for comedy. The program underwent many changes; it became a vehicle of topical satire, expanded to an hour, and ultimately reverted to a half-hour. Despite the star's ill-health, which forced him to take an extended rest in 1943, and despite the vagaries of sponsors and network censors, the show remained one of the constants of radio. Some of those sponsors assumed that Fred Allen was a comedian too highbrow for the mythical average man. But Allen, who was really as plebeian as a pot holder, attracted a weekly audience of three out of four radio households, an estimated twenty million coast-

to-coast listeners. The reason for his acceptance was fundamental: the man, the times, and the medium coincided. "People tuned in Allen for relief," Bryan conjectured. "They
discovered he was funny. He continued to be funny, and they
continued to tune in."

The comedian's national popularity soared even further in
the immediate postwar period when he perfected the format
called "Allen's Alley," introduced in 1942. On each program
Allen would start with a topical question for the evening. Together he and Portland would stroll down an alley where four
contrasting types lived — a bombastic southern politico, a tart-
tongued New England farmer marinated in luxuriant under-
statement, a Jewish matron given to antic malapropisms, and
a bibulous Irish coot — and, after knocking on their doors in
sequence, hear their answers to the question. The characters
received equal billing with the star, but he was the puppet-
master who, on April 7, 1947, received the accolade of a *Time*-
magazine cover painted by Ernest Hamlin Baker. Like Hamlet
contemplating the skull of Yorick, Fred Allen contemplated a
microphone above the cryptic but evocative phrase "this
drudgery, this sham, this gold-mine." The cover story,
"World's Worst Juggler," began in the magazine's "Radio"
section and described the program from warm-up to sign-off,
the studio audience rocking with laughter at every quip: "They
were with him. They had been with him all over the United
States for fourteen years. But never before this season has he
had a greater volume of enthusiastic listeners. Twice this season, for the first time in Fred Allen's radio career, his show
has ranked first in the Hooper telephone poll of listeners."

Allen was an institution that spring when *The Best Years of
Our Lives* played the movie houses, and eighty-three-year-old
Henry Ford died among the kerosene lamps and flickering
candles of his historical reconstruction, Greenfield Village, and
the Salsbury was selling so fast Northrup proclaimed it couldn't
keep up with the demand.

THE WEEK OF *TIME'S* COVER, *The Fred Allen Show,* sponsored by Royal puddings and Shefford cheese, began as it always did with Allen and Portland stepping through the curtain

at Studio 8-H in Radio City for the preliminary warm-up. He was no more reconciled to the studio audience than before, but during the interval before airtime he always won over the tourists and casual visitors who flocked to watch the program. John Crosby later pointed out that a considerable amount of humor simply resides in telling the truth, and the truths Fred told were unadorned: the audience still had time to get out, the NBC ushers would provide a military escort. The audience laughed at everything. The importance of the warm-up, though, had less to do with wit than with the bond established between the performer and the audience; in those moments he was addressing them rather than a radio audience, and while they had come to see the broadcast, they were pleased to be taken into the star's confidence, part of a backstage complicity.

During the warm-up there was good-natured kidding with the orchestra leader, Al Goodman — an old vaudeville custom — then gestures from the control room, the actors taking their places, silence, a red light, up-tempo music, followed by announcer Kenny Delmar's voice. The guest star was Hollywood director Gregory Ratoff. And now . . . Fred Allen!

The opening, between Delmar, who doubled as Senator Claghorn, and Allen, contained the kind of fanciful imagery (in this case, suggesting a folktale hero rescued by guardian animals) that distinguished Allen from other comedians.

KENNY: I read *Time*'s story on you, Fred. It was very interesting. When you were a boy in Boston did you ever feed the squirrels on the Common?

FRED: Yes, Kenny. If it weren't for those squirrels I wouldn't be here tonight.

KENNY: How do you mean?

FRED: Well, when I was a little boy, every day during the winter I used to stop and feed the squirrels on the Boston Common. Some years later things were bad in vaudeville. One New Year's Day I was sitting on a bench in a Palm Beach suit. One of the squirrels recognized me. He saw me shivering. He scampered away and came back with two-hundred other squirrels. The two-hundred squirrels climbed all over me and made like a fur coat.

With my new fur coat I was booked on the Keith circuit. And I've been an actor ever since. The moral is — always be kind to a squirrel, Kenny, and some day he may take you off the nut. But I digress —

This was the cue for Portland's entrance.

PORTLAND: Mr. Allen!
FRED: Portland! (*Applause*) Pull up an old executive and sit down, Portland. Kenny and I were talking about *Time* magazine.
PORTLAND: Mama says with your picture on *Time* —
FRED: Yes.
PORTLAND: This week — *Life* can be beautiful.
FRED: That's Luce talk. Henry, that is.

The Alley question that week revolved around the opening of Jamaica racetrack. Titus Moody, the Down East farmer played by Parker Fennelly, used the question as a pretext for a saga about a rube who comes to the big city and winds up scanning televised horse races through a liverwurst wrapped around a telescope. Senator Claghorn was more interested in music.

CLAGHORN: The Mobile Philharmonic — the only band in the world with a hound-dog choir. Plays all the Southern classics: The Flight of the Boll Weevil; Poet and Sharecropper; Rhapsody in Gray . . .

On that program, when the Allen show led all the rest, Mrs. Nussbaum (Minerva Pious) and Ajax Cassidy (Peter Donald) answered the racetrack inquiry without straying from the topic.

FRED: Mrs. Nussbaum.
MIN: Nu?
FRED: Nu?
MIN: Fifth Avenue — all day I am parading.
FRED: Tell me, Mrs. Nussbaum. How do you feel about horse racing?
MIN: On account of horses, where am I living? Here in an alley.
FRED: You mean your husband, Pierre?

MIN: Always he is betting. Always he is losing.
FRED: Really?
MIN: I am taking Pierre to a psychiatral.
FRED: A psychiatrist.
MIN: A doctor.

Ajax Cassidy:

FRED: How do you feel about betting?
PETER: You can't win, me boy. Now take Feedback Finnegan. All his life bettin' on horses.
FRED: Really?
PETER: If you had a charley-horse — he'd bet you which leg it was in.
FRED: What happened to Feedback Finnegan?
PETER: He died as he lived. Out of the money. They had to pawn his only suit to pay the undertaker.
FRED: Gosh.
PETER: Finnegan was buried in his underwear.
FRED: I see.
PETER: How is it goin' to look when Gabriel blows his horn? Feedback Finnegan floatin' through the air in his union suit?

ONE YEAR LATER, the first week in April 1948, *The Fred Allen Show* sounded the same. The guest star was Basil Rathbone, the British-born actor who played Sherlock Holmes on the screen, and who was then on Broadway in *The Heiress,* adapted from Henry James's story "Washington Square." (Rathbone appeared in a skit both as Holmes and hardboiled shamus Sam Spade.) There was a new sponsor, Ford, but otherwise the format seemed unaffected. The Alley question concerned truth in advertising — in particular, the ubiquitous Burma-Shave jingles that motorists saw in sequence as they drove through the countryside; each line of a ditty adorned one of the separate tiny billboards arranged in succession alongside the road. Titus claimed to have profited from the longest Burma-Shave poem in the country.

> *John McGee*
> *Had a long goatee*

> *When he combed it out*
> *It hung down to his knee.*
>
> *Today John's happy*
> *He married a Wave,*
> *His goatee's gone*
> *Thanks to Burma-Shave.*

FRED: Say, that is long.

PARKER: The poem starts half a mile down the road.

FRED: I see.

PARKER: It comes in my gate — goes once around the house.

FRED: Uh-huh.

PARKER: The last line is on my back door — on the inside.

FRED: You have to open the door to read the last line of the Burma-Shave poem?

PARKER: That's the trick.

FRED: Trick?

PARKER: As you open the back door, my wife's sittin' there sellin' the stuff.

In every respect, *The Fred Allen Show* remained the same program that enthralled the nation a year previously — but the ratings had sagged, and in popularity the show dropped to twenty-eighth place. Never before had it finished out of the top ten. Was this attributable to the impact of television or the success of the giveaway game program, *Stop the Music,* competing against Allen? These were part of the answer; all the same, by 1948 the country had only 172,000 television sets, mainly in bars and lounges, and *Stop the Music* exhausted the entertainment possibilities of greed within the next five years, although it spawned similar giveaways that abide into the present. What happened to *The Fred Allen Show* was postwar America. The satirical attitudes so relevant in the thirties, when listeners reveled in Allen's gibes against "molehill men" and functionaries responsible for hard times, and in the early forties, war years when he also embodied values of tradition and continuity, no longer seemed pertinent.

He was, after all, in many ways a representative American of a generation born in the 1890s. He held automobiles and most

technologies suspect, conducted a vast personal correspondence, believed in the restorative powers of self-improvement
and moral earnestness, and preferred to spend his leisure in the
company of friends rather than cultivating anonymous useful
contacts. A few years later, beginning his autobiography,
Allen cited advice from John Steinbeck: "Don't start by trying
to make the book chronological. Just take a period. Then try
to remember it so clearly that you can see things: what colors
and how warm or cold and how you got there. Then try to
remember people." It was advice Allen had always heeded.
Remembering people meant for him celebrating their eccen-
tricities, and in those postwar years when conformity was becoming a watchword, he delighted still in unique and compelling individual chronicles. The urban world of his boyhood (a
world now becoming increasingly fragmented and complex)
was not altogether remote from the pastoral Hannibal, Missouri,
of Mark Twain. Ten years older than the comedian, Harry
Truman might recognize in Fred Allen's career a similar self-
education, but a contemporary generation, back from the war
and about to embrace the corporate society Allen had so long
ridiculed, hesitantly reserved judgment on his comic genius.
The denizens of Allen's Alley, summing up the ethnic humor
of vaudeville, belonged to an earlier era, and it is impossible
to enlarge upon the dialogue of the Basil Rathbone sketch in
racially sensitive late-twentieth-century terms. As the famous
Asian detective One Long Pan, Allen's entrance line was "Ah,
gleetings and sholem aleichem, kiddies. One Long Pan, Chinese
Dick Tlacy."

The sudden turnaround of *The Fred Allen Show* in the months
between 1947 and 1948 involved the replacement of one view
of the world by another. It is doubtful if Allen himself realized
what happened. Radio, the medium par excellence for speaking to a mass audience on a personal basis, had been his element for fifteen years. Throughout his career he had chafed
under front-office authority: the business of show business had
always been big business, the vaudeville bookers and circuits
and blacklists, the monopolistic Broadway producers, the fatuous admen and sponsors, but never before, with radio as he
knew it vanishing, had American comedy seemed to him so

thoroughly manufactured, a product as bland and anonymous as sliced bread. In the stale vaudeville routines that constituted television comedy ("Imitation," he said, "is the sincerest form of television"), no one was speaking to anyone, and at the age of fifty-four, Fred Allen, radio's foremost wit, was obsolete.

The Jack Benny program could survive change because its central figure was changeless; Allen's comedy, based on sparkling wordplay and topical reference, depended on listeners who shared his frame of reference. By 1948 they were not clamoring for the Salsbury motor scooter; they wanted the new DeSoto, which they could drive without shifting, or the Hudson, which boasted it was the only car in which you stepped *down* to enter. Men of late middle-age have often felt the same loss of direction, so it was perhaps natural for Allen, his performing days over, to take stock, consider writing his own story, and go back to the beginning.

2 | One Boy's Boston

He was born on the border of Cambridge and Somerville, Massachusetts, not far from Harvard Yard, May 31, 1894, and christened John Florence Sullivan. ("I passed through the university," he liked to say, "on the way to visit my grandmother.") Family tradition maintained that the Union Street house in which he was born stood on the Somerville side, and until he sent for a copy of his birth certificate at the age of twenty-two, he considered himself a native of Somerville. But Somerville has no record of his birth; one later turned up in Cambridge City Hall without a street address — a blunder John attributed to his father's tipsy rejoicing. There is another plausible explanation; the elder Sullivan spent considerable time in the Cambridge homes of his parents and four brothers, so it is also possible he registered the birth at the most convenient location.

The infant's unusual middle name indicates his family had emigrated from west Munster, where Florence is both a male and female designation. The name does not derive from Saint Florence, as might be expected, but from *Fingin,* meaning "fair birth" or "fair offspring," pronounced "Fineen" and anglicized as Florence. John's paternal grandfather, Florence, arrived in Boston from County Kerry on the twenty-first of October, 1852. The maternal grandfather, John Herlihy, a County Cork stonecutter, landed in New York at the age of twenty-two in 1850. From his wake, in 1896, his two-year-old grandson retained one of his first hazy memories, a parlor and a coffin and man's face beneath the glass rectangle atop the coffin lid.

The grandfathers who bequeathed their names to John shared similar backgrounds. They had become citizens at separate naturalizations during the early 1870s, each flanked in a Cambridge courtroom by a pair of friends who attested to their good moral character and their attachment to the principles of the Constitution of the United States. Then they had pledged "to renounce all allegiance and fidelity to every foreign Prince, State, Potentate and Sovereignty whatsoever — more especially to Victoria, Queen of the United Kingdom of Great Britain and Ireland." The ominous pothooks of the word *Victoria,* rendered in Gothic letters glowering upon the page, stood apart from the rest of the text.

Of Cecilia Herlihy, John's mother, nothing survives save her faded signature on a handful of legal documents. Born in Cambridge, June 20, 1869, she died in Cambridge, February 19, 1897, having contracted pneumonia only a fortnight before. The dates exhibit a lapidary reticence, the symmetry of a brief, obscure life spent within the boundaries of a single place. Her children came to adulthood without tangible memories of her presence.

John Henry Sullivan — known as Henry — attempted to rear his sons, John Florence and Bob, John's younger brother. Theirs was a turn-of-the-century New England Irish-Catholic upbringing, nurtured by faith, ritual, and the admonitions of the parish priest, the ancient rhythms of the ecclesiastical calendar, first Fridays, novenas and retreats, and tangible reminders of a peasant past. At Sullivan family wakes, the kitchen table was heaped with mounds of tobacco alongside clay pipes called "T.D.'s." The initials, impressed in the clay, probably referred to the manufacturer, although the pipes, having been made in Newburyport, Massachusetts, were sometimes called "Timothy Dexters" after that town's eccentric Federalist-era merchant-prince, a self-styled "Lord." T.D.'s were cheap and fragile and almost invariably offered with the verbal formula "Drop it, and you won't have to pick it up." The male mourners retired to the kitchen, tamped their pipebowls, poured a glass (or "jar"), and reminisced about the departed. "As the night wore on," Allen remembered in his autobiography, *Much Ado about Me,* "the tobacco fumes cast a blue haze over the kitchen, glasses were filled and refilled, the talk changed to other subjects, stories were told, occasional laughter rang out, and a good time generally was had by the many friends who had gathered to see the host off on his final journey."

The voices and faces swirling in the smoke were the voices and faces of Cork and Kerry, but Boston's idioms tinged their talk. The Irish, whose sense of community had hitherto centered about tenements, urban churches, schools, and ward political clubs, were now fanning outward into suburbia and composed a substantial segment of the middle class. Yankees maintained a slackening but tight grasp on the social and economic levers of power, however. The doings of the Irish filled the segregated society columns of the Boston papers, where a firm editorial line demarcated Irish and Yankee births, marriages, and deaths. Henry belonged to an enclave of Irish-American bookbinders who had settled in literate Cambridge, although he himself worked as a "book forwarder," wrapping and packaging books for delivery in the bindery of the Boston Public Library. His employment was sporadic. Sober, he cut an elegant figure, a tall, slender Victorian gent, "rather artistic-looking," brown hair cut in a pompadour, a large elk's-tooth gleaming on a gold watch-chain looped across his vest. After Cecilia's death he began drinking, and while he remained on the roster of library employees from 1898 to the winter of 1901, his name thereafter vanishes. Earning $19.23 a week during periods of full employment (he appears to have worked at intervals thereafter), he could not support a family. Hard times further diminished Henry's meager talents as a provider; the stock market crash during the Panic of 1893 had wiped out five hundred banks, sixteen thousand businesses, and the vast railroad combinations; and by the following spring, when John Florence was born, 2½ million men were unemployed.

Throughout adulthood Fred Allen deflected references to his father; that memory was too painful. Henry, though seldom a physical influence, dominated almost every moment of his sons' upbringing. Once, at the age of fourteen, Johnny entered a junior marathon, the feature of a church field day. "As the starting gun was fired I saw my father standing in the crowd. As the race progressed and I ran through the neighborhood streets, trying to keep up with the pack of kids, it seemed to me that my father suddenly started coming out of every saloon we passed, shouting encouragement. While I was trying to figure out how my father was able to come out of a number of saloons in different sections, and virtually simultaneously, I lost the race." Sullivan *père,* of course, had perused a map, noted the watering holes along the marathon course, and charted his shortcuts. Like an hallucination, there he was in all directions at once. The impulse of every boy to endow his father with herculean attributes was superimposed upon the absurdity of the figure lurching from the swinging doors, an apparition all the more terrifying in its banal goodwill.

A family photograph shows Henry with his sailor-suited boys perched on either knee. The image, which ought to express the warmth of a family portrait, is cheerless. The boys are sulky, the father awkward. His lachrymose mustache droops; he stares glumly at the camera, as though interrupted while enjoying an affable drink. The boys remind him of Cecilia, and when he thinks of her, dead at twenty-seven, he wipes his eyes and fills his glass. She used to sing "Love Me and the World Is Mine." He hums the tune and again wipes his eyes and fills his glass.

"My father was a stranger," Fred said. "When I grew older, people often told me how funny he was. At that time he didn't seem funny to me. He squandered most of his fun away from home." Fred, in the first draft of *Much Ado about Me,* wrote: "Being my father was a hobby with Mr. Sullivan. He was a bookbinder by trade. He went all through life binding books and trying to make both ends meet. He was good at binding books." The bitterness of an alcoholic's rejected son is manifest, but in the manuscript's final draft Fred moderated his reproof, and even achieved a conditional reconciliation with the past. Conversing on radio with Gilbert Seldes and Clifton Fadiman about the topic "What Would You Do With Your

Life If You Could Live It Over?" Fred alluded to the gregarious aspects of his father and uncles. "They had the Irish thing: they could make people laugh."

Henry's family ignored his plight. Cecilia, however, had left a sister, Elizabeth F. Lovely, "Aunt Lizzie," who assumed a matriarchal role not uncommon in turn-of-the-century Irish-American households: the self-sacrificing female relative uncomplainingly holding the establishment together. Aunt Lizzie, eleven years older than Cecilia, agreed to make a home for the widower and his boys. She faced domestic problems of her own: Michael, her husband, a plumber suffering from lead poisoning, paralyzed and bedridden, his condition deteriorating; her other sisters, Mary and Jane, and her brother Joseph, living upstairs with the Lovelys in a duplex at 35 Bayard Street in the Allston-Brighton section of Boston, just across the Charles River from Cambridge. Each adult — Mary worked in a shoe factory, Jane at the haberdashery counter of the Jordan Marsh department store, and Joseph sold pianos — contributed five dollars a week toward the housekeeping.

The bereaved but inebriate Henry brought his boys there, along with an upright Emerson piano and a sewing machine. This decreased the space (parlor, dining room, two bedrooms, kitchen, and bath on one level, four small sleeping cubicles in the gabled attic above) shared by six adults and two children. The piano in the small parlor personified respectability; the sewing machine in the bedroom answered need. Fred Allen joked in vaudeville that "we were so poor, my bean bags had patches on them," or alternatively, "the rats ran around the house with tears in their eyes," but shabby gentility prevailed, borderline poverty rather than a grim struggle for survival. Aunt Lizzie did the sewing, washing, ironing, shopping, and cooking; she baked the bread and provided her brother and sisters with three meals a day, which included packing lunches; she managed the accounts of iceman, grocer, landlord, and the utilities; she nursed her ailing husband, wiped the smudged faces of her little nephews, dressed them and sent them off to school, recited their nightly prayers, and remained one of the most ardent communicants of Saint Anthony's parish. Only the scope of her piety exceeded her domestic versatility. Henry's sister, Aunt Mame, was equally devout if somewhat less charitable. She took to lowering the top of her bedroom window in the event the Blessed Virgin should decide to visit her through the window; and after Henry died, Mame tried to repossess the piano.

On Saint Anthony's parish hall stage, Johnny made his theatrical debut at the age of seven in a Christmas pageant. Portraying one of the Magi, he spoke his first histrionic lines.

> *Myrrh is mine — its bitter perfume*
> *Breathes a life of gathering gloom . . .*

Sunday afternoons he and Bob accompanied their father to Cambridge. Henry and his brothers regularly visited their parents for midday dinner and a chat about the day's news. It was a convivial ritualized gathering, and each adult Sullivan brought along a pint of whiskey. Members of Yankeedom's Colonial Club in the Henry James mansion at 20 Quincy Street (today, the address of the Harvard Faculty Club) could, if so inclined, witness a curious weekly spectacle: a tall man, not a Yankee, and two children passing quietly up the street, then returning in a raucous tousle a few hours later. John and Bob steered their stumbling parent three miles through the twilight. "We looked like two sardines guiding an unsteady Moby Dick into port" — a sight not calculated to improve the forebodings of the members of the Colonial Club — and the trio lurched past the elms of Harvard Yard and the trolleys of Harvard Square, over the rickety wooden struts of the Boylston Street drawbridge, down North Harvard Street and Bayard Street, until at last Henry flopped into bed beneath the troubled gaze of Aunt Lizzie.

CLASSMATES at the Thomas Gardner Elementary School called Johnny Sullivan — a tall, scrawny, jug-eared kid, all arms and legs and adenoids — "Sike" or "Twit." "I tried to reach the age of discretion," he said, "but I had short arms." The class cutup, though not a problem student, he made friends quickly, and his inseparable pals, from the same Allston neighborhood, were Ernest "Tug" Lalley, and Leslie Rogers, later the librarian of the Boston Symphony Orchestra. Johnny, like every schoolboy, hero-worshiped Teddy Roosevelt. Strenuous living was not confined to his example: the world into which a boy was born at the century's turn in Allston-Brighton meant the Abattoir, the Charles River, and the electric streetcars that brought inner-city excitement within reach.

The "Abattoir" or "slaughterhouse" reflected the consolidated communities' past as the Wild West of Boston. (Allston, a segment of Brighton, was known as Little Cambridge until the postal substation was renamed for the painter Washington Allston, who seems never to have visited the place.) Farmers had begun herding animals there in order to supply the Continental Army during the American Revolution, and one in seven Brighton families soon earned a livelihood from butchering. By 1869, Estelle Winwood Wait reported, "fifty-odd slaughterhouses dotted the town, zoning laws unheard of. A butcher thought nothing of building and operating his slaughterhouse within full sight of the fine house next door — whose occupant might well be doing the same thing within close range of someone else's house."

The pervasive stench, wretched drainage, and pollution of the Charles River and other streams alarmed even the laissez-faire authorities of that lax public-health era. Fearing an epidemic (one-third of the town's deaths in 1869 were ascribed to unsanitary slaughtering practices), Brighton representatives framed a state law that prohibited slaughtering within six miles of the Massachusetts State House except in a new central facility, the Brighton Abattoir. This in effect gave the incorporators, Brighton butchers all, a monopoly. Their inspired choice of a high-sounding French word to gloss over their sanguinary activities prompted one enthusiast to exclaim: "If it will not make slaughtering a fine art, it will at least place it high above its earlier position."

No Allston-Brighton boy grew up without indoctrination into the stockyards' bloody mysteries. Today the zone where sixty arid acres once sprawled beside a bend of the Charles is an industrial park and highway; but in the 1870s the Abattoir almost made the district hog butcher to the world. Gustavus Franklin Swift, founder of a meat-packing empire in Chicago, started out in Brighton and probably would have stayed had not the refrigerator freight car transformed the industry.

At the Abattoir you could milk a cow for a dime — a consideration for immigrant families as hard-pressed as the Lovelys of Bayard Street. When freight cars crammed with squealing pigs were unloaded during the summer, large semiliquid ice slabs remained; the pigs had sprawled on these lest they suffocate. The neighborhood boys would lug the slabs home and, inserting layers of paper between each layer of ice, put them in the cellar. Even in a heat wave, many Allston families near the Abattoir had no need to display the rectangular window card that informed the ice-wagon of their requirements. Johnny Sullivan played in the cattle yards like the others. Jack Whyte, a neighborhood boy, has left a vivid account:

> On Saturday morning, we'd go down and we'd have to find this herd of pigs, sheep and cattle. They'd give us maybe a quarter to herd them with a stick. In the afternoon, things quieted down and we'd have milk fights. We'd go into the pens, grab the teats of one cow and squirt each other. I'm not a great milker, but they were so full of milk! Then we'd ride — we were crazy! We'd get on the back of the steers and ride them around the pen. And we'd have fights with each other on the steers.

The stockyard reek of blood, sand, and offal hovered over Allston on windless days, and hardly less noxious was the Charles River. Henry Wadsworth Longfellow had written of "the bright and free meadows of Brighton," but, lined with wharves, warehouses, and factories, the tidal Charles served as a malodorous catchment. The Allston-Brighton section, over four miles and spanned by five drawbridges, was perhaps the most heavily polluted portion because the sewers of both Brighton and Cambridge emptied upstream and the sewage washed out with the tides. Until 1908, the river's swift-running currents rose and fell daily almost ten vertical feet. The Charles attracted boys who awaited the tidal shift and then splashed along the banks where midstream tugs pulled coal and lumber barges toward Watertown. Swimming by night and in the nude was popular. Low tide, however, transformed the pastoral flood into a muddy gulch threaded by glistening brooklets and releasing a noisome miasma. The damming of the river and development of an embankment, lagoon, and basin — in emulation of the water-park of the Alster River in Hamburg, Germany — changed the character of the Charles that Johnny Sullivan first knew.

Allston-Brighton proper at the turn of the century was turning away from Cambridge and the river toward a future as a streetcar suburb. Johnny's earliest childhood ambition, in fact, was to be a motorman. The neighborhood — first stop on the Boston and Worcester Railroad, the pioneer passenger-line railway in the United States — was a traditional transportation hub; the filling-in of the Back Bay during the 1850s and 1860s ended its physical separation from Boston. Annexed in 1873, Allston-Brighton gravitated toward the central city: electric streetcars, which began operating in 1889, ran from Park Square in Boston to the Allston railway depot; carbarns soon covered acres, a web of street railway systems traversed Brighton, and it was possible to ride for a nickel from Oak Square to City Point in South Boston. On Sunday afternoons, children sat up front and through the artful use of transfers tried to go round-trip to suburbs as distant as Stoneham. The motorman's forward post and the sides of the cars were open spring and summer, and the operator prudently placed a raincoat and umbrella on a seat in the event of a cloudburst.

The spread of the "electrics" would affect John Sullivan's early show business career, since he would shepherd troupes of amateur performers to amusement parks, small zoos, and resorts clustered near the end of the trolley lines. Traction companies supported the dance halls, rinks, theaters, and excursion facilities of the terminus. Norumbega Park, for example, with its carousels and vaudeville performances, was an hour from Brighton, and the round-trip fare was thirty cents.

Now and then, in adulthood when he had established himself, Allen's correspondence harked back to his Allston-Brighton boyhood. He alluded to the Abattoir as a "lost opportunity," a site where he might retire and become a knife-sharpener, slot man, or knacker, an honorable enterprise compared to the lot of one forced to cope with the machinations of network radio vice-presidents. The comedian's store of slaughterhouse jokes was of necessity slender; death may have its ironies, its sardonic melancholia, its derisive rictus, but slaughter only connoted the gruesome. On the other hand, without its sibilant first letter, the word has a different look.

WHEN JOHN turned fourteen and thus met the minimum legal requirement for employment, his father secured him a job as a Bates Hall runner at the Boston Public Library. The boy was embittered at first, feeling he had been sold into bondage, but in time came to relish the job. Working Sunday afternoons and from six to nine three nights a week, he received twenty cents an hour, less a nickel trolley fare each way Saturday mornings when he was obliged to visit City Hall downtown and sign the payroll.

Bates Hall, the main reading area, gave architectural focus to eleven other separate reading rooms and thirty-four miles of shelves holding almost two million books. Readers filled out a slip; then the runners fetched the books. In the hierarchy of the library, a stack boy outranked a runner. A runner might spend his entire shift trotting through the corridors, but a stack boy could finish his homework (or not) in tranquil isolation beneath a sliver of green-shaded light at a desk deep in the crypt of a Great Pyramid of print. Fred Allen recalled that he became a runner in the Boston Public Library in the summer of 1908. Official records first carry John Sullivan as a part-time employee on September 3 of that year. He may have substituted for boys who didn't turn up; a library job could be taken lightly during the vacation months. That summer, however, marked the end of schoolboy play.

The architectural landmark of the Boston Public Library, facing H. H. Richardson's Trinity Church in Copley Square, was only a year younger than John, though the institution itself, America's oldest free library, dated from 1852. The apotheosis of Boston culture, it symbolized the august achievements of early-nineteenth-century New England letters. American literature was for the most part now written elsewhere, but architect Charles Follen McKim's stately palazzo also commemorated the grandeur of human achievement. The Boston Public Library's copper-crested, red-tile roof, tall arched windows, and granite facades inscribed with chiseled lists of the awe-inspiring names of Western philosophy, science, art, religion, and statesmanship, proclaimed the transcendent tasks of knowledge. Above the main staircase, toga-clad figures painted by Puvis de Chavannes gazed down upon recumbent stone lions commemorating Massachusetts soldiery in the Civil War. The setting called for lordly brass fanfares rather than limber soft-shoe steps, trombone smears, and the impudent banter of vaudeville.

Of how many comedians can it be said that their careers were launched in a public library? (A subsequent Bates Hall runner was poet L. E. Sissman.) Wit, a category skipped by the chiseled roll-call outside, intruded upon studious pursuits, and John Sullivan's chances of receiving billing on a stone marquee appeared remote. The library, nonetheless, would serve in roundabout fashion as the nursery of his talent.

ONE SPRING EVENING in 1907, Henry announced that he planned to remarry, taking the piano and sewing machine with him. The announcement did not occur spontaneously; Aunt Lizzie made sure it would be a penitential rite. Henry would have something to say, she declared, but not for twenty-four hours. The next evening, after supper, Henry stood up among the parlor's fringed lampshades and antimacassars, before the assembled household, and said it. Confronting crisis, Lizzie followed an instinct that signaled her to protect the family. John also responded instinctively: he transformed rejection into a joke, humiliation into farce. As he recalled the scene, diffident Henry hung his head and addressed the elk's tooth on his vest, and "each word appeared to lie in state on his lips before it tumbled out into space."

John Henry Sullivan's second marriage proved ephemeral. The strains of "Love Me and the World Is Mine" seldom strayed from his thoughts. Five years later, he died in the home of his parents, 7 Emmons Place, Cambridge. The medical examiner set down the cause, acute alcoholism, and the age of the deceased: forty-three years, six months, and twelve days.

WITHOUT A SEWING MACHINE or Henry's household contribution, Aunt Lizzie needed to retrench, and John went with her to an attic apartment in the Savin Hill neighborhood of

Dorchester rather than with his father and Henry's bride-to-be. Neither of the boys had seen their prospective foster mother, and "young as I was, I felt I owed something to a wonderful woman who had been a mother to me for some twelve years. I said that I would stay with my Aunt Lizzie. I never regretted it."

Uncle Joe and Aunt Mary took other lodgings, which left Lizzie and Mike and Jane and John sharing the attic. The return of Bob, whose foster mother had begun to tipple, meant a further constriction of space. The attic's view, however, opened onto the tributaries of a salt marsh and the flicker of shorebirds; Dorchester retained rustic vestiges, as Bacon's *Dictionary of Boston* (1883) indicates: "The most famous and fashionable of all the suburbs lie to the southward and westward, with beautiful rural estates of Boston's merchant princes. Milton, Brookline and Newton, in particular, stand in the front rank in this respect, although but little ahead of Dorchester and West Roxbury."

In their Savin Hill "penthouse rookery," the Lovely clan joined an influx of Irish-Americans streaming into Dorchester's two- and three-family houses. Until the mid-nineteenth century, Dorchester's remoteness and economic segregation had guaranteed the residents — Yankees fleeing inner-city pressures — insulation from immigrant society. An 1842 petition of the town meeting, for example, begged the state legislature to avert "so great a calamity to our town as must be the railroad through it." The mirage of seclusion disintegrated as the metropolis pushed outward. The charms of Dorchester real estate enticed immigrants who had saved enough cash to leave central Boston. Trains invaded the marshes, annexation was voted, and reform legislation of the 1870s made lower-class three-decker construction more profitable for speculators than slum landlordism. An efficient trolley system presently gave the newer ethnic groups swift access to the city: Dorchester developed a maze of neighborhoods, each with a distinct identity.

The marshy coast where Aunt Lizzie resettled her brood was a relatively undeveloped section of this complex network. The parish line — the boundary between Saint Margaret's parish,

Dorchester, and Saint Augustine's, South Boston — defined territorial limits. Streets and sidewalks were mostly unpaved, and the spring mud coursed over boot tops. Although many farms and grazing lands had yielded to urbanization, the process was incomplete. Growing up on the edge of Dorchester Bay meant you might know a neighbor with a herd of back-yard cows or a squatter who lived on a houseboat in the midst of the reeds. Franklin Park, a gem in the "emerald necklace" envisioned by landscape designer Frederick Law Olmsted, shone at one end of Dorchester's enlarged Columbia Road (1893), and at the other end glimmered the blue crescent of sail-studded Marine Park in South Boston. Daddy Clap's nationally known pear-and-apple orchard (guarded at night by a truculent mastiff) sloped toward the ocean near the Russell Boiler Works, a brass foundry and a supplier of mannikins for department stores; and behind the foundry spread Haystack Marsh.

Determined that Johnny would find future security as a solid businessman, Lizzie sent him to the Boston High School of Commerce for Boys. The school, opened in 1904 and modeled upon the New York High School of Commerce and similar high schools of commerce in Europe, was a pet project of Mayor John F. "Honey Fitz" Fitzgerald — a vocational equivalent of the Boston Latin School, which prepared academically gifted youngsters for college. If Boston Latin signified the promise of a meritocracy, Commerce fostered the hope of a job. (Year after year, the school produced a substantial portion of Massachusetts's certified public accountants.) At both all-male institutions, the students bypassed neighborhood schools for the sake of specialized training.

In 1909 Commerce was temporarily situated in Roxbury, two miles from Johnny's home. "I worked my way through high school as some fellows work their way through college," Fred Allen soberly remarked years later. Days in class and nights at the library stretched him to the limit. Aunt Lizzie would pack two meals for John on nights he reported for work. The first lunch was consumed at school, the second at his locker on the library employees' floor. When school was over, he walked four miles from Roxbury to Boston, an enjoyable hike, and prior to six o'clock, sat in one of the reading rooms and finished his homework. Then he spent the next three hours as a runner among the corridors of stacks. Coming off duty, he tried to avoid the gastronomic temptations of the Waldorf Cafeteria near Copley Square, but an adolescent who has been jog-trotting all evening in marble corridors is ill-equipped to resist. After he had wolfed down a trilby — a fried-egg sandwich that resembled an oval cap — and a glass of milk, John compensated for the dime it cost him by returning on foot to Savin Hill, six miles away. Altogether, he covered approximately twenty miles, not counting his itinerary in school. Even in a generation of pedestrians (walking remained a popular recreational activity despite the evolution of the horseless carriage into the roadster), he was exceptional. He would never own an automobile or learn to drive one, and he took taxis only when walking was out of the question.

Although his schedule left him scant time for extracurricular activities, he was a high jumper on the track team and played as a forward on the junior basketball team that won the interclass championship in 1910. Most of his marks were A's and B's, in the middle-upper range of his class; he disliked algebra, and his best subject was English. Burlesquing the style of popular *Boston Post* newspaper columnist Newton Newkirk, Johnny began publishing a home room daily paper, the *Bingville Bugle*. Like other efforts of its kind, the *Bugle* was amateur-improvisational, a single sheet of paper folded down the middle to form four pages. In typing class, enthusiastic accomplices reproduced the original, using carbon copies, and he added diminutive caricatures of teachers and students. John chose the news items and commented upon them — a forerunner of the formula he would employ on radio. Moreover, his multiple roles as writer, artist, editor, publisher, and distributor forecast various adult roles as writer and performer.

That same typing class allowed him to demonstrate an exhibitionist flair for bringing the audience into the act. Whenever the teacher, a Mr. Connell, stepped out, leaving students busy with an assignment, John slipped into his place in the front of the room. Hands poised like an orchestra conductor, he announced that he would lead the class in a demonstration of typing to music. Then he launched into a ditty: "Down went the old maid to the country fair, to sell a load of 'taters and a pair of hare." At the close of each stanza (ribaldry was probably too dangerous to attempt), he sounded a refrain, "dum-tiddy-dum-dum," accompanied by the boys keeping time with the space bars of their typewriters and shifting their carriages in unison. Briefly and furtively, the future comedian emerged at such moments from the insurgent schoolboy.

The family moved again. Because he had been appointed Sunday director of the children's department (on the recommendation of his predecessor, Cornelius McGuire, later an eminent economist), John found himself prosperous by library standards, and he was now earning as much as $3.10 for Sundays alone. He saw his first play, Denman Thompson's *The Old Homestead*. On the second floor of the three-decker at the corner of Buttonwood and Grafton streets, he had once and for all a bedroom of his own. Worried about his treadmill of work and school and his relative isolation in their new Dorchester neighborhood, Aunt Lizzie insisted that he take back enough each week for a ticket to a vaudeville show. John had become interested in the origins of what made people laugh — an interest that came about by chance one evening when, as a stack boy, he idly took down from the shelves a book about the history of comic performance. The book gave Johnny an idea. In Salesmanship, the teacher, Mr. Grover, urged pupils to prepare and deliver five-minute talks once a week on any subject. A sales pitch prefaced by a funny story, Mr. Grover said, relaxed the prospect and lowered his resistance; then, by way of illustration, Mr. Grover told a series of jocose but tired anecdotes, each more excruciating than the last. John felt he could better these, as well as the clumsy efforts of the class, including his own previous effort about a cargo of elephants shipped across the Euphrates River. Why not a talk about comedy itself?

The class enjoyed the talk, but Mr. Grover contradicted his Salesmanship doctrines and announced there was a time and place for everything. The subject was undignified. For the first time, John realized that laughter involved recognition: Mr. Grover's mildewed jokes were hilarious to the teacher, if to no one else, because the teacher recognized them as funny. The incident inspired the novice salesman to think further about the nature of humor, and before long — exactly how it came about was impossible for him to recall — he took up juggling.

He may have been imitating the vaudevillians he saw each week, since the best jugglers in show business played Boston. W. C. Fields, who claimed to have conceived the notion of a tramp juggler after seeing a tramp magician, was then demonstrating his peerless pantomime on the Orpheum circuit. Unlike the confidence sharpster of his later movie incarnation, Fields, billed as "The Silent Humorist," was a shy man with a bad stutter. He had at this point spoken only once onstage; his solo mime routine achieved a universal pathos comparable to that of Chaplin's variation on the same character, the Little Tramp. Dialogue by slow degrees trickled into Fields's act: "The hardest trick I do," he told a contemporary reviewer,

> is that in which I toss a silk hat on the rim of which lies a lighted cigar, from my foot, balancing the hat as it falls on my nose, while I catch the cigar in my mouth and go on smoking. Half the time I fail to do it on the first trial, but by means of a lot of little extra comedy turns following the failure I usually succeed in making my audience believe that my failure is intentional. I also keep the bass drummer pretty busy while I am on the stage, and I suppose he more than makes up for what I don't say. At any rate, though my regular time on the stage is twenty-one minutes, I rarely get through in less than twenty-five or twenty-six minutes; the additional time is taken up by laughter.

Audiences responded to the patter more than the juggling, and Fields developed his idiosyncratic, whining, corner-of-the-mouth style as another rein on his stutter.

Fields and his near-double, the tramp-juggler billed as Harrigan, emphasized the dramatic importance of a juggler's mistakes as foil to his triumphs. Harrigan wore comic hooligan makeup, including a shaggy beard; Fields, who may or may not have patterned his tramp makeup on Harrigan's (the latter claimed he did), used similar ramshackle props. The act depended on Harrigan missing trick after trick and contriving elaborate excuses for botching each attempt. Finally, upon releasing a despairing wail, "This is the time I never fail to miss!" he brought off a prodigious finale.

John studied each vaudeville juggler passing through town and memorized his jokes. In algebra class he piped up, "Let X equal my father's signature." He noted the idiosyncrasies of the trade, such as the successive layers of vests each juggler wore: if a trick was fumbled, the juggler decoyed audience attention by peeling off another vest. From a book on juggling, he learned to juggle three tennis balls and three tin plates. Three silk hats were added to the repertoire; he purchased them at a magic shop where the proprietor assured customers theatrical juggling hats must be specially weighted and balanced. The extra ballast justified a charge of three dollars for each secondhand chapeau. John carried home the glossy silk hats and juggled them above his bed so that if he missed he wouldn't dent the crowns. Only with experience did he find that any hat could be juggled. The professionals purchased theirs at the Salvation Army store, which had a bargain basement filled with silk hats large and small selling for fifty cents.

Constantly rehearsing his tricks, he carried a pocketful of golf balls for odd-hours practice. Frank Masterson, who worked with John shelving fiction, was impressed by his tobogganing-book routine.

> He'd balance a book on his right forearm and let it slide toward the floor, seeing how close he could let it fall before he caught it with a flip of his right hand. He finally got to the point where he could make the catch just before the book was about to strike the floor. He juggled pencils and derby hats, too. He had such nimble, long fingers, with perfect coordination between his darting eyes and hands, that it was fascinating to watch him. And he was always doing or wearing something different. I remember the day he came in wearing one of those newfangled notch collars, the latest thing in 1910. He was the first youngster in the library to wear tan shoes; most of us still wore somber black footwear.

The summer of 1911, following his graduation from Commerce, John accepted an invitation to participate in *High Jinks,*

the library employees' amateur talent show. Once he agreed
to appear, however, his confidence drained away; he had
watched enough vaudeville to realize that he needed an act. He
began to link his tricks together: tin plates, tennis balls, top
hats, and cigar boxes, along with a garnish of hopeful jokes.
The patter opened with the line, "Well, summer is going, and
winter drawers on," and built toward, "I could tell you a secret about a can of condensed milk, but I'm afraid it would
leak out." Suppose he received no applause? He had a safety
net: "Who spilled embalming fluid in here?" But John's con-
cern was unnecessary; the talent of the other library employees
was confined to singing and dancing, and though one of his
oranges wobbled out of sync and struck a member of the audience, his juggling routine outshone repetitive clog-step ba-
nality. A knot of admirers surrounded him and a girl in the
crowd said: "You're crazy to keep working at the Library.
You ought to go on the stage."

Her words would reverberate; it was all the advice he needed,
and in future years he would playfully embroider the incident.
If she had kept her mouth shut that evening, he said, "today I
might be the librarian of the Boston Public Library," or, in
another variation, "I might be in full charge of the Encyclopedia Britannica, Volume Six, Coleb to Damasc." Like another traveler on the road to Damasc, Johnny Sullivan had
experienced revelation — but it was easier to imagine a stage
career than to launch one.

THAT FALL Uncle Joe obtained his nephew his first full-time
job — errand boy for the Colonial Piano Company opposite
Boston Common, at eight dollars a week. Johnny opened the
store at 8:00 A.M., swept out the showroom, polished the front
windows, dusted the keys, pedals, and lids of the pianos on
the floor, and undertook miscellaneous chores. These included
delivering cartons for one of the owners who raised hens in
suburban Newton, and who sold surplus eggs to office workers. The undemanding job provided plentiful opportunity to
observe that business practices at the Colonial Piano Company
did not resemble the classroom ideals of the High School of
Commerce. Customers were lured into the store by a micro-
scopic classified ad offering a bargain-priced, "slightly used"

instrument bearing a patrician label such as Steinway, Chickering, or Pleyel. Escorted past shiny, cheaper Colonial pianos, the prospective buyer at length encountered the bargain in a shadowy corner of the basement. The instrument — what could be seen of it — was in visibly wretched shape. The prospect, primed for the moment of truth like a Spanish fighting bull softened up by the banderilleros and picadors, now confronted the matador-salesman. He flourished his assurances like a cape. If the client responded with a small down payment, he would find a gleaming new Colonial piano awaiting him when he arrived home. "The prospect might wriggle away," Allen recalled years afterward, "but not before he had left his address with the salesman. With this, the potential owner was really in trouble. The instant the company knew where he lived, my Uncle Joe or the other outside salesman started calling at his house on the half-hour until, in self-defense, the subject weakened."

Upstairs, the Colonial Piano Company, with its unctuous salesmen and musically glib house virtuoso, Mr. Morse, who could perform anything from ragtime to Mozart, was a milieu of glowworm promises, fallible impressions, and half-truths; but downstairs three Swedish craftsmen and a tuner overhauled pianos salvaged from errant customers. Laboring in the timeless realm of honest craftsmanship, the Swedes took snuff, which, they claimed, prevented them from swallowing airborne particles of dust and felt. They indoctrinated John into the mysteries of how to dismantle the parts of a piano and how to chew tobacco. Years later, the comedy team of Clayton, Jackson, and Durante was performing a famous cabaret routine that culminated in the sledgehammer demolition of a grand piano, an act so wanton in its assault on high culture that the chaos reduced audiences to hysterics. Had Durante instead sent out for help, one of his fellow comedians possessed the technique of removing and reassembling the frames, the action, and the keyboard — a vocational skill of somewhat limited but impressive possibilities, like mastering the engineering of an igloo.

The snuff-chewing of the Swedes served as a rite of passage. Snuff nauseated John, however, so he began chewing a medicinal licorice cut like a plug of tobacco. To the others, he appeared to be an adept, and this, he thought, enhanced his status. Soon he put away childish licorice for the real thing, and tobacco chewing became a habit. He defended his preference for Tuck's nickel plug: "When you smoke cigars you're likely to burn yourself to death; with chewing tobacco the worst thing you can do is drown a midget." A letter written in the 1930s to the *Waterbury Republican* reminded the citizenry of Connecticut that he, Fred Allen, had done his personal best to keep Waterbury's brass foundries clanging out cuspidors. Tobacco chewing, nevertheless, is a proclivity associated with baseball dugouts, ward heelers, and the law west of Pecos, not with entertainers and their immaculate, smiling public faces. Even for devotees, the tactile appeal is offset by visual drawbacks, and if hard-bitten Broadway columnists took Fred Allen's chaw in stride, squeamish backstage interviewers found it daunting. The visitors sometimes found him working in shirtsleeves at a card table over which the pages of a script were scattered; he wore a felt hat, there was a bulge in his cheek, and from time to time he scored a bull's-eye in the bottom of a wastebasket. Those expecting a Rudy Vallee–like sanitized image of the performer found the unequivocal spectacle disconcerting. During a rehearsal for the 1928 musical *Polly,* Allen was enthusiastically chomping tobacco when summoned to sing a number; he couldn't get rid of the plug, and the stage director assigned the song to someone else. The off-putting visual impact of chewing tobacco occasioned compromises. Allen abstained in public and smoked cigars, or in his radio years favored a wad of gum. A coming-of-age in the basement of the piano store, Tuck's plug symbolized Johnny's adult status.

As he became a trusted Colonial employee (he still worked nights at the library), the management delegated him to go out and enact a charade meant to intimidate piano owners who had defaulted on their installment payments. Standing at the owner's door beside two husky piano movers — one had a coil of rope and the other a block and tackle — John threatened repossession unless the delinquent account was settled. The performance was pure bluff. If the customer proved defiant, "we gave the person one more chance, and withdrew with the coil of rope, the block and tackle, and as much dignity as we could muster under the circumstances. We then came back to the Colonial Piano Company empty-handed. This was not good, but it was, we knew, better than the alternative: to come back to the Colonial Piano Company with a Colonial piano."

The Simon Legree of the rented piano (days) and library stack boy (nights) should not indulge vagrant fancies, but he continued to hear in the back of his mind the voice of the young woman after the *High Jinks* performance. Was he crazy to go on working at the library? He practiced fresh material based on experience. "A month ago I couldn't sing a note, and now I'm moving pianos." His juggling improved, his jokes too, but he would never know if he ought to go on the stage unless he tried. So in the spring of 1912 he applied to Sam Cohen, the kingpin booker for New England Amateur Nights, and Cohen agreed to give him a spot on the April 1 amateur program at the Hub Theatre. (*The Prince and the Pauper* was opening on the other side of Boston that same night, as was the classical scholar Gilbert Murray, lecturing on "The Forms of Greek Drama.") The seventeen-year-old juggler took the subway to the theater. Half-paralyzed by stage fright, he contrived to execute his routines, recite his jokes, and bow off to a smattering of applause. The theater manager came to the dressing room at the close of the performance and remarked to Cohen that no one could hear the juggler's half-swallowed lines. "Bring him back some week and tell him to talk louder."

Amateur night was a bogus contest; no one received prize money and the envelope held above the heads of the performers was empty. Sam Cohen paid singers and dancers fifty cents; acrobats, jugglers, and novelty acts received a dollar. The impresario had more singers and dancers than he required, but could book a juggler everywhere in his empire of thirty-odd theaters.

To Aunt Lizzie's distress, the erstwhile stack boy and Sunday librarian of the children's room now spent his spare evenings in the Cohasset Town Hall, the Medford Armory, the

Winthrop Lodge of Elks, juggling top hats and cracking wheezes from Joe Miller's jestbook. "I left home to play a circuit of amateur nights around Providence, Rhode Island," he afterward told Broadway columnist Ed Sullivan. "Lived there in a furnished room for three weeks until I ran out of amateur nights." Benny Drohan, composer of "Southie Is My Home Town," hallowed tavern anthem of Irish–American Boston ("We buy pie-anners for one dollah down / God help the collectah when he comes around"), who performed a song-and-dance act with his wife, Marty, was a year younger than Johnny Sullivan but already a veteran. As a professional he appeared on numerous bills with Johnny and the amateurs, and recalled him as "a sort of pimply-faced kid, very thin, who always looked undernourished." George Libby, another vaudevillian, met him during the same period at Congress Hall, a small upstairs theater in South Boston, and was also struck by his boyish demeanor. "Johnny appeared one night with Sam Cohen's group, and had his hair shaved close to his head with just a bit of a pompadour brush in front."

Spectators at amateur nights liked to boo, heckle, shout, and feel superior to the novice performers. Entertaining the groundlings was akin to poking your head through a canvas as a human target for the baseball-throwing patrons of a carnival booth. Professional vaudeville required a modicum of talent, but amateur nights welcomed everyone and provided experience for a young self-taught juggler. Sam Cohen himself took part in the shows as master of ceremonies. Hearsay credited him with the invention of "The Hook," a wavering pole that emerged from the wings to yank unfortunate acts offstage; more certainly, he had formulated a potpourri of practical jokes, comedy signs, slapstick sounds, and squirting seltzer bottles with which to insult maladroit players. Despite his sadistic showmanship, gruff Sam was humane and affable, a former circus strong man who dealt honestly with his hirelings.

The performer willing to learn could take advantage of the opportunity to break in a routine, evaluate audiences, study other acts. Shameless amateurs directed crass appeals to the gallery, sang sentimental ballads on crutches, and, tattered as street beggars, blurred distinctions between the theater and a charity ward; but embryonic talent occasionally emerged and bathos yielded to inspiration. While Johnny fumbled through his act one evening, the stage manager stalked from the wings and asked, "Where did *you* learn to juggle?"

John drew a deep breath and said, "I took a correspondence course in baggage smashing."

The audience roared at his cheekiness. It was his first on-stage ad-lib, and from that moment he decided the act needed more topical gags.

The knockabout democracy of the amateur circuit appealed to him. Stowing his juggler's cardboard suitcases in the basement of the Colonial Piano Company, he looked forward to every evening's renewed challenge. In this period he also may have tried amateur boxing. Benny Rubin, afterward a headliner as a Yiddish-dialect comedian but then a clog dancer trying to augment his income with occasional boxing bouts, met him on the amateur circuit. "Johnny could box," Rubin recollected. "He won about every boxing match he went into. So I, too, went in, and achieved an unbroken record — thirty-eight fights, no wins."

With more booking dates than he could supervise personally, Sam deputized John to escort amateur units via streetcar to suburban theaters. His responsibilities were multiple. He informed the theater manager which of the acts were "lemons" — simply a service to prepare the management for possible turmoil — and filled Sam's role as master of ceremonies. (Sam supplied the frayed jokes.) In addition, John performed his juggling routine, ran the climactic contest, and handled financial transactions. After distributing trolley fare to each act, he then returned to Boston to hand over Sam's profits.

The summer of 1912, John spent his two-week vacation from the piano company with a Sam Cohen group booked into amusement parks and resorts across northern New England. His era of apprenticeship had begun; over the next two years, Johnny would perform in virtually every small-time theater from Nova Scotia to Connecticut. Touring was a festive experience for a boy who had never been away from home, a panorama of small-town boardinghouses, fickle audiences, and picaresque encounters with all sorts of players, from fiercely competitive zealots to talentless amiable ciphers. The vogue for amateur nights was fading and Sam was destined to suffer reverses, but before the vogue disappeared, John met a journeyman vaudeville juggler named Harry LaToy. They perched on the counter stools of the Royal Lunch on Hanover Street, where a meal of baked beans, bread, pie, and coffee cost ten cents, while LaToy recited the saga of his vaudeville triumphs. The triumphs were imaginary; he was what the bookers called a "coast defender," a Boston-based act forever fated to roam New England as though in expiation of an ancestral curse. LaToy, who had changed his name from Shepard in order to be mistaken for Paul LaCroix, a big-time juggler, performed a trite Harrigan-like tramp-juggler routine. John was impressed, though he noticed that his mentor never picked up a check.

The National Theatre, a B. F. Keith house in Boston's South End, decided that fall to inaugurate a program of "Professional Talent New to Boston." To underscore the professionalism, the management advertised the event as "Not an Amateur Night"; outstanding performers would get dates on the Keith circuit. Since LaToy was known under his own name in Boston, he agreed for five dollars to appear on the tryout bill under a pseudonym, "Paul Huckle, European Entertainer." A day or so thereafter, making the rounds of the smaller booking offices, he unexpectedly received an offer of three weeks' work. If the small bookers knew of his connection with the tryout show, they would cancel his engagement. He hit upon a solution: Sullivan would appear as Paul Huckle and they would split the five dollars practically fifty-fifty, three dollars earmarked for LaToy. The opportunity to make a professional debut looked tempting, and Johnny accepted.

Just before eight, Friday evening, October 9, John identified himself as Paul Huckle at the National Theatre's stage door and lugged his cardboard suitcases to his first separate dressing room. Like the amateur shows, the five tryout acts would succeed the regular program. The manager scheduled him to follow Long Tack Sam, a Chinese novelty acrobatic team, and while he waited, he rehearsed his tricks and monologue.

Through the walls drifted the sound of the distant orchestra —
amateurs usually had to settle for a pickup band or a piano —
and the laughter and applause of the crowd. Six months of
amateur nights had conditioned John to derision, and he hoped
this house was more indulgent. On his entrance, however, he
was unprepared for the audience's alarming outburst of cor-
diality. Mockery fueled amateur-night popularity, but tryout
audiences sought to encourage talent. The same jokes that in-
cited whistling, jibes, and groans from Sam Cohen's regulars
were now hilarious knockouts. Mercifully, John did not realize the audience regarded his strident jokes and butterfingered
juggling a travesty of a conventional juggling act. He milked
the applause, took too many bows, collected the five dollars,
and divided the proceeds with LaToy at the Royal Lunch. LaToy
listened indifferently to the account of his excited partner.

The next morning, though, LaToy's insouciance faded.
Checking the Keith office, he found the bookers agog over
Paul Huckle's performance. Where did he come from? They
wanted to sign him for the New England territory. LaToy
instantly mustered his not inconsiderable improvisatory gifts.
Paul Huckle, he announced, was a big-time juggler from the
Far West, and he had agreed to appear on the National's bill
as a personal favor to his friend, Harry LaToy. Paul was booked
solid out west; he probably wouldn't be interested in playing
Boston for peanuts. Actually, his name wasn't Paul Huckle —
Into LaToy's mind flashed an image of the Saint James Hotel,
a vaudevillian's seedy rendezvous in Bowdoin Square. The name
was St. James, he said, Fred St. James.

John Florence Sullivan used five stage names during his
vaudeville career: the one-night Paul Huckle billing, Fred St.
James, Freddy (sometimes rendered as Freddie) James, Fred
Allen, and Benjamin Franklin. All were dictated by professional necessity, and this was by no means unusual. George
Burns, for example, often changed his name because of bookers' threats of blacklisting or cancellation. Born Nathan Birn-
baum, he acquired the neighborhood designation of George
Burns since his family lived close to the Burns Brothers coal
yards, and he would stuff his pockets with coal from the wagon.
When he broke into vaudeville, he employed a diversity of

pseudonyms. "The booker," he said, "would never give me another job if he knew who I was." Once he met a man named Eddie Delight, who had just had two thousand business cards printed announcing, "Eddie Delight, in Vaudeville, 1922." Eddie's vaudeville career ended before he exhausted the supply of cards; Burns inherited the cards and promptly changed his name to Eddie Delight. After the cards ran out he was Billy Pierce, Captain Betts, Jed Jackson, Jimmy Malone, Williams of Brown and Williams (they tap-danced on roller skates), Burns of Burns and Jose, Glide of Goldie, Fields, and Glide (he named himself after one of his favorite dance steps), and, to compound confusion, in an act called Burns and Links, he was Links. It is simpler to refer to John Sullivan as Fred Allen from this point, although he performed as Freddy James for another five years.

The bookers begged LaToy to find Fred St. James; he would be a sensation on the Keith circuit. LaToy left, promising to produce the phenomenon by Monday. Around noon, on lunch break at the Colonial Piano Company (it was Saturday, but the six-day week prevailed), Fred stepped outside and almost collided with LaToy, who had been lurking outside the entrance. The older juggler explained the situation. He was interested in disentangling himself from his straitjacket of lies, but those lies, incredibly, had yielded a contract: Fred St. James could open at the Scenic Temple in East Boston a week from Monday.

Before meeting the bookers, he would need Fred St. James lobby photographs. Buoyed by LaToy's enthusiasm, Fred accompanied him to White's photographic studio. The lobby photographs looked thoroughly professional — so persuasive, in fact, that LaToy pinched a stack for himself. The following year, when Fred arrived in Halifax, Nova Scotia, to tour the Ackers circuit, he was threatened with cancellation because LaToy, having preceded him on the circuit a few weeks earlier, had used Fred St. James's pictures. Mrs. Ackers, the owner of the theaters, said she couldn't send out the photos again; people from Sydney Mines to Shag Harbour would assume they were getting a repeat performance. She had no choice but to cancel the act. Then, taking pity on the victim of a swindle, she relented and lent him photographs of another juggler so that Fred could complete his tour.

LaToy for the next forty years would remain true to type, cadging handouts while picking his benefactor's pocket. "Dear Friend Johnnie," his entreaties always began, and though disillusionment about LaToy had long since overtaken Friend Johnny, the epistolary pleas for money were never denied. Now, a date at the Scenic Temple and a professional future ahead of him, he decided to resign from the piano company and the library; the contract's compelling figure, thirty dollars a week, justified the risk. (For now-obscure bureaucratic reasons, his name lingered on the library's payroll until July 2, 1914.) Vaudeville opened before him, a broad stretch of opportunity so luminous, seductive, and strange he never sensed it gliding past, gathering speed, dissolving.

VAUDEVILLE

Milton, I guess my secret ambition is to go back to vaudeville again.

> — to Milton Berle, on the radio
> program *My Secret Ambition*

3 | In the Footsteps of Baby Alice

Benjamin Franklin Keith's first show starred Baby Alice. Billed as a midget, Baby Alice was a monkey dressed in female clothing. Keith shaved the simian face, trained the creature to walk in high-heeled shoes, and charged Bostonians a dime to gape at the spectacle. The monkey tottering across an improvised stage in a vacant store became Keith's first entrepreneurial success. A few years later, in 1894 — six weeks before the birth of John Florence Sullivan — he was able to unveil, next door to the site where he had started, a dream pavilion of vaudeville, his first B. F. Keith's Theatre, which appropriated the incandescence, the magic fire, of grand opera.

A native of Hillsborough, New Hampshire, Keith had drifted into the impresario's trade through a medley of jobs, including purser aboard a steamer, carnival tout, and candy butcher of a circus for which his future partner, E. F. Albee, handled legal problems. Back on the farm, Keith's New Hampshire relatives received letter after letter from their prodigal, each message outlining a new visionary scheme: all he needed was seed money, the idea would be a sensation. Keith (Frank to his family) seemed rootless, a futile figure duped by the extravagance of his pitchman's spiel.

As he told his cousin at a dinner party years afterward, he was between circuses and down to his last five cents when he reached Boston in May 1883.

"He slept on Boston Common on a bench," reported the cousin, Mrs. A. E. Little. "The next morning he went to the Adams House, found a razor on a washroom shelf, and cleaned up. Then he took two of the five cents and put a stamp on a letter. The hotel gave the stationery free. The letter went to my father-in-law Lyman Gerould, who was an officer in the gas company in Manchester, New Hampshire. It was the usual request for a loan."

How Keith survived on his remaining three cents was not explained by Mrs. Little; even by the standards of the 1880s, the sum looks excessively frugal. In any event, Gerould met Keith at the Adams House, Frank promised liberal interest, and continued, "Listen, there's a vacant store right here underneath us. If I can get $300 I'll rent it and put in Baby Alice. She'll certainly draw a crowd and I'll make good." Gerould, future confidential secretary to William Randolph Hearst, agreed. "Lyman had been ready to risk $500, anyhow."

At first Keith and another partner, George H. Bacheller, ran the store as a dime museum divided into two parts: a ground-floor hall malodorous with animal cages, and the upstairs theater, where the audience occupied 123 straight-backed kitchen chairs. "Keith himself introduced the acts and Mrs. Keith kept it clean," declares the only eyewitness account. The word *museum* signified uplift, a justification for miscellaneous clutter, whereas *theater,* still dogged by its racy reputation, meant sin. Keith, a seasoned midway grifter, had a carnie's esteem for respectability and initially enhanced Baby Alice's act by installing a blood-testing mechanism. (As a barker glorifying freak shows during his midway days, he had extolled the wonders of blood-testing machines.) Keith had other and more original notions, however, foremost among them the revolutionary idea of continuous performance.

The inspiration for the "continuous" struck him around 1885. He may not have been the pioneer; other dime museum operators also claim the distinction, but he was undeniably the most successful. "Come when you please," he advertised in the Boston papers; "stay as long as you like." Sam K. Hodgdon, his stage manager and lecturer, considered him daft. Keith envisioned a successive twelve-hour show without reserved seats; the headliners would appear twice and the other acts three times. Hodgdon, who opened the show with a lecture titled "The Arctic Moon," using relics from the Greeley Relief Expedition, protested that people who had heard the lecture would walk out on him. "I hope they do," Keith replied. They walked out, but others flowed in, and the theater prospered. Tedious acts, known as "chasers," came to occupy the tail end of the bill and cleared the house of all but the most resolute customers.

When Bacheller decided to collect his profits and depart, Keith summoned Albee. They had many traits in common, even to sharing the same middle name: eleven years younger than Keith, Edward Franklin Albee, from Machias, Maine, had the same farm-bred foxiness, the same background in the florid circus life. An "outside ticket" or "sixty-cent man," his specialty was the selling of tickets in excess of established prices to people tired of waiting in line. Infinitely more hardheaded and aggressive than Keith, who remained throughout his life a combination of clodhopper and con artist, Albee preached and practiced a doctrine of pragmatic business acumen. He looked over the situation, removed the animal cages, persuaded Keith to offer a pirated (and profitable) version of Gilbert and Sullivan's *Mikado,* and soon became the dominant partner.

Since Albee preferred a backstage role, accounts differ about his contributions to vaudeville. The policy of refined entertainment in patrician surroundings is sometimes attributed to him, sometimes to Keith's meekly following the directives of his pious Catholic wife. According to vaudeville chronicler Joe Laurie, Jr., Albee wanted to build a palatial theater, and Keith, always close-pursed, objected, so Albee borrowed the money from the Catholic diocese of Boston, assuring church officials of his penchant for respectable family entertainment. Both Keith and Albee as personalities remain slightly enigmatic, the former never losing the bumpkin streak in his unfathomable character, the latter cast in the mold of the classic robber baron but choosing to operate from the shadows. As showmen they were late-nineteenth-century heirs of P. T. Barnum; and Albee, for all his rapacity, was to prove in time no match for the sharklike twentieth-century business maneuvers of Joseph P. Kennedy.

It was Keith, at any rate, who implemented the doctrine of gentility, posted signs backstage ("Don't say 'slob' or 'son-of-a-gun' or 'hully gee' on this stage unless you want to be cancelled preemptorily"), and personally stood up in the gallery at the opening of his first Philadelphia house and lectured customers on appropriate behavior in a theater. No smoking, spitting, or rowdyism would be tolerated — and Keith backed up his words with a pair of strategically placed bouncers. In a study of male-female comedy teams, Shirley Staples points out that Keith's "deference to upper-middle-class canons of taste was but one expression of a broader social phenomenon." The arbiters of late-nineteenth-century America's Victorian high culture, founders of imposing art galleries, libraries, and symphony orchestras, solicited the support of popular-culture pacesetters, potential torchbearers of a high-minded message to the masses. Patrons from diverse ethnic and social backgrounds recognized and endorsed the attitudes illustrated by the vaudeville house. Keith's accent on the rules of etiquette reflected the upward mobility of his city audience.

Of course, American vaudeville existed long before Keith and Albee materialized as its Prince Charmings. A by-product of the honky-tonks, dives, free-and-easies, beer gardens, and concert saloons of the pre–Civil War era, variety shows gradually sprouted from a low-life mulch of drinking, gambling, and prostitution and blossomed into a postwar aspect of leisure. Competing semirustic forms, the minstrel show and the riverboat, lost relevance; the circus, constantly on the road, never prospered in a metropolitan setting, and the growing sophistication of audiences foretold the demise of the dime museum.

Antonio (Tony) Pastor, antedating Keith in promoting wholesome entertainment, separated variety from the stag-night atmosphere of the saloons. His "beautiful Temple of Amusement," Tony Pastor's Opera House in New York, was planned as "the Great Family Resort of the City." To attract women, he set Fridays apart as Ladies' Night, and when such high-mindedness didn't abolish the stigma of the concert-saloon past, he devised giveaways: sewing machines, silk dresses, bonnets. Eventually, he wore down prejudice, but the struggle was lengthy. The genial and generous Pastor, composer of more than a thousand songs based on current events — he could take any newspaper headline, from a homicide to a hurricane, and turn it into a ballad — was impresario, creator, and performer, a man personifying the ornate spirit of his era. Appearing onstage to sing from his enormous repertoire, he sported a ringmaster's boots, frock coat, and top hat. Although Pastor anticipated vaudeville, a variegated entertainment in opulent theatrical settings, his performing style represented a throwback to variety in the honky-tonks. An innovator in making the saloon respectable, he offered old-fashioned turns, the legacy of earlier decades: banjo and bones solos, blackface acts, comic and sentimental ballads, terpsichorean interludes, acrobatics, farcical playlets. Indeed, he objected to the very word *vaudeville,* which, he maintained, merely stood for clean variety.

Neither the acts nor the audiences of vaudeville turned genteel overnight. Racial and dialect routines (Dutch and Irish to begin with, then other stereotypes) were earsplitting and crude, duplicating the urban frictions of immigrant struggle. The success of *The Black Crook,* the 1866 musical spectacle featuring skimpily clad female dancers; the faddish Parisian cancan that animated the 1870s; the double entendre songs and jokes; the physical comedy of rough-and-tumble clowns — all indicate the primitive frontier flavor of the pre-Keith era. Nevertheless, by the 1890s the boors were banished to the balcony, and a different type of patron, prevailingly lower-middle-class but as sensitive to vulgarity as Keith himself, supported vaudeville. For such patrons and their families, Keith (or Albee, as the case may be) constructed Keith's New Boston Theatre, designed by the New York architect J. B. McElfatrick, whose remodeling of the Metropolitan Opera House had been widely praised.

The theater, a landmark of American playhouse architecture and prototype of the vaudeville and movie palaces that succeeded it, dazzled the public. Albee and Keith had lavished the

then-astonishing sum of $600,000 on the sumptuous structure.
At the opening, Easter Monday, 1894, the press regilded
workaday adjectives to describe the glories of the Italian-
marble grand staircase, the mirrored lobby, the ivory-and-gold
cupids bearing crescent lamps, the magisterial proscenium, the
nymph-twined dome, the costly oil paintings, the stained glass,
the bric-a-brac, the wainscoting, the statuary, the bronze fixtures, and the polychromatic architectural details of an interior
that proclaimed itself an enchanted space preserved from the
humdrum world outside. Even so, the thirty-six hundred guests,
invited to wander through the house from eleven in the morning to almost eleven at night, found themselves less awed by
these features, splendid though they were, than by the elegance of the basement engine room. A marble staircase descended from the main entrance, and you passed along a cream-
colored corridor toward a marble switchboard covering a
complete wall. The switchboard circuitry suggested industrial
dynamism, as did the generators inside the boiler room. Keith's
was the first theater in the city to employ electric lighting and
it made an extravaganza of it. From a gallery with a nickel-
plated railing, visitors watched firemen at work. Coal spilled
down a burnished brass tube to a mechanical stoker. The firemen wore clean, white uniforms and used silver shovels that
twinkled above the crowning touch, a red brussels carpet val-
ued at eighty-nine dollars. Reporters marveled at the carpet —
"in an ordinary establishment covered by grime and soot,"
but pristine at the New Boston Theatre — and their stories
repeated its price like an incantation.

The red-carpeted engine room demonstrated Keith and
Albee's grasp of the medium. "When the managers of vaudeville stumbled onto the concept of the 'continuous show,' they
created a theatrical counterpart of the powerful rhythm of
modern city life," historian Gunther Barth has observed. Keith
and Albee and their competitors regulated entertainment as they
would a turbine; vaudeville circuits spread across the country,
generated a steady flow of performers, and established the
booking agent as the engineer of the performer's destiny. Every
Wednesday in later years, conferences were held at the Palace
Theatre at which Keith managers and bookers determined the

fate of performers. Douglas Gilbert's *American Vaudeville* describes such a meeting:

> From a pile of memoranda one would draw a slip and call out the name written thereon — "Joe Blotz." "No interest," someone would answer. Two words, and the poor chap was ruined for Keith time. Sometimes the response would be — "pick up." This meant that, if the actor's agent's sales talk was plausible, maybe they would give him a chance. The great words were "give him a route." This meant from forty to eighty weeks straight time. And the performer was made.

The idioms of vaudeville actors attested to the importance of industrial concepts in their lives: they played the Pantages, or Pan "time," the Poli "circuit," the "two-a-day." Even their billings, separated by the ubiquitous ampersand, resembled the logos emblazoned on freight cars. Theatrical illusion was contingent upon a throbbing dynamo of industrial energy. Before vaudeville, aspiring actors went on the stage; now they went into show business.

But human beings, not to mention vaudevillians, thwart industrial regimentation. The autocrats of vaudeville — has there ever been a more piratical-sounding combination than Klaw and Erlanger? — tried with varying success to make them act like automata. Albee founded the East's United Booking Office and broke performers' strikes; John J. Murdock developed the Western Vaudeville Managers Association; Marcus Loew fought William Fox for control of the eastern small time; Alexander Pantages battled Sullivan and Considine; William Morris, Martin Beck, Percy Williams, and F. F. Proctor, an old-time foot juggler, took on the behemoth Keith-Albee organization. Only Morris proved resilient enough to survive. The brassy candor of *Variety,* the show business weekly founded by Sime Silverman in 1905, provoked Albee's wrath, and for fifteen months he barred from the Keith circuit any actor who advertised in the publication (the initial victims were Burr and Hope, a pair of English small-timers who took out a twenty-dollar ad), or who was seen reading it or was caught with a back-pocket copy. The overlords used the blacklist as a weapon in an industry where they controlled labor as well as supply and demand; meanwhile, out front, Bert Williams played his captivating pantomime poker game and Eva Tanguay sang, "It's all been done before but not the way I do it."

Lacking the traditions of the legitimate stage, plebeian vaudeville inspired critical condescension. A few prominent intellectuals endorsed it. President Woodrow Wilson was a fan; so was William Dean Howells, who attended shows twice a week. The painter Marsden Hartley wrote eloquently, "Why, for instance, should a fine act like the Four Danubes and others of their quality be tagged onto the end of a bill, at which time the unmannerly public decides to go home or hurry to some roof or other, or dining place?" Better than any other medium, vaudeville expressed the immediacy of change in a changing society. Gifted performers seized the passing moment, shaped fashion, and sketched symbolic roles, and yet vaudeville's panorama of possibilities unfolded within a form as inflexible as the length of a sonnet: the eight- or nine-act program.

Nonverbal acts opened and closed a bill, allowing latecomers to find seats and jackrabbits to beat the crowd to the exits. An overture incorporating the popular songs of the day introduced a "dumb act" — acrobats or novelty hoop-rollers, magicians, animal routines, wire-walkers, trick cyclists. Waltzing on roller skates, Earl Reynolds and Nellie Donegan, who initiated a 1909 craze for skating pavilions, were the ideal "dumb" act, because they could also close the show with a dazzling assortment of costumery and dance steps.

A male-female song-and-dance team or a singer settled down the audience and lent contrast to the preceding mute displays of skill. The second spot took place in front of the curtain, or "in one," while the backstage scenery was prepared for the number-three turn. The initial act always opened full stage, and the rhythm between full stage and "in one" afforded some of the subtler examples of the alterations of pace. Coming on second was a formidable task — the audience still showed restive symptoms — and many performers avoided "deucing." Fred Astaire dubbed it "the lousy number-two spot on the bill," and in general black performers worked in the number-two spot unless they had a big-time following like that of Buck and Bubbles. Yet for scores of big-time song-and-dance teams the second position also allowed them freedom to try out their act, polish their repartee, and devise more elaborate effects.

The number-three billing, "the sketch position," was the canonical part of the program. Here a one-act play or a full-stage revue built up to an effective curtain and sought to astonish the audience through clever staging, dialogue, or a "flash" (the illusion of grandeur). Sketches, comic and otherwise, entered a heyday at the century's turn when vaudeville audiences relished entertainments borrowed from the legitimate stage. Victor Moore and his wife, Emma Littlefield, for example, toured in *Change Your Act, or Back to the Woods* from 1903 through the late twenties, and similar sketch duos pursued their outmoded careers until the close of the vaudeville period. Dramatic sketches featured such headliners as Ethel Barrymore in James M. Barrie's *The Twelve Pound Look,* and Nazimova in *War Brides,* the bane of every comedy act that followed this patriotic tearjerker. By the midteens, "flash acts" tended toward specialty routines, singing and dancing, and girls.

The fourth and fifth acts had to be solid enough to guarantee that the audience would talk about them during the intermission. Since the fourth position was "in one," it was frequently a popular musical turn not deserving the cheerless number-two slot. "Song-and-piano teams" provided a solution; Dolly Connolly, with her husband, songwriter Percy Wenrich, at the keyboard, did a routine in which she sang five numbers with a costume change for each, and during the changes he riffled through medleys of his infectious tunes, "Put On Your Old Gray Bonnet," "Moonlight Bay," "When You Wore a Tulip," which everyone knew from sheet-music scores. If number four was musical, closing the first half with a comedy headliner would leave the audience in a buoyant frame of mind, although reversing the situation was common, a name performer and then a jazz band or imposing dance number.

Intermission generated the problem of an "in one" sixth act. How does the act sustain momentum without overshadowing the acts to follow? Once again, seating the audience rendered performance difficult; six was not a spot for subtlety or smart banter. A juggler sometimes appeared, or sophisticated dancers, or a romantic duo on the order of George Whiting and Sadie Burt. They took a dreamier approach than the ragtime-oriented Connolly and Wenrich. The composer of "Strolling through the Park One Day" and (with collaborator Walter Donaldson) "My Blue Heaven," Whiting had a forgettable voice but an extraordinary empathy with song lyrics. With Sadie Burt he often appeared in the coveted next-to-closing role — a rare distinction for a singing team. The alchemy of a vaudeville program permitted incidental variations on the basic recipe.

A big-name full-stage sketch or musical specialty reached another visual plateau preparatory to the appearance, anticipated by the audience, of the comic headliner. Singular or plural, the comic routines in the eighth position, "next to shut," completed the orchestration of the bill amid the light-footed atmosphere of laughter and general euphoria. Then it was "shut," the ninth and foreordained act: Fink's Mules ("Vaudeville's Equine Joy Fest," they once shared the same bill with the "Jersey Lily," Lily Langtry); Gillette's Baboons and Monkeys, who were jockeys in their "Day at the Races"; White, Black and Useless, another mule act, about the shoeing of Useless; Rhinelander's Pigs, where the trainer wore a butcher's apron and whetted a chopper whenever the pigs drilled in less than perfect formation; Beautiful Jim Key, the educated horse who played the organ in the Sousa road show; or, if the audience was lucky, the return of Reynolds and Donegan. An eight-act bill could be trimmed anywhere, but generally observed the same conventions.

Vaudeville theaters, like vaudeville itself, exemplified the big time, small time, and small-small time. The two-a-day theaters meant neat dressing rooms, sanitation, a full orchestra; but the five- and six-a-day piano-and-drummer houses had primitive facilities at best. Allen noticed that the smaller the theater, the less consideration management showed the actor. Had it been possible to crop expenses further, piano and drum would have given way to a comb-and-tissue-paper or kazoo accompaniment. There were theaters without plumbing, theaters rancid from neglect, theaters with cellar and boiler-room

dressing cubicles; on a higher level, the movie houses present-
ing vaudeville could be intimate or cavernous, seating audiences of three thousand or more, and playing these theaters
required exemplary vocal projection. Legitimate theater stars
had more prestige than vaudevillians — "legit" was deemed
high art, "vaude" folk expression — but earned lower salaries.
If stage performers often dropped in and out of big-time
vaudeville, the small-timer seldom attained Broadway. While
the small-time performer hammered on the castle gate of the
big-time, waiting for the drawbridge to lower, he or she dreamt
of playing the Palace, where dressing rooms One and Two on
the first floor were repainted twenty or thirty times a season.

Fred Allen embarked on his career during vaudeville's waning years. He had no reason to suspect the medium would not
endure. Silent movies, after all, hadn't replaced live performance; the silent film substantially enhanced the contrast between the screen's somnambulist shadows and vaudeville's vital exuberance. At once, though, he noticed the vaudevillian's
total self-absorption. Regardless of their billing, small-timers
gravitated toward each other, even spending their off-season
summers (theaters then lacked air-conditioning) in colonies
where the incessant refrain was vaudeville, vaudeville, vaudeville. The narrowness of the performer's outlook is suggested
by an anecdote of which Allen was fond: "A vaudeville actor's
wife had died and he ranted and cried around Campbell's as
the body reposed there before the burial. After the funeral, a
friend said, 'I saw you at Campbell's. You were wonderful.'
The actor said, 'You should have caught me at the grave.' "

The small-time actor's egotism was born of insecurity. "All
the human race demands of its members is that they be born,"
Allen declared. "That is all vaudeville demanded. You just had
to be born." Aside from the cultivation of skills and attributes
often as bizarre as the bound feet of Chinese concubines, they
had no other stock in trade; the talents of a contortionist may
be useful to a burglar or second-story man, but otherwise must
be enjoyed for art's sake. Performers on the road congregated
in the same dowdy boardinghouses and hotels. Boston's were
situated around the city's tenderloin, Scollay Square, a hiving
crossroads of theaters, nickelodeons, restaurants, pushcart

hawkers, and hotels. The Old Howard, a theater of graceful Federalist design originally called the Howard Athenaeum, staged clean and lively burlesque shows patronized principally by sailors from nearby Charlestown Navy Yard. The sailors ogled young women in tights just as their descendants (once burlesque standards degenerated) ogled young women without the tights. The Rexford Hotel at the end of Howard Street, a massive building with bars on the windows like a jail, was a raffish hostelry that hovered between the institutional (sheets, pillowcases, and blankets were stenciled "Property of the Rexford" in bold, black lettering) and the Dionysiac. Comedians, animal acts, singers, musicians, and chorus girls rehearsed in perpetual motion throughout the night, and at 3:00 A.M. — so it was said — a bell rang and everybody had to go back to his room. In hot weather thirsty actors cooled themselves on the roof and "rushed the can." Each sunbather tossed a dime into the can, which was lowered by a string to an accomplice on the street. He filled the can and took a long gulp, his commission, before sending the beer to the roof.

Although the small-timer was self-centered, he was also resourceful, skilled in the techniques of survival. Backstage retained a domestic air; a young bachelor like Allen shared the same Pullman with husbands, wives, and their families, and along with them was awakened by a squalling infant in the middle of the night or a fretful troupe of midgets in an upper berth. A sepia-hued album snapshot of Fred Allen amid a costumed group of small-time players is captioned "Dallas." Beside him, with an arm flung over Allen's shoulder, is a middle-aged man with a puckish expression, white top hat, knee breeches, vest, and frock coat. Nothing in the picture suggests late-twentieth-century Dallas — no oil wells, no skyscrapers, no downtown hubbub. The snapshot reveals only a low building and space and a frisky cluster of vaudevillians on alien ground. They don't appear flustered or out of place, however, for wherever they travel they bring their own environment with them, the one-night stands, split weeks, long-sleeper jumps, hard knocks, and fulfillment of vaudeville. Nomads, they would look much the same in Hyderabad or Hoboken.

Marian Spitzer, chronicler of the Palace Theatre, has made an astute distinction between the legitimate actor's sensibility and the vaudevillian's. The legitimate actor is always performing a role, but the role of the vaudevillian is himself.

He is always sure that he is the best acrobat or the best hoofer or the best mammy singer in the business. If some other fellow is getting along better than he is it's not because the other fellow's work is better, but because the other fellow has a pull with the booking office. . . . This attitude, in spite of its externals, cannot be classified as conceit in its ordinarily accepted meaning. In "The Song and Dance Man," that wistful and moving piece of theatrical hokum by and with George M. Cohan, the essential vaudevillian stands perfectly revealed. He explains the whole thing in a paragraph. It is not exactly conceit, he says, that makes every song and dance man, no matter how obscure, feel sure within himself that he is the best song and dance man in the whole world. It's just his song and dance man's heart. If he didn't feel that way he couldn't be a song and dance man.

Alfred Lunt, whose theatrical debut occurred in vaudeville on the same bill with Lily Langtry and Fink's Mules, was fascinated by this quality, and he used to stand in the wings at every performance watching the other acts. An inexperienced twenty-one years old, but the romantic leading man in a sketch in which he played opposite a woman of sixty-three, Lunt responded to the sincerity of vaudevillians and their determination to perfect their routines. The condition of the comedian's material was crucial; the twelve or fifteen minutes of a performer's act constituted his career. A good act meant "a good route" on the circuit, playing big-time houses featuring two performances a day.

Opening in three a day at the Scenic Temple, Allen thought of himself as a juggler with a monologue to go along with the tricks. The act could be improved, but what act couldn't? If he persisted, he would learn vaudeville's ins and outs. Vaudeville was many things. It was Hamm's Scollay Square Peri-

odical Store, where on spring and summer evenings the actors
congregated beneath a streetlight, the singers falling into close
barbershop harmony and the dancers holding informal com-
petitions. It was jargon such as "Fally Markus," meaning a
small-time booker who paid low salaries (actors used "Fally
Markus" dates to test new material), or "civilian" (anyone not
in show business), all the phrases peppering brash verbal exchanges and stamping vaudevillians as a clan apart. It was the
mind reader who advertised the mental vibrations of his act by
wearing a wired helmet — short-circuited by stagehands in
Detroit; the sketch actress who inveigled customers into the
theater by playing trombone solos in the lobby (on the bill she
portrayed Camille); the Cleburne, Texas, theater with hitching
posts out front, managed by a female impersonator. Vaudeville was the great black monologist Charlie Case, who in beer
halls and dives had perfected an act consisting entirely of compelling talk, yet was so nervous that he couldn't work unless
he had a piece of rag or twine to twiddle in his hands. It was
Hindu Sam, the fire-eater; Major Doyle, the baton-twirling
midget; and Diamond Doll Falardeau and her glittering smile
(the diamonds inlaid in her front teeth prompted Allen to dub
her "a flash in the pan"). It was Fred and Adele Astaire, the
Marx Brothers, and Will Rogers. "If you care for the irides-
cence of the moment you will trust vaudeville as you are not
able to trust any other sort of a performance," Marsden Hartley
asserted. Sam K. Hodgdon, the critic of Keith's idea of continuous performance, fell under the spell of vaudeville so absolutely that in time he became the only person to have a funeral
service in the Palace Theatre.

Fred St. James's debut at the Scenic Temple, however, was
foundering. During the painful silences with which his jokes
were greeted it was borne in on him that when a juggler is
billed, audiences expect prodigies of juggling. Three times a
day he realized that he was only — and probably would never
be more than — a coast defender.

The next week, booked into the Superb Theatre in Roxbury, he wore a red fright wig and clown makeup. A veteran
performer on the Scenic Temple bill had sold him the costume, guaranteeing hilarious results. The outcome was a fi-

asco. At the opening matinee, the theater's manager recognized the former amateur behind the clownish greasepaint and fired him instantly. The Superb Theatre offered professional entertainment; amateurs need not apply. The Keith office received a manager's report that meant cancellation of the contract, the thirty-dollar salary, the future.

Allen said good-bye to Paul Huckle, erstwhile phenomenon from the Pacific slopes, crumpled up the red wig of Fred St. James, packed his juggling equipment, and walked home with his cardboard suitcases to Dorchester's Grafton Street.

4 | World's Worst Juggler

I meant to be the world's greatest juggler and went into training, and had got past balancing a lighted candle on my eyelashes when I met Cinquevalli, and he bought me lunch. I hadn't seen "Cinq's" act, so after lunch he took me to see him practice. He did things with a cannon ball, feather and spring-dray that made me feel like a man in a hospital. The same afternoon I met W. C. Fields and went with him to a matinee. He juggled two bicycle tires, a lighted lamp and four penny stamps simultaneously. I got cold feet on the "best" juggler business and swore over a whisky cocktail to become the "worst."

The content of the interview was imaginary, of course, though it made quotable copy, but Fred Allen's explanation of how he evolved from juggling to comedy is substantially accurate. Jugglers rated each other by the number of balls they kept in the air, and he sensed his inadequacy:

If a juggler had spent as many hours practicing a musical instrument as he had to spend mastering his tricks, he would have been a concert artist. When I saw the really great jugglers — Cinquevalli, Rastalli, Kara, Chinko, Sylvester Schaffer and others — I was discouraged. I could juggle four balls; Frank LeDent juggled eleven. I handled silk hats clumsily; Paul LaCroix featured his dancing hats. There was no comparison at all.

No comparison, and no stage work, either. Having burned his bridges at the library and the piano company, Allen consulted the Help Wanted ads and landed a job as an eight-dollar-a-week stock boy with Carter, Rice, a wholesale paper distributor. His heart was elsewhere. During his lunch hours he walked to Scollay Square hoping to see actors, and outside Hamm's or on Howard Street loitered near the fringes of the crowd simply to hear vaudevillians talk. While the former Fred St. James languished at Carter, Rice, surrounded by paper and cardboard samples, he paid less attention to cutting rooms and case prices than to the phantasmal twinkle of vaudeville marquees. Then, out of the blue, Harry LaToy phoned from a theater in suburban Waltham; he had come down with rheumatism and needed a substitute. Although it was the customary LaToy arrangement — if Johnny would do the last two shows, LaToy would get paid for three days — Fred saw it as a chance to redeem himself after the Superb Theatre disaster.

The jokes seemed to go over well; so well, in fact, that he was encouraged to start making the rounds of the bookers again. They rebuffed him, but he kept returning, and at length received a fraternal-lodge date here, a small theater there. Once he had pieced together two weeks, he resigned from the Carter, Rice stockroom. Afterward, however, his vaudeville bookings were infrequent. Relying on such lines as "A young widow is like an eclipse; she doesn't stay long in black," or "How did that sausage last night agree with you? I think it hurt my liverwurst," he knew he could not long contribute toward the expenses of Aunt Lizzie's household.

During 1913 Allen alternated humdrum jobs — clerking in the basement of Raymond's department store, packing hardware for a Federal Street firm — with random dates in clubs and theaters. He rehearsed his act in the loft of the hardware company at noon while the other employees fetched their lunch buckets, gathered round, and applauded. The most significant event of that year for Allen, though, was seeing the English juggler named Griff.

The act, at the Academy of Music, which later became the
Orpheum Theater, was billed as "a mono-dramo-singo-danco-
ventrilo-juggo-logue." The middle-aged but manually adept
Griff could summon up a six-ball "shower," but his act was
unlike any other juggler's — it was really a monologue full of
amusing digressions. He parodied a tightrope walker; imitated
a ventriloquist (someone else sang offstage while he held the
dummy on his knee and drank a glass of water); performed a
dramatic sketch in which he assumed every role; and essayed
several juggling tricks in which he missed connections but explained that he had done the tricks the night before and the
audience should have been watching then.

Allen carefully analyzed Griff's routines, impressed by the
deceptive ease with which he achieved his effects. Burlesque
juggling could compensate for fumbled top hats. Griff, poking
fun at the mechanisms of the ventriloquist, was a star because
of his comment and comedy, not because of his juggling. Excited by this revelation, Allen began to study comedians even
more closely and copy more jokes and situations in his notebook. His transition from juggler to comedian did not occur
all at once: juggling would remain important in Allen's act
until 1917, but Griff had made a lasting impression.

One evening, homeward-bound on the elevated train, Allen
bumped into a theater owner who had seen him as an amateur,
and who offered him three days' work. There must be other
manager-owners a fellow could approach directly, Allen
thought, so he mounted what was in effect a one-man booking campaign. A few blocks from Grafton Street, in Uphams
Corner, was an upstairs movie theater, Winthrop Hall; so he
went to Winthrop Hall and convinced the manager of the wis-
dom of booking a neighborhood actor. Then Allen approached a South Boston theater owner and received dates in
a pair of South Boston theaters on the strength of his booking
at Winthrop Hall. How far his local strategy might have extended is problematic, but he had another fortnight of vaudeville booking, enough to encourage him, in February 1914, to
quit shipping hardware. His first monologue, influenced by
Griff, ran throughout the act, and his new billing read, "Freddy
James, Almost a Juggler."

Simultaneously, his stock began to rise among orthodox bookers. Realizing he was reliable, they sent him on one-nighters around Boston, then to split weeks in Waterville, Maine, and Norwich, Connecticut, and in Gloucester, Massachusetts, and Rutland, Vermont. Dropping the "St." — he was now Freddy James — Allen purchased a symbol of his regained professionalism: patent-leather, high-button shoes. He played town halls, armories, clubs, school auditoriums, and fairs, anywhere an audience assembled. Most of the theaters were small and decrepit. Three weeks in Nova Scotia at $45 a week left him with $23.75 weekly after expenses. In Yarmouth, where the tiny theater featured only one act, he pulled up the curtain and handled the lights, performed his act, and lowered the curtain for the movie. Often he was out of work, but all in all, the life of a small-time vaudevillian was more interesting and profitable than packing machinery.

Summer approached; and amusement parks offered the vaudeville actor seasonal employment. These were the same parks, subsidized by streetcar companies and featuring zoos, boating, a sylvan atmosphere, and a theater, to which he had escorted Sam Cohen's amateurs. The family audiences were not overly exacting. That summer at Norumbega, in Auburndale, and Sabbatia Park, in Taunton, Allen met acts who usually performed in New York. They assured him he was polished enough for the big time and should find New York bookings when the fall season opened. The positive reactions were encouraging, he didn't want to be a coast defender forever, and yet he hesitated. Suppose he went to New York and didn't land a job? Aunt Lizzie, notwithstanding her views concerning the grasshopper existence of actors, depended on him as the household's main source of support. He couldn't afford to stay out of work.

Ordering stationery, he altered his billing slightly:

FREDDY JAMES
"The World's Worst Juggler"
12 Minutes in One

LaToy soon appropriated the "World's Worst Juggler" title and the theft would remain a wellspring of discord between them for years. The stationery, with the provocative phrase, was intended to dent the collective managerial consciousness by circulating the name of Freddy James around New York. Beneath, he appended gags or snippets of comic verse. The campaign succeeded; each Manhattan booking office responded to the unusual publicity barrage, and Allen resolved to work in New England vaudeville only until he saved one hundred dollars. Out of this, he would bank forty dollars, a reserve fund in case he had to put his dreams of the big time in mothballs, return, and start building a sensible High School of Commerce future. John Murphy, a close friend from the library, agreed to stand by. Once he heard the stake was exhausted, he'd send the return fare.

Allen saved the hundred dollars, informed Aunt Lizzie that he was performing out of town, and gave Murphy the emergency fund. From *Players,* a theatrical weekly, the twenty-year-old comedian clipped an ad for Mrs. Montfort's boarding-house on West Fortieth Street. Mrs. Montfort's was once an address of consequence, but standards had sagged over the years: room and board were a dollar a day. On Friday, September 18, 1914, carrying a suitcase for his belongings and a black patent-leather sample case crammed with props, he walked into South Station and boarded the train for Fall River and the overnight boat to New York. He was leaving a past whose values he would essentially never leave, embarking for New York and the big time, the landfall of previous explorers.

THE HEADLINES that day were inky and ominous. "Wild bayonet fighting with Kaiser's troops!" newsboys shouted. Battles raging across northern France shared attention (in Boston) with the signing of the Irish Home Rule bill. "REBIRTH OF IRELAND IS FORECAST OF LEADERS." Sir James M. Barrie had disembarked in Manhattan on behalf of the British war effort and announced that more Irish recruits were swelling the ranks of Britain's armies than those of any other nationality. The arrival of a small-time vaudevillian in the shabby foyer of Mrs. Montfort's could hardly be expected to catch the eye of the muse of history. On the other hand, that eye is notoriously roguish and the significance of any event is often as disguised as the *Boston Globe*'s daily puzzle that September 18, a camouflage-drawing captioned "Find the Music Teacher's Helper."

When he arrived at eight, Allen's room was not ready, so he parked his bags in the lobby and walked to Times Square and Broadway, where he breakfasted at the Automat. (He was to define the Automat as "the first restaurant to make it possible for the poor man to enjoy food served under glass.") Then, taking in the tourist sights, he sauntered down Broadway and realized he was passing the Putnam Building, a hive of vaudeville agents. Why not let them know Freddy James was in town? Inside, however, the halls were silent, the doors locked. The six-day week was evidently less popular in New York than at the Colonial Piano Company. An open door beckoned along one corridor, and while Allen hesitated on the threshold, checking his list of vaudeville agents, a man looked up from his desk and asked if there was anything he could do. He was an agent Allen had somehow overlooked. The young performer described the routine of the World's Worst Juggler and the agent chuckled. An act had just fallen out of the bill of the Keeney Theatre, in Brooklyn; Freddy James could go on as a three-day replacement. Agreement was instant, a contract signed, directions to the theater diagramed. The booker neglected to state that in Brooklyn the Keeney was in opposition to both the Loew and Keith circuits, and any performer playing the Keeney Theatre was automatically blacklisted by those chains. In a haze of euphoria, Allen left the Putnam Building. Three hours off the boat and he had already clinched a three-day contract! Against the early morning light, Mrs. Montfort's boardinghouse almost looked inviting.

"Fred loved cheap hotels," says Al Hirschfeld. "Absolutely adored them." As a radio star, of course, he could afford hostelries of a more comfortable order than Mrs. Montfort's, but his preference for fleabags had nothing to do with money. Having grown used to them, he felt comfortable in small-time lodgings, and held bona fide membership in the nomadic race of hotel dwellers. "He was a permanent transient," Arnold Auerbach has written, "with the transient's aversion to possessions and long-term leases."

Mrs. Montfort's lacked amenities on the order of bellboys or room telephones; its dismal splendor, however, inspired Allen to a celebration of lyrical squalor. Plodding behind the lobby clerk to the room, suitcase in hand, he marched down a dark and endless tunnel. "One small bulb on the wall furnished the only light; the feeble ray gave the impression that a glowworm had impaled itself on the wallpaper." En route he learned the new owners had discontinued serving meals so his rent had been decreased to four dollars a week. Upon entering the windowless room, the clerk turned on the naked ceiling bulb and "the darkness brightened a shade into gloom," Allen recalled. "The single bed looked like a frozen hammock." The room had no closet; a skewed wardrobe and old-fashioned marble sink completed the decor.

This hideaway became the sturdy basis of countless Allen radio jokes. "I had a room that was so small it had removable door knobs. If you wanted to bend over you could take off the door knob just in case. At Mrs. Brown's when you took a bath you had to keep singing. There was no lock on the bathroom door."

The small-timers who patronized the boardinghouse learned to cope with these vagaries. The flamboyant yet domestic pattern of their lives was self-enclosed. Mothers allowed their children to play in Bryant Park, across Sixth Avenue; the Olive Lunch nearby served a bowl of pea soup and three slices of bread and butter for ten cents. The guests smuggled oranges, cereal, and jam into the wardrobes, rye bread and cans of sardines into the wardrobe's bureau drawers. Allen met "chorus girls who could take a bit of face powder and two tears (placed on a dime) and cook up a tea biscuit over a gas jet. With a half dollar they could have made waffles."

Like the Scollay Square denizens of the Rexford, the occupants of Mrs. Montfort's rehearsed in their rooms. Some hadn't worked for more than a year. The Miller Brothers used the defunct dining room to prepare their Indian-club juggling act; an aviary containing Lamont's Performing Cockatoos and Macaws screeched in the cellar, and the Texas Tommy Dancers practiced their cyclonic routines as "chandeliers swung like tassels, and when the plaster stopped falling, it was impossible to tell the floor from the ceiling."

Pooling his resources with a Montfort neighbor, John Carbrey, Allen moved into more expansive quarters, a room with a window. Carbrey was a dancer who, with his brother, performed a conventional dance number until their finale. Then they donned a single billowing harlequin costume and executed intricate steps together, creating the illusion that one person with two heads was dancing. The Carbrey Brothers originated the two-person one-suit finale, inevitably duplicated by others who contrasted the sexes, sizes, or a bizarre relationship.

The Keeney Theatre engagement proved successful, but like a false stage-set door, opened onto a blank wall rather than an exit. Allen couldn't find work. He was not blacklisted, for he was so insignificant that neither Loew nor Keith officials had heard of him. Although friends from New England amusement-park summer vaudeville recommended him to their agents, he was such an unknown quantity no one was willing to take a chance on him. The big-time agents had big-time clients; the small-time agents wanted big-time clients, too. The "World's Worst Juggler" letters had been a clever publicity stunt rather than assurance of a future. Week after week, he sat around offices "talking to other acts who seemed to be sitting there because they, too, had no place else to go."

He spent days in enforced idleness, nights brooding about dwindling funds and how to shield Aunt Lizzie from the truth. Every week he sent her money. The fare at the Olive Lunch was varied by his discovery of the dime meal at another restaurant: liver and bacon and coffee and doughnuts. "Uncle Jim" Harkins, later the comedian's aide-de-camp, called this period "Fred's short-dollar days." It was meager solace to realize that half the guests of the Montford were unemployed; the accommodations resembled a rooming house less than a welfare shelter. Six actors slept on the Allen-Carbrey floor at one interval, and all eight performers lived on a stockpile of salami and raspberry jam in the bureau drawer.

The monotony of unemployment was interrupted twice — by a job in a Masonic Club show on Twenty-third Street, when no bookers appeared; and again at the Lexington Avenue Theatre, when Allen served as the back legs of a prop horse in a major comedy act: Fields and Lewis. The act opened with the horse hauling a hansom cab, the driver of the cab falling into argument with his passenger while the horse reacted to their harangue. Fields and Lewis's prop man lived at the Montfort and acted as the horse's front legs. "The night he asked me to help him," Allen recalled, "I joined him in the equine pelt. I appeared as the lumbar section. There was no money involved. I received no adulation. I was in a big act, appearing in a big theater, in front of a large audience, but nobody knew I was there."

Presently, money almost gone, he threw in the towel and decided to wire Johnny Murphy for the return fare. But when Allen left the Montfort and rounded the corner of Broadway and Fortieth Streets, a last-minute reprieve occurred in the manner of an old-time Hollywood musical where the understudy goes on for the ailing star. A young man from the booking agency in which the performer had spent so many futile hours came puffing up to him. An act had been canceled after the matinee at the Empire Theatre in Paterson, New Jersey, and the young man had been asked to find a replacement. The Poli circuit booker had an interest in the Empire. If the juggling act went over, Allen could get a route.

In Paterson, he performed his monologue between the acts of a stock-company melodrama. The audience was cordial, and, as predicted, he received a three-week booking on the Poli time owned and operated by Sylvester Z. Poli, a Greek immigrant who had made good as a showman. The Poli theaters, scattered across Connecticut and central Massachusetts, plus Scranton and Wilkes-Barre, Pennsylvania, played "family-time vaudeville" as well as star turns. Hartford and Springfield and the larger cities boasted two Poli houses, one for big-time, two-a-day performance, the other for the cheaper acts who performed three and four shows daily. The family-time theaters were called "presentation houses" because they also presented a feature film on a continuous policy. Family-time audiences exhibited a lesser level of sophistication, but did not grate on Allen's nerves as they tended to seven or eight years later. He was receiving sixty dollars a week, and after penury in the stygian depths of Mrs. Montfort's, it seemed a noble sum.

Mrs. Montfort's closed its doors forever shortly after he came back to New York. Allen and John Carbrey moved into a more comfortable boardinghouse on Forty-eighth Street, but missed the tatterdemalion warmth of the old address. Mrs. Lowery's seemed more sedate, although the building was owned by a legless professional beggar known as "the Seal," who propelled himself about on a small wheeled board. A momentous event, however, took place after Allen's Poli-circuit tour, when he met an agent named Mark Leddy. To this encounter the comedian attributed the success of his future career.

Mark Leddy, who worked for the Loew's circuit, offered distinct advantages over the bookers Allen had been courting. Young and ambitious, Leddy represented only five acts; he could concentrate upon his clients, help develop their routines, keep them employed, and, best of all perhaps, he was attuned to Allen's style of humor. Leddy booked him into the Loew's circuit around New York, and in December, three months after boarding the Fall River boat, Allen was performing on a Boston stage, Loew's Orpheum, where he had seen Griff. The audience included Allen's aunts, who were embarrassed by the laughter that greeted his botched juggling feats. They did not mention the act during his visit home. Besides, Aunt Lizzie had always maintained that Uncle Joe was the funny one in the family. On the other hand, the Howard Street coast defenders hailed the returning hero; and LaToy, confiding his own plans to storm New York, asked for a loan.

Under Mark Leddy's management, Allen performed steadily. With almost total recall he could summon up every vaudeville theater he had played, but in 1915 he worked so hard even he could not retain the dates.

"The smalltime bills I played that year? The Comedy, Amphion and Folly Theatres in Brooklyn — Hackensack — Gloversville — and those I can't remember, thank God." Leddy kept him scrambling throughout the winter. There was always a town ahead, another audience. You never knew where you were; the towns were defined by the sweep of vaudeville's unruly currents. A part of him preferred the role of onlooker, however, and sometimes Allen stood aside and absorbed the restless scene, relishing its vitality and fun. When that happened he was both observer and participant, with a critical double vision that assessed his performance while it was going on. He often used the word *fun* in connection with his efforts, but what, after all, made people laugh?

Reaching a landmark, his twenty-first birthday, he spent it on the road. Home again in New York, he took in the show at Hammerstein's Victoria, where the program consisted of twenty-two acts, with three silent acts opening the bill — a contortionist, an acrobat, and a juggler performing simultaneously. When they finished their performances, they split the one bow three ways. Into his notebook went the names of outstanding acts. Tim Thornton — Charlie Case — Harry Fox and the Dolly Sisters — Don, the Talking Dog — Dan Sherman and his Jay Circus — Bunny Granville — Joe Cook.

Allen's meticulously indexed joke file was expanding. Many routines, in the discordant style of the period, were ethnic, and he had a lurking fondness for Scottish anecdotes, such as the story about a female patient who needed a blood transfusion. A brawny young Scot volunteered. For the first pint, she gave him fifty dollars, and for the second, twenty-five dollars. After the third pint, she had so much Scottish blood in her veins that she merely thanked him. Then there was the Irishman who swore off drinking and had to pass his favorite tavern on his way home. As he approached the saloon, his willpower weakened, but he plucked up his courage and passed by. Ten yards farther, he stopped and said, "Well done, Murphy. Come back and I'll buy you a drink." Vaudeville stereotypes of this kind never entirely faded from his act, but in time Allen learned how to use them to create individual characters.

Despite his industry, he realized he was still far away from stardom. "Progress meant steady work, the chance to give my Aunt Lizzie more money, and to appear in better theaters before smarter audiences, and the opportunity to learn and improve." When the season started afresh, in September 1915, Mark Leddy revealed he had been negotiating with a representative of the Benjamin Fuller circuit in Australia. Allen, who till then had never been west of Philadelphia, was intrigued. Fuller's agent duly materialized backstage just before the matinee performance in a New York presentation house. The agent promised he would return after the show with his verdict on whether or not the act was suitable for Australian theaters. Thus encouraged, Allen went on, gave the routine his best effort, and finished with a flourish, but after bowing off, he looked in vain for the agent. At last Fuller's man reappeared and abashedly announced that he fell asleep during the movie and slept throughout the entire vaudeville program.

Allen forgot about him; there were problems more urgent than Australia, namely, improving the act. However, a report must have been relayed to the Fuller office in Sydney, for Benjamin J. Fuller himself — Sir Benjamin, as he later became — was struck by the "World's Worst Juggler" billing. Three months later, the Australian showman visited Chicago, combining his honeymoon with a search for American vaudeville acts. The war had curtailed Australian performers, never plentiful in normal times. Playing the McVickers Theatre, where Mark Leddy had booked him in his first Chicago appearance, Allen was on the bill with two headliners — Onaip, a virtuoso of the wire-suspended midair piano, and the prizefighter Battling Nelson. The latter was doing a celebrity turn in which he described his training regimen and then sparred two rounds. He had taken a shine to Allen's comedy juggling and watched every show, no doubt reminding the performer of John L. Sullivan, the Boston Strong Boy, former heavyweight boxing champion of the world. The two Sullivans once met at the Boston Public Library, where the pugilist had come to look up stories about himself. Skinny John F. pointed out to corpulent John L. the coincidence of their names. "Lots of guys named after me," John L. growled. Battling Nelson, cut from the same cloth, insisted that Allen wear the old, gray hat that he, Nelson, wore during his roadwork, because the hat, riddled like a sieve, would be instantly recognizable to a Chicago audience and get big laughs. No laughs were provoked by Battling Nelson's perforated hat. Coping with this delicate problem in etiquette, Allen inadvertently overlooked the note Benjamin Fuller sent backstage; but later in the week, a Mark Leddy wire announced that the Fuller circuit liked the act. If Allen agreed to terms, he could depart from San Francisco in February 1916.

Headquartered in New Zealand, the Fuller circuit was notorious for long hours and low salaries. Allen didn't know this; he agreed to take the $100-a-week offer, providing that Leddy arranged a route from Chicago, a series of bookings that would stretch over the ensuing weeks between the McVickers Theatre and pierside. Leddy agreed and thereby inaugurated a meandering odyssey through Cleveland, Saint Joe, Topeka, Wichita, Tulsa, Oklahoma City, Dallas, Shreveport — and then a jump from Shreveport to San Jose, California.

Benjamin Fuller came home after the first of the year and briefed reporters on the results of his American talent hunt. The magnate implied that he and Allen had met and conversed with each other: "I saw lots of acts, the perpetrators of which told me they were good. Most of them I found rotten. But this man told me that nothing could be worse than his juggling and that's why I booked him. That and the fact that he was making about fifteen-hundred other people around me laugh at the same moment."

Meanwhile, the latest Fuller acquisition pursued his errant itinerary toward the West Coast. The journey began conventionally enough ("He is on the order of Griff who was the first of the misjugglers," observed the Topeka critic. "Pretty good"), but then took on the characteristics of an obstacle course — two steps forward, three steps back. En route from Shreveport, Allen's train ran off the tracks near El Paso and scattered seven Pullman cars like matchboxes along the roadbed. Curiously, he had a premonition of the accident. Lying naked in his lower berth because the weather was sweltering, he began to imagine how he would cope with a train wreck:

I decided that if I was in a lower berth I would roll out into the aisle and grasp anything solid I could get my hands on. I had scarcely completed this plan in my mind when I felt the Pullman car bumping along as if it was off the track; I rolled out into the aisle and held on to the arm of the seat. The car careened along crazily, the lights went out, women started to scream, men began to shout, and then the car stopped abruptly, teetered, and tipped over on its side. The windows of my berth were resting on the ground.

Fortunately, casualties were limited to another passenger's broken leg. Whether or not Allen's premonition was psychic, the train wreck reveals his reflexive response toward misfortune — "to roll out into the aisle and grasp anything solid I could get my hands on." Haphazard as his life had been, in an emergency he reflexively discovered supports: Aunt Lizzie, the church, the sorcery of words. As he lay in a berth at his most vulnerable, however, on a train bearing him toward a foreign place where he could not depend upon the support of an extended family of American vaudeville performers, he had begun almost instinctively to imagine catastrophe and weigh his course of action. The odds against him were formidable; it was wise to anticipate the worst.

Once a relief train was procured, Allen proceeded onward. His trousers, which he had draped over the hammock beside the window just before the accident, were slashed by broken glass, and with two safety pins holding the rips together, he arrived in San Jose. The importance of his wardrobe to a vaudevillian cannot be underestimated; the impromptu adjustments suggest that Allen owned only the single pair of pants. A jiffy repair job later, he played his last date, and presently discovered the charms of San Francisco. If "every city west of Chicago was a Hackensack," San Francisco looked "like New York with a hill in the middle of it." The city's cosmopolitanism appealed to him, but he had only two days to appreciate it. He attended a show, bought two fifteen-dollar suits and other articles of clothing, and, on impulse, a ventriloquist's dummy in a store window. What use did he have for the dummy? "I had no use for it," he remembered. "A psychiatrist would probably have said I was lonely." Booked into second-class aboard the SS *Sierra,* a ten-thousand-ton steamer, he boarded the vessel and located his cabin.

Save for cramped conditions, seasickness, tedium, sunburn, and a petulant missionary, the Pacific crossing was unmemorable. Allen shared quarters with an elderly New Zealand sheep rancher who nightly submerged his dentures in his cabin-mate's water glass. The young man made the acquaintance of other American actors aboard, and a contingent of professional boxers. Time passed. The *Sierra* ploughed on, stopping at Honolulu and Pago Pago. Weather changed. Twenty-one days out of San Francisco, Sydney's opaline harbor, sparkling and flecked by sails, widened before them beneath the cloudless paradox of a February summer sky.

5 | Australia, 1916

Sydney. The beautiful harbor, the dumpy theater." No snapshots of the harbor embellish the
scrapbook titled "Freddy James, Acting for Money"; Allen
aimed his camera instead at a peeling trash can backstage in
the National Theatre. The National was billed as "The Home
of Clean Vaudeville." Always conscious of the gulf between
stage illusion and the gritty conditions of the performer's life,
he was nonetheless surprised by the primitive creature comforts of the small-time Australian circuit. When, years afterward, he wrote that he was playing a theater so deep in the
woods the manager was a bear, he exaggerated his circumstances only slightly. A kangaroo rather than a bear for an
Australian audience — yet he would still be embroidering upon
his sense of otherness, his distance from the urban amenities
of stateside vaudeville.

Few Americans played Australia, and those who did were
mainly from California, although American performers had long
been fixtures on the Australian stage. W. C. Fields only two
years before had completed his third tour, and Fields was following a procession. Joseph Jefferson, Dion Boucicault, and
Maud Jeffries had trouped across the continent; in 1854,
American actors Joseph Wyatt and the Wallers, husband and
wife, opened Sydney's Prince of Wales Theatre. They were
joined by Edwin Booth, who was taking the high aesthetic
line, although he ran afoul of the occupational hazard of tra-

gedians in the provinces: he himself was admired but the house was sparse. Stranded, he accepted his return fare from tycoon George Francis Train, who singled out Booth in his memoirs as an authentically ungrateful man. Even John L. Sullivan had toured the continent, his fistic celebrity enhancing his role as a blacksmith in *Honest Hearts and Willing Hands*.

Australia imported her entertainment, and it was artless. Minstrel shows played Sydney, Brisbane, and Melbourne long after minstrel shows had fallen out of fashion elsewhere, and hoary comedies prospered, the broader the better. Indeed, *Struck Oil,* a comedy brought to Australia in 1874 by Americans, became the basis of an Australian theatrical domain still in existence. James Cassius Williamson, an actor-manager, and his wife, Maggie Moore, had purchased the piece from a California prospector, and Williamson, tired of playing a bloodhound in *Uncle Tom's Cabin,* decided to present their farce. It was a boisterous success. The couple took it to London, where *Struck Oil* also met with British approval, and from manager Rupert D'Oyly Carte, Williamson secured the Australia and New Zealand rights to Gilbert and Sullivan's operettas. He appeared in *Pinafore* as Sir Joseph while Maggie Moore played Josephine, but they were beaten to the Sydney premiere by Kelly and Leon's Minstrels, featuring a female impersonator as Buttercup. Ultimately, the Williamsons went to court, barred pirate competition (most notably a *Wreck of the Pinafore,* perpetrated by one Horace Lingard, in which the characters of Gilbert's libretto, castaways on a desert island, performed out of character), bought four theaters (two in Melbourne and one each in Sydney and Adelaide), and established "the firm." The Williamson Theatres have dominated the Australian stage ever since.

Conformism in 1916 saturated Australian life. "The firm" substantiated Williamson's conviction that only tried-and-true fare pleased the public (the influence of "the firm," which flourished by importing sanctioned hits of the West End and Broadway, has been frequently debated), and Williamson understood his patrons. They venerated propriety. By observing convention, they repudiated their geographic solitude, their doubtful national identity, their fears of racial and economic upheaval. Conformism also encouraged political submission; Australians had loyalties to country and Commonwealth, and ties to Britain were expressed at the conclusion of every civic gathering with "God Save the King." The swarming crowds of street toughs known as larrikins (Austral-English for "larking," though the word may derive from the French *larron*, a thief), more numerous than similar gangs in the factory cities of Europe and America, hewed out their own peculiar standards of group behavior. Larrikins affected a peculiar style of dress, a uniform, like the punks of the early 1970s, and organized themselves in rival gangs, or "pushes," who fought the police and each other and preyed on respectable citizens.

"Australians remained notorious for their disapproval of individuals who behaved in ways which offended against the unwritten laws of the tribe," historian C. M. H. Clark has observed.

> Street hoodlums in the cities and larrikins in country towns imposed their own check on any grotesqueries or eccentricities of dress in either men or women. Howling and jeering mobs pursued all those who risked appearing in a get-up in any way novel or different from that of their neighbors. Idle and mischievous loungers were the allies of Philistines in high places — both acted as unpaid censors of eccentricity. People who essayed the fanciful in Australia exposed themselves to the brutality of the larrikin and the frowns of the men dressed in black.

The latter, known as "wowsers," were members of dissenting Protestant sects, a minority who cherished a puritanical dislike of sports, amusements, and pastimes. George "Doc" Rockwell, an American comedian on the Tivoli circuit when Allen toured Australian small-time houses, was struck by the provincial environment. American vaudeville actors with their flashy wardrobes were instantly recognizable and "people would follow you down the street hoo-hooing and flapping their arms."

Sydney-siders considered themselves egalitarians representing a credo of robust individualism, but the rules had changed. As Clark put it, "the mighty bush, the cradle of the noble bushman, of mateship and equality, of the prestige of the male values of pluck, resource and physical strength . . . was coming under the influence of industrial civilization." Inflexible class distinctions defined an English pattern of hierarchy. Robert Hughes has pointed out that the obsessive cultural enterprise of the nation was the obliteration of its convict origins. One of the ways to purge that anguished history was to erect a barrier of bourgeois respectability between the past and the present. "Australians showed a cheeky deference to those in authority over them," continues Clark, "and a coarse insolence to those they loathed or deemed inferior." Of all classes, the men and women of the stage were deemed least respectable and were quarantined from normalcy.

Aboard the *Sierra,* caste lines were drawn early. The vaudevillians on the ship were destined to play either the Tivoli (or big-time) circuit or the Brennan-Fuller (or small-time) circuit. All had been given secondhand tickets; but when the Tivoli acts realized they would have to associate with the Fuller acts, the former promptly moved into first-class accommodations, paying the difference themselves. To pass the time, they lounged against the first-class deck rail and looked down on the Fuller people, who leaned on *their* rail and looked down on the steerage passengers. Allen mused, "Who knows: the steerage passengers were probably sitting on their bare deck practicing class distinction by looking down at the porpoises because they weren't even on the boat."

In Sydney he dressed for the debarkation: pipestem trousers, double-breasted vest, flaring jacket, patent leather shoes with gray canvas uppers fastened by white pearl buttons. The crowning touch was a leghorn hat of finely plaited straw, the brim curled down fore and aft in the dashing manner of a photoplay leading man. His sartorial flair would have been regarded with envy at home, but he was out of season for Australia, and he sent the stevedores on the dock into paroxysms of mirth. They looked so absurd themselves that Allen and a friend began to laugh and in the subsequent confusion walked off the gangplank and onto the pier without surrendering their documents. Allen had no papers to surrender, for in the flurry of departure the steamship company had promised to forward his birth certificate and passport. Neither had arrived, but no one seemed to care.

American acts usually opened in Sydney because Fuller could inspect them there and proffer suggestions. Since the impresario had already endorsed Freddy James, he was directed to Brisbane by rail. Frank Herberte, "The Descriptive Vocalist," whose act consisted of slides thrown on a screen while he sang, went along and showed Allen the routines of an Australian train — the trip took two days and a night — as well as guiding him to the Menzies Hotel and indicating the location of the theater. Coming into Queensland, the train rolled past towns with names like Nudgee and Pinkenba and Wooloongabba ("place of the whip-tailed wallaby"), past stilt houses where banana stalks and Moreton Bay fig trees interrupted the triangular geometry of galvanized iron roofs.

At the hotel the guest was taken to the rear of the building and shown the outhouse; on the dresser of his room stood a candle that would light his path privy-wards. Brisbane, a semitropical city of 300,000, had no sewerage, and the forces of progress did not approve. "Anything more degrading to a fine city than soil carts parading the streets at night or nightmen being met on the stairs of a stately hotel, polluting the air with an abominable stench, cannot well be imagined," declared the *Australian Builder and Contractors News*.

Australia did not in 1916 otherwise resemble the States. Private cars were owned for the most part by wealthy drivers, horse-drawn hansom cabs could sometimes be hailed on city streets where omnibuses and cable trams rattled, and bulb-horn taxis frightened horses and wagon drivers. Sydney's rackety green-and-yellow trams often ran in jointed pairs, which prompted an English visitor to compare them to copulating butterflies. Engines seldom disturbed the quiet of the bush where dray horses, camels, bullocks, and manpower helped move heavy goods. Until 1924, the legendary stagecoach outfit Cobb and Company operated leather-springed Concord coaches that bounced across alkaline desert wastes with passengers and mail just as the same coaches were doing in American western movies of the same vintage. Telephones and typewriters still retained a fading gloss of novelty, and in business offices male typists operated the machines. Phonographs had begun to adorn up-to-date parlors; ice chests served the housewife; but there was a shortage of headache pills and powders, which had been a German monopoly, and of beef and mutton, commandeered for the duration by Britain. Visiting vaudevillians preferred to receive their wages in gold rather than the war-inflated Australian pound. Picture palaces showed the films of Chaplin and Mary Pickford, subject to rigorous censorship exerted by commonwealth and state governments; also subject to puritanical examination were books, recordings, and other material entering the country from abroad. Hotel bars and pubs closed at six o'clock, but "sly-grog shops," operated by shady proprietors, catered to an after-hours clientele. Tall buildings were uncommon, space abundant: most people lived on separate blocks of land large enough to accommodate a dwelling, garden, and outhouse.

While these social manifestations gave Australia its pastoral tranquility, they were deceiving. The nation was steeped in war. The storming of the Gallipoli heights and the Dardanelles campaign of 1915 had cost the Australian Imperial Force 7,818 men, killed in action or dead of wounds and gas poisoning. Lengthier casualty lists were in store. Australian troops headed into action in France, and the symbolic significance of the ordeal at Anzac Cove was not lost upon the home front. Dinkum Aussies had stood up to Johnny Turk, a tough and formidable foe, and the diggers had proved themselves possibly the finest fighters in the world. Images of the oafish, undisciplined colonial, the First Fleet landing its rabble of petty crooks transported from England, the untamed frontier elements of Australian existence, yielded to patriotic pride. "THE EMPIRE CALLS," proclaimed a large banner draped across the ornate wooden facade of the Empire, the Brisbane theater where Allen would make his debut. "ENLIST NOW."

Under the circumstances it was small surprise that he felt qualms — a young man of military age about to perform a comic routine before an audience separated from him by idiom and behavior. "Without the protection of the formal mask of a narrative drama, without a song, dance, or any other intermediary to create distance between performer and perfor-

mance, the stand-up comedian addresses an audience as a naked self," social commentator David Marc points out. "Good
actors can be singled out of bad plays; good singers can put
over bad songs. But in the case of the stand-up comedian,
there is no dividing medium from message; the mask cannot
be pried loose from the face of the performer."

Australian vaudeville, too, observed different conventions.
The bill frequently comprised a full-length play followed by a
half-dozen acts. The fondness of Australian audiences for com-
binations of legitimate theater and vaudeville harked back to
turn-of-the-century America and the format of earlier entertainments of the Anglo-American stage. Theatrically, it was
like the menu of a Victorian banquet, piling a farcical after-
piece onto a tragedy preceded by a ballet. The antipodal supply of acts was limited, yet the audience didn't mind. At two
shillings sixpence for the best seats in the house, or one shilling for the worst, a theatergoer could drop in, see a favorite
act, leave, and repeat the experience night after night. There
were no split weeks. Compared with the frantic pace of American vaudeville's three- and four-a-day performances, Australian vaudeville was a gavotte. Audiences saw but one show a
night, plus Wednesday and Saturday matinees.

The "World's Worst Juggler" billing piqued the audience as
it did Benjamin Fuller, but at the opening, a Saturday matinee,
Allen went through his "front-cloth" routines with apprehen-
sion. Would anyone understand him? Most Americans did
nontalking acts. To make matters worse, at every opening
matinee the girls from the local brothels were permitted to
occupy a box. "Any sap can find a pearl in an oyster, but it
takes a smart girl to get a diamond out of a nut." Some of his
lines floated into silence; still, he managed a good finish with
the silk hats. He had to fret away the hours through Sunday,
awaiting the verdict of the Brisbane critics, and when the
Monday-morning papers appeared, he turned to the theatrical
pages.

Freddy James, The "World's Worst Juggler," is one of the
best of Ben J. Fuller's Yankee acts. The act consists of
trying to "make believe" he is not clever. Freddy's trick

with three hats is a sure laugh-getter with the smarter
portion of the audience; but the other half — or three-
quarters — really believe he does something wonderful
when he throws two hats up and sneaks the other one on
his head from his right hand.

The reviewer captured a rare specific image personifying
Allen's early performances: the trick with the three hats. It was
self-reflexive rather than illusionistic; Allen was poking fun at
the trick itself and at those who treated its naive mechanics
literally. The members of the audience who caught on without
delay were not only paid the compliment of being treated as
sophisticates but became, in a sense, collaborators of the performer. In effect he was implying that they were not just
watching an entertainer, but someone who shared their intel-
lectual values — an onstage partner. A variation of the hat trick
came back to the States with him in the vaudeville season of
1917–18: Allen produced a hoop and announced that he was
going to roll it clear around the stage; he then spun the hoop
into the wings and a few seconds later a stagehand rolled another hoop onstage from the opposite wing — only the disc
was smaller and unlike the first. The conventions of the routine were similarly expressed still later in a sketch that Allen
performed in the movies with Ginger Rogers and on radio
with Tallulah Bankhead. Portraying a syrupy morning talk-
show couple, they commented upon current events and cued
in mawkish commercials. The parallel half of the sketch revealed their actual responses: they were hostile toward each
other, surly about the charade they were enacting, and nauseated by the treacle they were hawking. The contrast between
rhapsodic illusion and things as they are is a perennial staple of
comedy, and in American humor inspired some of the brightest — and some of the darkest — passages of Mark Twain.
 "Freddy James comes from America to demonstrate to Bris-
banites that he is the worst juggler in the world," another review began. "To the vaudeville fan there is one glaring fact in
James's offering; it is the welcome fact that every bit of his
chatter is new and pointed." Still a third review declared,
"Freddy James, billed as the 'World's Worst Juggler,' was the

laughing hit of the Empire program on Saturday." The notice concluded, "Give us more front cloth acts of the same calibre, please, Mr. Fuller."

The act was accepted, he could relax, but Allen kept tinkering with his stage business in order to bring in Australian allusions and jokes. It meant listening closely to the variety of Australian voices around him. Before he could tune his ear to the swing of the spoken language, however, he awoke one morning with violent chills and a temperature. The hotel manager summoned a doctor and the doctor diagnosed and prescribed for dengue fever, a species of malaria. Although Allen could scarcely walk, he managed to drag himself to the Empire that evening and to nightly martyrdoms thereafter. Somehow he survived and reached the end of the week, shaken yet recuperative.

His Australian tour was rife with boredom and loneliness. "The actor when well has little opportunity to know the city or to participate in its civic or social life," he reflected, a spectral presence among others going about the world's business. The illness in Brisbane enhanced his sense of the performer's nomadic seclusion; life goes on elsewhere while he travels from one alien city to another. He purchased a tall ledger of the Accounts Receivable kind and lettered his name across the boards of the marbled cover. Inking the capitals, he added a bold graphic flourish. The applied decoration of the title, "Freddy James, Acting for Money," suggests that time dragged. A snapshot captioned "Gone Are the Days When He Did Three Shows a Day" depicts him as a fashion plate, his close-cropped reddish-brown hair bristling while he poses before a wardrobe mirror in that most characteristic setting of the itinerant actor, a hotel room indistinguishable from a closet.

The pages of the ledger repeat a motif, the scissored cutouts of two young women. Sloe-eyed vamps of the period, they may have also played the Empire: Estelle Wordette and Company, a two-person act, opened the program in "their original playlet, 'A Honeymoon in Catskills,'" and the bill included distaff song-and-dance numbers. The pressures of life on the road allowed a young juggler scant opportunity for anything but arriving at the next theater on schedule. To Henry J. Kelly,

a vaudeville friend, searching in the twenties for a female partner, Allen confided: "As regards the girl, I am keeping my
eyes on all chambermaids, waitresses, manicurists etc., without results up to now. I have never been much of a success as
a lady's fellow, which explains my inability to rush the address
of some eighteen or twenty members of the opposite sex who
are open for employment." Now that he finally had time for
a semblance of social contact, there was nowhere to go. Brisbane was named for an army protégé of the Duke of Wellington whose true passion was astronomy rather than the draco-
nian regimen he enforced during the convict period — in other
words, the general's attention was centered light-years away
from the settlement nominated after himself. Not much had
changed. On a short stroll after his recovery, Allen discovered
that all the streets running parallel to the main artery, Queen
Street, bore female names, while those streets running at right
angles were male. That more or less exhausted the possibilities
of Brisbane sightseeing, and like the general he turned his
thoughts elsewhere. More specifically, to his career as a Bates
Hall runner in the Boston Public Library.

> I started to read. I realized that I had a lot to learn about
> comedy. To study the methods two famous authors had
> used in developing characters and comedy situations, I
> started reading Dickens and Mark Twain. During the eleven
> months I worked in Australia (plus two months in transit
> across the Pacific) I spent all my spare time reading. I went
> through Shakespeare, Artemus Ward, Bill Nye, Eli Per-
> kins, Josh Billings and the works of all the current British
> and American humorists. All the English humor maga-
> zines were new to me. I discovered *Punch, Tit-Bits, Lon-
> don Opinion, Answers, Pearson's Weekly,* and the others.

> He assembled a new joke file, but more important, his in-
> tensive reading stirred latent ambitions.

> This interest in jokes and comedy led to my first desire to
> write. My early efforts were crude. My High School of
> Commerce education hadn't prepared me to weld nouns
> and verbs together in acceptable literary patterns. I have

always had a great respect for writers, and even today I stand in awe of the person who can clothe his thoughts in words. Before I left Brisbane I resolved that, with the time I had to study as I played the Fuller circuit, I would try to improve my act, my jokes, and my writing.

These comments suggest Allen's respect for learning, the discouragement he felt at his fledgling efforts to emulate Dickens and Twain and "acceptable literary patterns," his sensitivity to the scantiness of his formal education. The choice of books is revealing since "literary" humorists like O. Henry, an author Allen later listed as his favorite, go unmentioned. In general the titles focus upon writers onstage — Shakespeare, Dickens, and those nineteenth-century Americans who had built up their reputations by performing on the lyceum platform. Then as now, humor, a second-class genre, received condescension; onstage it was different: writing could become performance and the pragmatic demands of the act absorb whatever inadequacy a self-taught author might feel.

Reading did not occupy every moment; in March he returned by boat to Sydney, and on the fourteenth appeared in a twelve-act Australian Imperial Force benefit at "White City" stadium. It was the beginning of many similar patriotic appearances punctuating a strenuous tour. The texture of Allen's travels soon began to resemble a timetable film montage in which the audience watches him in close-up performing his act while superimposed railroad signs race past — Melbourne, Adelaide, Fremantle, Perth, Auckland, Toowoomba. The montage, however, does not chug like a locomotive, but jerks, falters, and before gathering speed stops in a drawn-out sigh of steam. Passengers in those days changed trains at the state border. Only in 1970 did Australia complete a transcontinental railway system with standard track gauges. The Irishman in charge of planning Sydney's first railways in the 1850s, Wentworth Shields, had spurned the English gauge, 4 feet 8 inches wide — said to have been the distance between Roman chariot wheels — in favor of the Irish gauge of 5 feet 3 inches. Then Shields resigned and his successor reverted to the English gauge. He neglected to inform the other states, and had he done so that probably would not have mattered, for the colonies were rabidly competitive. Queensland instituted a narrow gauge, 3 feet 6 inches; Victoria and South Australia contrived a hodgepodge of widths varying from locality to locality; and in the Queensland sugar fields, workmen picked up sections of double track and arranged these to fit the occasion.

As he meandered along the Fuller circuit, traipsing from gauge to gauge, Allen was not entirely lost in the Australian outback. At the Princess Theatre, Fremantle, he was reviewed as "another quaint Yank," and "Freelance" in Sydney called him "the best of the new Yank acts." On the circuit the small-time actors kept crossing paths, from Fuller's Bijou in Melbourne to the Princess in Dunedin, New Zealand — Estelle Wordette and Company; Frank Herberte, the Caruso of illustrated ballads; Alsace and Lorraine, a musical act who practiced electrolysis as a sideline; the Human Frog, Mankin; and Doranto, the "Chinese Musical Novelty featuring 'The Human Xylophone.'"

An anonymous vaudeville newsman reported: "Doranto, who makes up as a Chow, is a wonder. Last Sunday we went to Redcliff and entertained the soldiers there. Glanmore Jones, Doranto and Frank Herberte did all the entertaining whilst Freddy James and Jake Mack gargled all the liquid refreshments."

The same diffident gossip offers another beguiling social glimpse: "Freddy James buying ices for the panto girls at Jimmy Boyle's cafe."

In Australia Allen cemented friendships with comedian Doc Rockwell, later a perennial guest star on the radio broadcasts, and "Uncle Jim" Harkins, a jovial performer some seven years older than the relatively inexperienced comedy-juggler. Harkins and his wife, Marian, teamed on the Tivoli circuit, did not have the pretensions of big-time vaudevillians, and their warmth compensated for the isolation American acts experienced.

Doc recalled one of Allen's rare practical jokes, precursor of a popular graffito fifty years afterward. Outraged by Woodrow Wilson's pacifism, audiences had begun to boo American performers. "The ordeal of getting in and out of there [Australia] was terrific," Rockwell said. Allen responded to the mounting tension with his own offbeat comment. "He found a couple of sheets of rubber and cut out footprints and made a rubber stamp." The footprints climbed the wall and marched out the window. Hotel lavatories throughout Australia displayed identical footprints prowling from the sink to the bathtub and the rim of the drain.

Nonsense of this sort assuaged the monotony of trouping vast distances. England had been the chief source of Australian entertainment, but stepped-up submarine warfare meant that if Australian theaters were to remain open the country must rely on domestic and American talent. Vaudevillians had their contracts renewed and were dispatched again toward theatrical backwaters. The route from Shreveport to San Francisco was a hop and a skip compared to the jump from Fremantle, Western Australia, to Auckland, New Zealand. Across the Australian Bight, one of the roughest maritime reaches in the world, wallowed the vaudevillians' nightmare, SS *Dimboola,* unfit for transport duty. It "rolled and tossed through the Bight, pitching in the water day and night like a mammoth whale with insomnia," Allen said. Mention of the *Dimboola* never failed to tickle theater audiences; they were familiar with the vessel's name, thanks to endless onstage gibes. From Perth to Adelaide aboard the steamer took five days; from Adelaide to Sydney by train required another three days and two changes of train; Sydney to Wellington used up five days on a different boat; and Wellington to Auckland was overnight by train. "I had traveled two weeks to play two weeks in Auckland," Allen remarked. "It wasn't very profitable. My fares and meals were paid, but I got no salary while in transit; I was just an unemployed actor going from billow to billow." Returning to Sydney, he reported to the Fuller office wearing a sailor hat.

While he enjoyed the company of Americans destined to become lifelong friends, he also became popular among Australian colleagues. He had begun his small-time peregrinations wondering if audiences understood him; after the juggler's second visit to Brisbane, "Al," the author of "Brisbane Notes," announced, "Freddy James now knows the local slang as well as any Australian," and described him as "juggler, humorist and general good fellow." But another observer cautioned: "[James] specializes in 'cod' [that is, 'spoof'] juggling and should censor such phrases as 'some people spit like a shilling,' which are unfit for the feminine ear.' "

Mastering Austral-English distinguished Allen from other American acts and suggests his broad range of linguistic reference. On *Town Hall Tonight,* his radio program of the 1930s, he would capture the vernacular cadences of American dialects, high and low, and when he created the ethnic types of Allen's Alley in the forties, he did not poke fun at their ethnicity but instead relished their essential idiosyncrasies of speech. After all, he was not only the performer whose "act consists in trying to 'make believe' he is not clever." At the Opera House in Auckland, where the playbill motto reflected Australian and New Zealand democratic sentiment ("Here Genius, Not Birth, Your Rank Insures"), Allen performed on the same program with Van Hoven, "The Dippy Mad Magician," whose act mocked the pretensions of the stage illusionist; and in Perth, at the Melrose Theatre, Allen's billing even appears appropriated by "Merlyn, The World's 'Worst' Magician," though no controversy ensued as it did when LaToy pinched the "worst" title. The parodic approach of Griff, Edwin George, Merlyn, and other performers could be emulated, but not verbal energy and style.

Apart from studying comedy and buying ices for the panto girls, he attended prizefights. The passion for boxing awakened earlier lasted throughout his life, and Allen's odd conjunction with pugilists, starting with the Boston Public Library visit of John L. Sullivan, included, later on, weekly YMCA workouts with a professional, Joey LaGrey. Like American actors, American boxers had been trekking across Australia for generations. It was a two-way traffic: Australia welcomed American champions on the downgrade, and, encouraged by success against aging pugs, Australian boxers journeyed to the United States, where the pickings were leaner. Albert Griffiths, for example, "Young Griffo," described vividly by ring historian Nat Fleischer as "the Fastest Thinking Brainless Boxer in the history of pugilism," won eighty-two victories and added twelve more in America before losing to the lightweight champion, Jake McAuliffe. In 1908, the first officially recognized world heavyweight title bout in Australia matched the black champion Jack Johnson against the white Canadian title-holder, Tommy Burns. Johnson won handily despite the abusive conduct of the racist throng; Jack London covered the bout for several American papers, and his wife broke the gender barrier by gaining admittance.

Sports mania peaked in Australia just before the war. Gambling, of course, was illegal, but every town had a clandestine "two-up school" (for those who wagered on the popular game of "two-up") and "S.P. bookie" (starting price bookmaker). In tennis, horse racing, track-and-field events, cricket, and boxing, the country had gained international renown. The biggest boxing stadium in the world, a mammoth timber oval at Rushcutter's Bay, Sydney, also presented vaudeville, and here Fred Allen may have met Les Darcy, a legendary Australian pugilist. On the voyage across the Pacific, at any rate, the stable of prizefighters aboard the *Sierra* was managed by a Pennsylvanian, Jimmy Dine, who was training George Chip, a prominent contender, to fight Darcy. Chip lost, and no doubt this helped fire Darcy's Yank ambitions. He lacked enthusiasm to swell the casualty statistics on the western front, and in 1917, rather than volunteer for military service, stowed away on a ship bound for the United States, hoping for a shot at the title. On the contrary, reviled as a draft dodger, Darcy was denied bouts and died of pneumonia shortly thereafter. Such had been his popularity, however, that rumor spread that the Americans arranged his quietus, and his memory was soon assimilated into melancholy folk song.

> *The critics by the score said that they had never saw*
> *A boy like Les before upon the stadium floor.*
> *Oh, the Yanks called him a skiter*
> *But he proved himself a fighter,*
> *So they killed him — yes, they killed him*
> *Down in Memphis, Tennessee.*

This unquestionably reveals more about the Australian psyche circa 1917 than it does about Les Darcy or Fred Allen; but, interestingly, in the first draft of his autobiography, Allen pen-

ciled "Les Darcy" beside a passage describing the hostility of
Australian audiences. The outlaw had once been an Australian
folk hero; now all at once American actors were outlaws without glamor. The battle of the Somme opened July 1, and five
weeks later, 23,000 Australians were dead. Indeed, the casualty
rate for Australian troops (68.5 percent) was higher than for
any country involved in the war; of 330,000 troops sent over-
seas, 59,258 were killed in action. Australia's volunteer army
lost as many men as the forces of the United States, a country
twenty times more populous. The labor movement proclaimed its conviction that the working class was financing the
war and a Britain hoarding her own manpower used Australians as shock troops. Debates over conscription raged from
Sydney to Perth (the rich and respectable endorsed it, the lar-
rikin poor objected); the silver-lead miners struck, so did the
coal miners and sheep shearers, intimating the turbulence beneath the surface of a society unified by war.

Joking and juggling, Allen tried to survive the gallery's hostile stamping and whistling. Every week he mailed Aunt Lizzie her allowance. Some of his Australian friends, he thought,
might have been stars in England and America if they had not
been hesitant about leaving home. He played with Roy Rene
and Jake Mack, Jewish comedians who could have rivaled Willie
and Eugene Howard; also ranking with the best were Nat
Phillips and Stuffy the Rabbit, Leonard Nelson and Charlie
Verne of Vaude and Verne. The majority of Australian comedians acquired their routines through plagiarism. Without
writers to supply songs and patter, they watched foreign acts,
memorized these, and when the acts sailed away, performed
their material. Particularly unfortunate was the English or
American star who had made a phonograph record; disem-
barking, he found the song or monologue already copied and
done to death throughout the country.

By the brash standards of American vaudevillians, Australian performers dressed understatedly. Prudent foreigners emulated them. Anything that smacked of Teutonic origins, a
handlebar mustache, a penchant for bratwurst, earned public
disapproval. Two Bulgarian performers billed as the Musical
Balkans shaved off their Kaiser Wilhelm mustachios and opened

their act singing "America, Ve Loff You!" and Allen got rid of his Prussian pompadour and plastered down his hair with Vaseline.

Why not extend his tour around the world? Mark Leddy set to work and sent a projected route through India and Africa, concluding with four weeks in London; but the ominous shadow of the war fell everywhere. Maimed or embittered servicemen now dotted the audience, shouting insults and tossing pennies at the male performers. Women pinned the coward's white feather on suspected shirkers. At length a disturbing incident in Sydney convinced Allen that it was time to go home.

"I was chatting with an Australian friend in the theater lobby when two young women came up. 'Are you the juggling act?' said one. 'Yes.' She murmured that I could juggle these — two white feathers. The other fellow took a medal out of his pocket. He had received it for heroism in the Dardanelles. They backed off in confusion."

It was the medal that abashed them, not the Yank. Neutrality in the eyes of many Australians was tantamount to cowardice.

Not long after this distasteful episode, the Australian government passed a law that aliens traveling in the country must carry identification. Allen suddenly realized he had never bothered to send for his credentials, so he went to the American consul in Sydney. The consul advised him in view of the likelihood of American involvement in the war to acquire the necessary documents and return to San Francisco. When Allen cabled his brother, Bob, to forward the birth certificate, Bob could not locate it, owing to the mix-up over the Cambridge and Somerville birthplace. Aunt Lizzie then applied directly to Mayor James M. Curley of Boston, and the mayor contrived a solution, as he always did for his working-class constituency, and supplied a birth certificate card showing that Allen had been born in Boston.

Awaiting the card's arrival, Allen closed out his Australian year at the Elite Theatre in Toowoomba, a backwater some ninety miles west of Brisbane. The Elite reminded him of the tiny theaters around Boston. Once again he handled the lights and curtain; but there was a well-defined difference between his earlier theaters and the Elite: in Toowoomba, the only American in town, he was a nonperson.

Nobody mentioned the war to me, because nobody talked to me. The waitress at the pub where I stopped brought my food silently three times each day. She resented the Yank. The other people around the pub ignored me. The audiences at the theater tolerated my act. They neither laughed nor applauded. Every show to me was a soliloquy. When I walked down the main street, I might as well have been invisible. People passed me by as though repudiating my existence. Throughout the six days I spent in Toowoomba I was ostracized completely. Every day I went through the same routine. A silent breakfast, a long walk alone out into the country with my books, a reading session, a long walk back to sit through a silent lunch, another walk, another reading session, a silent dinner, and then to the theater to revel in the concerted silence that prevailed during my act. After the show, a deathlike walk back to the pub. Another week suspended in this social vacuum and I might have started talking to myself.

Outsider though he was, he felt a pang of regret when he presently boarded the *Sierra* again. The Pacific crossing promised to duplicate the trip of the year before; also on the passenger list was Chuck Wiggins, a middleweight who had lost to Les Darcy. Allen liked egalitarian Australia despite the stress of the war, and he was leaving behind a tangible part of himself — the act that would be purloined as soon as he vanished over the horizon. Australia gave him an invaluable opportunity to measure his ideas against the classic standards of comedy; it was a breathing space, a chance to read, write, and meditate; and it was a proving ground. He had arrived in Australia a juggler; he left Australia a comedian.

6 | A Young Fellow Trying to Get Along

"What's a juggler?" he maintained. "A pair of hands. And you never get anywhere working with your hands."

Toward the end of his Australian tour, revisiting the same cities and wondering how to refresh old routines, Allen opened his trunk and hauled out the ventriloquist's dummy he had purchased in San Francisco. Instead of making an entrance as a juggler, he'd come on as a ventriloquist. Jake, as he christened the dummy, was a strange, pop-eyed contraption; in derby, bow tie, cardigan sweater, and check trousers, he was a chip off a totem pole partially devoured by termites. For weeks Allen practiced a conventional "vent" routine in his dressing rooms, but the techniques of throwing his voice were too demanding. Then he recollected Griff's treatment of his dummy. The problem was solved as Allen "solved" his juggling inadequacies, by satirizing ventriloquism, speaking to the audience directly.

To begin with, he dressed like Jake, their derbies and over-sized shoes comprising visual rhymes. Their similar costumes enhanced the opening announcement, "If you are wondering which one is the dummy, this is the dummy on your left." The relationship between a ventriloquist and his dummy, often eerily ambiguous and Frankenstein-like, was an early point of departure. Allen used flour-white makeup, a mime's stylized mask that could be spotted from any area of the house. Next he gave a voice-throwing demonstration, and when he interrogated Jake, ushers stationed at intervals around the theater yodeled the replies. This worked, and he determined to preserve it, but, going straightaway from the *Sierra* to every vaudeville show in San Francisco, he realized that new routines demanded new jokes. The mossy gags guaranteed to get big laughs in Perth wouldn't do for stateside consumption. Eventually, Jake sat on a table and sang a duet — beneath the table was a concealed phonograph — with Allen as the other singer and alleged ventriloquist. When Allen paused to sip a glass of water, Jake kept on singing solo in Caruso or John McCormack's recorded tenor until a Sousa march intervened. The dummy, still singing, proceeded to disintegrate, and so did corresponding portions of Allen's costume — shoes, shirt cuffs, the crown of the derby — until the table also collapsed, disclosing the phonograph.

The routine was hilarious, but Allen felt the need for a different finish guaranteed to stop the show. A monologist always needed a rousing exit. He had purchased an old banjo in Australia and learned a number of chords. "In vaudeville, there was an audience psychology that never failed," he noted. "If a comedian walked onto the stage holding a violin, a saxophone, or a banjo, the audience assumed he was a musician. The comedian could tell jokes for ten minutes, occasionally tuning his violin, blowing a note on the sax, or strumming his banjo." Rounding off his new act with a musical flourish somehow didn't seem right. Meanwhile, it was more important to begin shelving old material and building up a fresh comic repertoire.

For three days in his hotel room Allen studied newspapers in search of topical material, and after reconditioning the act, he adopted a new billing, "Freddy James and His Misses." The "Misses" were his mistakes. Still known as a comedy juggler, he permitted juggling episodes to survive in the monologue, but the new billing promised an elastic style. He wired Mark Leddy for a route back to New York — one less strenuous than the Shreveport–to–San Francisco bookings — and a few days later Leddy had arranged several weeks at seventy-five dollars a week on the Western Vaudeville time.

The Western Vaudeville time was more accurately the Mid-western vaudeville time, covering fifty small-time theaters in eight corn-belt states. Allen opened in Cedar Rapids, where the manager of the Majestic Theatre, a frustrated theater critic, purchased space in the local newspaper in order to voice his unvarnished personal opinion of each performer. Freddy James wrung from him a laconic estimate: "Pretty good." The new act played Rockford, Terre Haute, Saint Louis, Evansville, and in and around Chicago. After the unhurried pace of Australia, the tempo seemed frantic. The Western Vaudeville Managers Association flung the actors like mail sacks from one desolate and deserted train platform to the next. The circuit specialized in split weeks; Monday to Wednesday in one town, Thursday to Saturday in another, and three shows a day on Sunday in an extra town. Seldom did the itinerary involve direct connections. Scrambling to meet schedules, Allen especially disliked the jumps that took seven or eight hours to reach a destination only a few direct hours away. He claimed that some of the towns he played were so small the Fire Department was a man with a water pistol. The rigors of the Fuller time, the jumble of Australian railway gauges and the lilliputian theaters of rural New Zealand, began to assume a cheerier glow. "Through the years," Allen looked back, "I have spent a hundred nights curled up in dark, freezing railroad stations in the Kokomos, the Kenoshas, and the Kankakees, waiting for the Big Four, the Wabash, or C.&A. trains to pick me up and whisk me to the Danvilles, the Davenports, and the Decaturs."

Because of his prolonged absence from American vaudeville, he started to advertise; otherwise, managers and bookers might forget his name. He sent out black-edged stationery announcing the death of his act at the Parthenon Theatre in Hammond, Indiana; he took small ads in the trade papers: "Hunger Strike Ended! (I start to work next week), Freddy James." For weeks he mailed hundreds of "Actor's Reports" styled in the manner of official manager's reports about actors received by booking offices in Chicago and New York. Edward Albee, sovereign of the Keith circuit, read one of the reports and advised Leddy to "have that young man discontinue making fun of our theaters." The lampooning of authority, which

had begun with his father and persisted through the regi-
mented typing classes of Commerce and the sailor hat incident
at the Fuller office, still remained an integral part of Allen's
comedy. He had an attitude not calculated to flatter. From Saint
Louis he mailed vials of murky water labeled as "Perspiration
Taken From the Body of Freddy James After Doing Four Shows
Today at the Grand Theatre."

There was another reason why he wanted to advertise: háv-
ing purloined the "World's Worst Juggler" billing, Harry LaToy
was using it in New England and taking out advertisements
for himself. To counter this, Allen had a batch of announce-
ments printed:

STOLEN

A smalltime Novelty Artist, calling himself Harry
LaToy, has stolen my billing —

WORLD'S WORST JUGGLER

I, Freddy James, am the Original "World's Worst Juggler." I have made good my claim to the above title from
Coast to Coast for the past five years.

FREDDY JAMES

N.B. A recent X-ray taken of Mr. LaToy positively
proves that there is not an original bone in his body.

The dispute crackled for months. In the April 19, 1917, issue of *Vaudeville,* Allen penned "An Open Letter to Harry
LaToy":

Please stop using my billing. I am the original "World's
Worst Juggler."

If you had played a city during the past four years, you
would have heard from me, as I am known from Coast
to Coast as Freddy James, "The World's Worst Juggler."

P.S. Owing to the fact that moving pictures hurt my
eyes, I shall never be able to see your act.

LaToy's answer assumed wounded dignity.

On Oct. 9, 1912, Mr. James played a "show" date at
the National Theatre, Boston, from which date he started
a career of juggling.

I had used the title "World's Worst Juggler" two years previous to that date and have been using it ever since.

This I can prove by bona fide statements before a notary, and the support of many recognized performers, and which I will do, providing Mr. James still insists upon accusing me of using "his title," which during his profession has borne such aliases as "Jesting Juggler," "Almost A Juggler," "The Talkative Juggler," "The Comedy Juggler," etc.

Of course LaToy never intended to validate his claim. Their relationship, so often entangled in acrid farce, would end in pathos. LaToy died a vaudevillian's death in Saint Louis, alone in a hotel room, in 1945, and his body lay unclaimed for a week, until a newspaper reporter working on an obituary recalled that Fred Allen too had been a vaudeville juggler and phoned him as a source for a possible lead. Allen promised that his office would take care of burial arrangements, but when they contacted the proper authorities, the reporter's story had been read by an ex-vaudevillian in the funeral business who as a charitable gesture volunteered his services.

ALLEN'S COMEDY ADVERTISING produced results; Mark Leddy succeeded in booking him on the Pantages, or Pan time, at double his salary. A twenty-week road-show contract on the Pan time, a western circuit, guaranteed that the act would not reach New York before the end of 1917. Traveling with a troupe that opened in Minneapolis, roamed through Canada, and closed in Denver, Allen appeared on a program headlined by Captain Sorcho and His Never-Equalled Monster Submarine Show. Captain Sorcho — who in publicity photographs sighted a sextant, stood at an engine-room telegraph, and gripped the spokes of a ship's wheel — gave a lecture about submarines. His act possessed authentic novelty; the sinking of the *Lusitania* and the depradations of U-boat wolf packs had aroused public curiosity about submarines, till then a subject for Jules Verne and other science fiction fantasists. A diver submerged in a huge glass tank of water illustrated Sorcho's talk, firing sham torpedoes, exploding a "mine," and disclosing the tactics of a submariner. Owing to the educational uplift of his turn, the Captain and his wife remained aloof from the entertainers, mere mummers all.

The only bachelor in the troupe that included an eight-member female song-and-dance revue (the young women, woeful hoofers, did a finale in red-white-and-blue costumes while a large American flag descended behind them), Allen was regarded with suspicion by the girls' chaperones. He submitted without protest to their disapproval since the Pan time represented the security of solid bookings. The show chugged through western Canada while he extended his repertoire of audience-tested jokes:

> "I was teethed on a dictionary and several times my mother took the words out of my mouth."
>
> "He didn't know what to send his girl for a birthday present so he sent her a suit of woolen underwear — she was tickled to death."
>
> "I dreamed I was eating Shredded Wheat. When I woke up the mattress was half gone."

In Calgary he recited a venerable joke that failed to register, but a local critic approvingly noted his quick recovery: "James says he nearly bit the nipple off the bottle when he first heard that one."

The newspapers covered the acts in detail in every town, and invariably the stacked subheads below the larger Captain Sorcho headline referred to the "nut" comic. The Captain's publicity was not uniformly favorable; in Great Falls, Montana, he couldn't appear because the water in his fifteen-thousand-gallon tank, filled from local hydrants using the Missouri River, was so polluted that divers refused to go down. A section of the tank cracked in Anaconda, Montana, and drenched the orchestra pit and half the audience. Assembling the tank and filtering the water at every stop was a nuisance. Captain Sorcho's act depended, alas, on overelaborate logistics.

Not so Freddy James and His Misses, which achieved resounding laughs through an economy of means. "To save wear and tear on the audience," he carried his own applause — four pairs of elongated wooden hands that carpenters made for him. Assistants thrust the hands in front of the curtain on either side

of the stage and slapped them together vigorously, an absurd-
ist device that poked fun at representational illusion. (The
clapping hands also broke the hush if the joke didn't succeed.)
After the clatter died down, Allen confided that some of his
comedy and tricks deserved applause, but he didn't want to
bother the paying customers. Occasionally, he planted an usher
in the orchestra seats and directed him to laugh during silences, whereupon Allen would remark, "He's just getting my
jokes." In a variation, he coined a comment destined to become a stand-up comedian's platitude. Coaxing laughs from a
cold audience, he greeted each tepid flurry with a tender "Thank
you, Mother." If latecomers appeared, he paused in mid-
anecdote, and once they were seated told the joke over again
for their benefit. The banjo provided a mild yet passable finish — then he thought of a strategy of beguiling simplicity.

The flag-waving females occasioned the idea of a patriotic
finale. He had earlier experimented with the patriotic motif in
a doggerel entrance (now discarded) with the dummy, Jake.

> *Ladies and Gentlemen — Look me over well,*
> *I'll ventriloque and jokes to you I'll tell,*
> *I'll try to make you laugh with my funny manner,*
> *And if you don't applaud, I'll sing The Star-Spangled*
> *Banner.*

If he winced when he recalled that entrance, he also perceived how to make it work. Immediately upon completing
the banjo number he would bow off, the stage would darken
and an oval picture of Abraham Lincoln would appear on the
screen. More applause. Then the lights would flash on and
Allen would reenter as though he had heard the applause backstage and was returning to take another bow. As soon as he
left, the lights went down and a picture of George Washington
joined Lincoln's. Still more applause. The lights came on, and
there was Allen taking his second bow. Down went the lights
again and the American flag joined the presidents. By now the
laughing audience knew what to expect, and cheered Allen's
final bow before the lights went off and a sign twinkled "Much
Obliged."

He modified the particulars (President Wilson instead of
Lincoln, "Thank You" instead of "Much Obliged"), but in

the phrase of his lobby photograph — Allen surrounded by his presidential collaborators — "We Get Applause On Any Bill."

The western tour over, he returned to New York and was surprised to find "the same two guys standing outside the Automat." Mark Leddy deemed the new material suitable for a big-time act. Of course, he would have to concoct a different billing. Freddy James had played the eastern small time for seventy-five dollars a week, and if he returned under the same name the bookers would give him the same fixed salary. Leddy ran a Loew franchise and couldn't book his client on the Keith circuit, but he persuaded the Bostock brothers, Claude and Gordon, who only handled top performers, to view the act; a split week was arranged at the City Theatre on Fourteenth Street. "Fred was up in the Fox booking office," Benny Drohan recalled, "and with him was a fellow by the name of Edgar Allen, who used to book the Fox theaters around New York." The City Theatre called the office, Edgar Allen described the act, "there was a mistake over the phone," and Edgar Allen's name got entangled with Freddy James's. Fred Allen did not invent his pseudonym — but for that matter, neither did Mark Twain: Twain simply inherited it from Captain Isaiah Sellers, a superannuated keelboat pilot, who, according to *Life on the Mississippi*, "used to jot down brief paragraphs of plain, practical information about the river, and sign them 'MARK TWAIN,' and give them to the New Orleans *Picayune*."

Reporting to the City Theatre for rehearsal, Allen saw his latest alias. He shrugged, accepting fate. "So many theater managers had mistaken me for one of the James Boys on salary days that I reluctantly changed my professional name to Allen as a tribute to Ethan Allen who had stopped using the name shortly after the Revolution." The nearby Keith theater considered the City "an opposition house," and the Keith management blacklisted the acts performing there. Twice a week, a Keith usher crossed the street and copied down the names of the City's acts from a lobby placard. He didn't see the show. The performers, therefore, adopted spurious identities: Keith's blacklisted a roster of fictive vaudevillians. Somehow Keith's didn't blacklist Fred Allen (that came later);

otherwise, he might have been obliged to resort to one of the preposterous names he enjoyed minting, such as Felix Rattan or Caldwell Fritter.

The Bostock brothers decided the act deserved the big time, but required a touch of "class." Always class-conscious, vaudeville in the waning years of the decade was renewing another of its upward-mobile ascents, and the Bostocks were trend setters. The accent on class would have curious results, as Abel Green and Joe Laurie, Jr., have pointed out:

> In 1919, acts tended to be pretentious, carrying their own sets, curtains, drops and, of course, wardrobes. By the following year even the acrobats were wearing evening clothes. There was a general feeling among vaudevillians that if your act had "class," it would rate more money as well as better position on the bill. So they "dressed" their acts.
>
> The effect of this sartorial vaudeville was so stultifying that managers were grateful to singers who livened it up with offcolor songs, despite the dangerous effect this had on the family trade, backbone of vaudeville.

Allen, measured for a custom-tailored suit, went out on the Fox and Poli time while the tailor prepared it. Claude Bostock also revised the billing; the twenty-three-year-old comedian was "Fred Allen, a Young Fellow Trying to Get Along." Slapstick was modified. The Bostocks wanted audiences to identify with a young, middle-class performer who incarnated the aspirations and energies of a Harold Lloyd. Allen wryly submitted.

> I had so much class I trespassed on the pretty. In my whole life I never looked as well on the street as I did on the stage. I still had the dummy, but the banjo had been changed for a guitar; the guitar had more "class." I couldn't play the guitar. I had to have the neck taken off the banjo and grafted onto the guitar; this enabled me to play the guitar using banjo tuning and banjo chords.

A vestigial juggling segment featured an iron ball and a turnip. The iron ball was conventional material; when Allen used the turnip, though, he threw it in the air and tried to catch it on a fork held in his mouth. After several tries accompanied by jokes, he tossed up the turnip, which came down and shattered on his head. This Harrigan-like routine never failed to make the audience whoop. The remainder of the turnip segment, however, was pure Allen. He stepped behind a screen and, throwing the turnip in the air twice to suggest his dogged effort to catch it, emerged from behind the screen with the turnip on the fork as though he had succeeded in catching it out of sight. The fork and turnip joined the vanishing top hats, the circumnavigating hoop, the clapping hands, and the patriotic slides.

For Allen's big-time bow, the Bostocks selected the Alhambra Theatre on 125th Street. He filled fourth position on the bill, an apparently auspicious spot. Unfortunately, the three acts preceding him were "in one" as well. Following a matinee debut, he returned that evening and was told he was no longer on the bill; the manager had no qualms about the act, but four acts "in one" were impossible, and he had decided to trim the program from the end. Allen went on the small time again for three weeks, then returned to play Proctor's Fifth Avenue Theatre, located whimsically not on Fifth Avenue but on Broadway. Before reentering the big time, however, he was solicited by an ad salesman for *Variety*. The publication emphasized the reviewer's probity, and editorial content was exempt from advertising pressures, but the missionary zeal of its representative may have blurred the distinction. When Allen pointed out that three days' pay at the theater amounted to $62.50 and a *Variety* ad cost $125, the salesman announced that Sime Silverman himself, founder of the journal and already a legendary Broadway figure, would cover the opening. Allen still refused to take the ad; Silverman attended the show, and in a marathon opening sentence drubbed the performance.

> If Fred Allen is his right name he should change it, and if Fred Allen isn't his right name, someone should tell him what it was, for this Fred Allen has copped and copped until he may think he has an act, but what he has is so well-known along the big-time routes that the very familiarity of it must push him back on the small time, even

though he could make the big time, which he might have done five years ago, but five years ago he would not have been able to cop what he has now. His first lift is the ventriloquial bit of Felix Adler's . . .

Sime cited other possible origins — Edwin George and Joe Cook — and found especially George-like Allen's assertion "that he can't take chances with an encore, so he'll do the encore now." Allen, he continued, "is merely a copy of other and better acts who have gone before him and will remain before him while he hangs onto this borrowed material." The seventeen-minute act could be summarized in a single prescient exchange between Jake and his master. The dummy sported an alarm clock strapped to one wrist, which caused Allen to remark, "I guess that's the only big time we'll ever see."

Numbed by *Variety*'s devastating review, Allen once again retreated to the small-time houses. Five years later, however, destiny arranged a pleasing irony: the comedian as columnist would find himself contributing to Sime's pages.

Rival trade publications ran dissenting opinions of Allen's Proctor's performance. "His act goes over in spite of his retiring manner"; "It is an act, simple in detail, but good enough for any bill that ever was played on any vaudeville stage." Even so, Allen, having clipped out Sime's diatribe as a chastening reminder of the disasters attendant upon the unwary actor, never expected the upshot — a phone call from the olympian E. F. Albee asking the young man to open the program at the Palace Theatre.

A Young Fellow Trying to Get Along getting along at the Palace? You don't begin at the top, in the vaudeville holy of holies, the preeminent, incomparable, peerless, unequaled, unsurpassed, ultimate theater. Yet that is what Mr. Albee wanted. The Supreme Autocrat of the Two-a-Day needed a favor from a small-time monologist playing Yonkers. Apparently Albee had forgiven Freddy James for his previous impertinence, or else did not associate James with Allen, or, more likely, the incident had vanished into the labyrinthine recesses reserved in the tycoon's mind for topics beneath notice. The City of New

York decreed that acrobats could not appear on the Sabbath in vaudeville. Mr. Albee had a troupe of flyers scheduled to open the Palace bill. Obviously, they were unable to appear. Could Mr. Allen substitute?

Albee's phone call is puzzling; the head of the Keith circuit could choose countless "dumb" acts as replacements. Opening the bill with a monologist as patrons were filing in flouted common sense. Nevertheless, Allen decided the response at the opening matinee was encouraging, although the Palace was almost empty when he began and half-full when he took his bows amid the presidential slides. The theater's manager disagreed; he deemed the satire too highbrow for his audience, and Mr. Albee or no Mr. Albee, he canceled the act before the evening performance.

The cancellation at the Palace, confirming Sime's tirade, must have been a humiliating blow. It is one thing to parry the catcalls of a Sam Cohen amateur night, another to suffer expulsion from every vaudevillian's eden. "Fred was canceled because he wasn't understood," said Uncle Jim Harkins. "The musicians laughed, the stagehands laughed, but he wasn't using the old gags. 'There must be some intelligent people in the world,' he'd say, and he kept on getting canceled." Zigzagging between the big time and small time became Allen's strategy of survival, even if the random sling or arrow penetrated his defenses and reemphasized his anonymity. "FRED WILLIAMS," proclaimed the addled headline of an affirmative review, "WILL GET ALONG."

Meanwhile, in early 1918, he received a draft notice from Dorchester, but was deferred since his brother Bob had enlisted and Allen remained the sole support of Aunt Lizzie and her paralytic husband. So Fred next played the Delmar time, a southern circuit, and, just as in Sydney, interspersed vaudeville appearances with benefits at army cantonments. The mood, too, reminded him of Australia — the regiments entraining for the front, mass hysteria, unruly confidence — and he watched the farewells again, not without trepidation.

The Bostocks hadn't given up; they managed to book him into the big-time Hippodrome in Cleveland. On this occasion his act went over, resulting in a succession of big-time dates across Texas and an appearance at Chicago's Palace Theatre, an auditorium deferring in importance only to its New York namesake. He was second on the bill, but the critics liked him: "When Allen trotted out the pictures of George Washington, Woodrow Wilson and the American Flag, the audience fell in with the spirit of this far from subtle dig at the proclivities of some artists to exploit patriotism, and cheered Allen lustily."

Jubilant, he purchased an ad from *Chicago Show World* in the name of "Fred Allen (The Non-Essential), Now Playing the Palace."

BETWEEN 1918 AND 1922, Allen performed in theaters, small time and big, returning home summers to Dorchester, Carson Beach, Hodge White's neighborhood grocery store, Grafton Street, and Aunt Lizzie. Baseball games at the "rubber ground" took place daily. The rubber ground beside Morrissey Boulevard held a sizable amount of peat mingled with cinders from an adjacent railroad; bouncing across this surface, the balls took skittish hops and tangents. Allen was a pitcher judged "pretty good" by players in those pickup games. Summers, when theaters closed, he haunted the rubber ground, and later donated equipment to the teams.

An engagement at the Keith Boston in 1919 enhanced Allen's neighborhood celebrity and he became known to the local gang as "the ackter." This pattern of the provincial and the cosmopolitan, like the big-time and small-time circuits on which he juggled, marked his early career; he returned to the old neighborhoods as if to rid himself of the shams of stardom. Vaudeville, to be sure, did not encourage those shams, although he appeared on the same bills in conjunction with authentic stars. Fred Allen and Lillian Russell, for example, the harbinger of a more sophisticated era of comedy and one of the last survivors of the age of the whalebone corset and picture hat, often played the same program. "The Venus Anno Domini of the American Stage," escorted by six husky U.S. Marines, Miss Russell sang her signature ballad, "Evening Star." Pioneer modern dancers Ted Shawn and Ruth St. Denis appeared with Allen at Shea's Theatre in Buffalo. He heard Fritzi Scheff sing her Victor Herbert specialty, "Kiss Me Again," which she had introduced in 1905. In Greenville, South Carolina, he received second billing to Niblo's Birds, and in Cincinnati came onstage after a performance of Eugene O'Neill's fo'c'sle drama *In the Zone,* which in the oxymoronic opinion of one reviewer, "holds interest but lacks dramatic punch."

Curiously enough, in the seasons before his first Broadway show Allen was sometimes admonished for off-color jokes. A comedian distinguished by the perfect pitch of his taste, he may at this point have been experimenting imprudently with his material. Aside from the lone Australian objection, critics had never faulted Allen for vulgarity, but all at once a chorus of tut-tuts greeted him. "A little shady in some of his humor" (Loew's Lyceum, Memphis); "A comic cuss who sings aimless ditties, comments impromptu on many subjects and strikes a few purple spots" (Poli's, Hartford); "Fred Allen offers some ancient jokes, some of which need an acid bath before presentation on a refined vaudeville program" (Academy, Charleston, South Carolina). In South Bend, Indiana, an indignant manager rang down the curtain on the act because of Allen's allegedly smutty gibes. What can be made of this? Douglas Gilbert states:

> In vaudeville Allen was . . . a clean nut comic who presented any ridiculous thing that occurred to him. He'd quit in the middle of a routine, sit flat on the stage almost in the footlights, and read his press notices to the orchestra leader. At one time he used a shapeless and dilapidated ventriloquist's dummy for a purposely atrocious ventriloquial specialty; another time he used a frightful banjo to accompany an equally wretched song. His dead pan was superb, making the foolish things he did get over the riotous laughter.

The persistence of the complaint, on the other hand, suggests that the managers were not excessively prudish. It is a peculiar and fleeting interval; the carping about alleged smut tapered off by the mid-1920s, and if there was indeed substance in the charges, Allen revised the act. Comic genius, like any other form of genius, sounds not only the depths of inspiration but the shallows of trial and error.

UNABLE TO LAND A LONG-TERM CONTRACT on the Keith circuit — notwithstanding his Chicago success — he again played the Loew time, then took another six-month western road-show tour with a Pantages unit. It included a pair of conceited gymnasts, the Haas Brothers; Lucy Bruch, a Viennese violinist who rehearsed her classical selections day and night; and Asahi and Company, Japanese illusionists. There was a girl act in the company, not quite as lavish as the song-and-dance show that accompanied Captain Sorcho, but provoking the same sexual tensions. Florence Lorraine, the star of "Girls Will Be Girls," became miffed because Tom McGrath of McGrath and Deeds, a comedy song-and-dance duo, had caught the eye of one of her chorines. She also disapproved of Allen, a pal of the sheik McGrath and Jack Deeds. By the time they reached El Paso, twenty-four weeks into the tour, Miss Lorraine had exhausted her tolerance. Her social friend, the district attorney, assured her that she need not fret, he would take care of the situation. The next morning he sent around a detective, who discovered Allen in his dressing room repairing the dummy. Jake didn't accompany them to the station, but in the ensuing brouhaha he would have been as articulate as many of the witnesses. Allen recalled:

> When we arrived at the police station, it developed that the detective had arrested the wrong man. The district attorney wanted either McGrath or Deeds, in order to avenge Miss Lorraine's grievance. However, it appeared that I couldn't be released gracefully, and so I was charged with using indecent language in Miss Lorraine's presence. I didn't talk to the woman and hadn't used any language in her presence for many weeks. The theater manager arranged for my release, and the next morning my case came up in court.

Allen now had been in a train wreck in El Paso and arrested on trumped-up charges there. His trial, chronicled in *Much Ado about Me,* eddied into a giddy masterpiece of farcical cross-purposes and misunderstandings.

> Miss Lorraine testified that McGrath, Deeds and I were disreputable characters, and that she had heard vile lan-

guage in El Paso, and that the language could have come from any one of us. My character witnesses were the Asahi Company, none of whom understood English too well; the Viennese violinist, who spoke with an accent; and McGrath and Deeds. They were all to testify to my exemplary behavior on the entire tour.

Prosecuting the case, the one-armed district attorney riveted the court's attention by rolling his own cigarettes with one hand and the stump of his missing arm — a fillip of Faulkner amid the ferment of Feydeau. The DA won the case and the judge fined Allen ten dollars and costs (thus possibly motivating sundry similar courtroom sketches on *The Linit Bath Club Revue*). The theater manager, sympathetic to Allen, settled the fine and costs and wired Alexander Pantages, overseer of the Pan time, explaining the circumstances. Exit Florence Lorraine and "Girls Will Be Girls" from the Pantages circuit.

By the close of this tour, the last vestiges of juggling had faded from the act. Allen had written a mock ballad, "The Electric Chair Is Ready," which required grotesquerie: whiteface, a derby, an inverness, ribless umbrella, large shoes, and white gloves. He had tried out the mock-ballad idea in Australia, standing in the footlight trough and reciting with tremolo stops a number called "The Rich Barber's Daughter." "The Electric Chair" added five minutes, so he pared his material, and when he finished, the juggling was gone.

Among small-timers he was known as someone who could fix an ailing act. The small-timer couldn't afford gagmen, and Allen's literacy and willingness to doctor material made him singular. Stanley and Birnes, a comedy song-and-dance team who had returned with him on the *Sierra,* wrote from the Waldorf Hotel in Toledo, enclosing a scrap of words and music: "The girls won't leave me / They're always chasing me. . . ."

Look the thing over Freddie and let us know if you can do anything in the line of material and give us a good idea something different from the average two-man act. We still wear the Beau Brummels and would like to if possible,

A turn-of-the-century gathering of the Sullivan clan in Cambridge. *Far right,* John Henry, the patriarch; three of his four brothers; his sons, Bob and John (*third from left*); and a niece.

Aunt Lizzie, who kept the Sullivan family together.

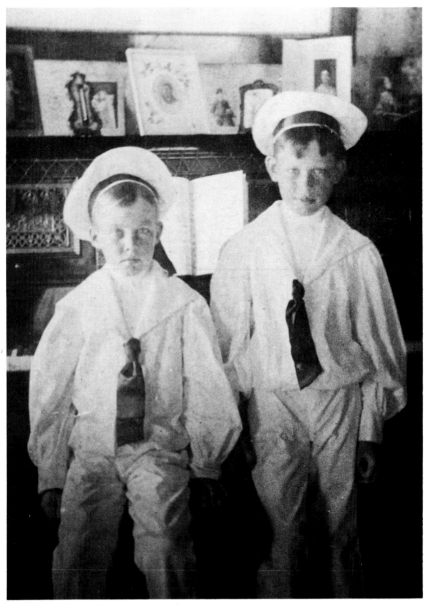

The Sullivan boys, Bob and John Florence (*right*), in the parlor of their Bayard Street house in Allston.

The 1911 graduating class at Commerce High. *Front row, center,* John poses with jacket unbuttoned alongside his best friend, "Tug" Lalley (*in light suit*).

Australia, 1916. The domesticity of small-time vaudevillians is evident at Dougherty's theatrical boardinghouse, where Fred (*upper right*) shared lodgings with the rest of his troupe.

A typical program on the Western Vaudeville circuit. Freddie James, "the World's Worst Juggler," obviously occupies a humbler spot on the bill than that of the headliners, Williams and Wolfus.

Only Fred (*far right*) looks almost conventional as he and a trio of vaudeville cohorts enjoy an offstage moment in Dallas around 1919.

Allen with the banjo used to accompany his jokes as his act
developed from juggler to full-time comedian.

The "Old Joke Cemetery" curtain conceived by Allen and drawn by Martin Branner for *The Passing Show of 1922.*

In "Disappointments of 1927," Fred opened at the Palace with his new bride, Portland Hoffa, on a program topped by Fanny Brice and the Gus Edwards Revue.

get away from the Tuxedo. We're your Australian strike me pinkers,

Stanley and Birnes

From "Garrison Hall, The Homelike Hotel, Garrison Street, opposite Mechanics Hall," Boston:

Dear Freddie,

No doubt you will be surprised to hear from us but I happened to see your name in the *Variety* so thought we would drop you a line. What our object in writing to you at this time is that we are looking for new material and we feel sure that you can write something for us and won't charge the same as Aaron Hoffman or you might do so for a peice [*sic*] of Pickled Herring so you can use it on the Sonoma. But all kidding aside Freddie I'll go through the routine we are now doing including the opening patter song and explain the dancing routine and perhaps from that you can get a good idea of just what to do.

Allen's literary chores among small-time vaudevillians went unrewarded. "I liked to write and see ideas take form and come to life," he said. "When I finished their acts for them, none of my clients ever paid me. I was lucky when they didn't borrow money from me to go out of town and break in the acts. I became a joke philanthropist." Nevertheless, his writing abilities helped lead to his first contact with Broadway, *Frank Fay's Fables*.

Fay was an inventive monologist and light comedian, best known to a subsequent generation as the star of Mary Chase's comedy *Harvey,* although he is credited with pioneering the role of the master of ceremonies in vaudeville. Fay asked Allen to collaborate with Jimmy Duffy, a gifted but alcoholic comic, who also wrote his own material. At this juncture Fay enjoyed a burgeoning career; the show's premises looked promising to Allen, and in rehearsal it displayed the earmarks of a hit. However, Fay could not stay on any conversational subject except himself, and as Elliot Norton, the drama critic, commented, Fay was "as elusive as a greased eel" when interviewed. The principal subject he was elusive about was money: *Frank Fay's Fables* lacked backers. Locating a pair of financial angels, he refused to let them have fifty-one percent of the show's stock, the controlling interest.

"At the rehearsal hall, when Fay had an appointment to talk with a prospective backer or the scenic designer, or someone he wanted to impress, Fay would borrow the tenor singer's camel's-hair coat for his business talks," Allen told interviewer Maurice Zolotow. "The tenor had to sit around the rehearsal hall until Fay returned." Still another prospective backer, a wholesale grocer, solved Fay's problem of paying the actors. Instead of salaries, the cast received cans of tomatoes and corn, which Fay stored in his apartment closet. When Duffy pleaded that his mother was starving, Fay offered him a wheel of cheese. Allen reported, "Duffy said his mother was hungry; she didn't have mice in the house." The show folded with $4,000 owed to the cast, but it instigated one of Fred Allen's enduring lines, "The last time I saw Fay he was walking down Lover's Lane holding his own hand." Long afterward, Allen observed: "I have known Mr. Fay for approximately twenty-five years. The fact that he only owes me $200 merely proves that he hasn't seen as much of me during the past twenty-five years as he has of many other people."

The Fay debacle sent Allen back to Mark Leddy, who informed him that the Shuberts, about to launch a new vaudeville circuit, needed acts. As always, there was a catch: whoever played the Shubert theaters would be blacklisted for life on the Keith circuit; Allen elected to take the risk. The Shuberts had a number of stars under contract. (Their shows had better talent, but over the long run could not compete with the Keith monopoly.) In September 1921, Allen started over the new circuit in a condensed version of *Snapshots,* a Broadway hit starring Lew Fields, of the venerable Dutch comedy duo Weber and Fields. The entertainment fell into two parts: five acts of vaudeville, including Fred Allen, and Fields's hour-long revue. For the Brooklyn opening of *Snapshots of 1922,* Fields brought in his son, Herbert, who made the sixteen-week tour as a spare actor. With him arrived a college friend, recently graduated from Columbia: Richard Rodgers, whom Lew Fields appointed musical director of the unit. Although the older pit musicians resented the cub placed in charge — Dickie Rodgers to them — he and librettist Herbert Fields and lyric writer Lorenz Hart would reshape the American musical theater during the next decade.

Playing the Shubert circuit of mainly eastern theaters, Allen was assigned a Nora Bayes unit in which he once more altered the opening of his act. To portentous chords from *Lohengrin,* the house went dark and a sign shot into the spotlight: "Mr. Allen Is Quite Deaf. If You Care to Laugh or Applaud, Please Do So Loudly." As the audience responded, he made his entrance, hand cupped behind his ear, and confided that his suit had been made in Jersey City — "I'm a bigger man there than I am here." (The same joke proved serviceable in *The Passing Show of 1922,* where New Rochelle replaced Jersey City.)

Today the "Quite Deaf" opening would draw fire from representatives of the hearing-impaired, but in 1922 it provoked no outcry, and Allen found the entrance effective. Nora Bayes, whom he came to admire, took the troupe around the circuit twice. The tour built up his reputation in certain locales, notably in New Haven, where Yale students kept clamoring for more. That season, working harder than ever, he played the Hyperion Theatre in New Haven four times. From the Hotel Touraine in Buffalo, he wrote his vaudeville friend Henry J. Kelly.

Just a line to let you know that I have been busier than a blind moth in the dressing rooms at the Winter Garden. . . . I am dizzy from rehearsing and despite the fact that the show opened well here on Monday, we are still going over new sketches and putting one in tomorrow night. There are two more to be tried out and then my troubles are over.

I have no news except that I feel lousy as usual and wish that I could have five minutes alone with whoever it was that encouraged me to stay in this business. It is all a colossal fake Old Man and you would realize it if you

could see me dancing in the show. I dance four choruses
with three other people and nothing has taken place yet.
Whatever is Mexican for Good Luck.

His contract expired all too soon, however, and it was back
to the small time. Blacklisted for life by the Keith office, he
steeled himself for a protracted stretch of cheerless dressing
cubicles, flyblown luncheonettes, and moribund hinterland
hotels: Watertown, New York . . . Red Bank, New Jersey
. . . Pottstown, Pennsylvania. Several split weeks passed before the deliverance of Leddy's phone call. J. J. Shubert, whose
glacial eye appraised theatrical diamonds and zircons, had
scrutinized Allen's act several times and pronounced it suitable
for the forthcoming Winter Garden attraction, *The Passing Show
of 1922*. Musical comedy, a dawning horizon of possibility,
swept into sight.

BROADWAY

VANCE: Now the murder was committed exactly at 8:32; rigor mortis set in at 8:33, habeas corpus at 8:44, with standing room only at 8:45. What was Death's instrument? Was it a banjo, a ukelele or a marimba?
CHIEF: I don't marimba.

— opening of *The Little Show*

7 | Follies and Fly Talk

The Kahn-Donaldson tune "Carolina in the Morning" remains the only faint echo of *The Passing Show of 1922,* ninth of a series inaugurated in 1912. The Messrs. Shubert, brothers J.J. and Lee, had constructed their Winter Garden Theatre as a showcase for a sequence of spectacular revues intended to surpass in splendor the *Ziegfeld Follies.* Florenz Ziegfeld had chosen to launch the first of his annual divertimenti on a sweltering July night of 1907, so the Shuberts, emulating him, likewise planned their annual *Passing Shows* for summer, supplementing them with opulent fall and spring productions.

The *Scandals,* the *Follies,* the *Vanities,* and other aptly named extravaganzas of the teens and twenties reflected the hedonistic spirit of an age of excess. Grandiose, sassy, and lush, they were intended for sugar daddies, flappers, and big butter-and-egg men, but the Rabelaisian mood stopped short of unbridled bawdiness and the garish exuberance contained a saccharine hint of the sentimental. Broadway musicals of the twenties were, more often than not, American versions of Viennese operetta such as Romberg's *Desert Song* and Friml's *Rose Marie.* The decade, invariably portrayed as an era of uninhibited whoopee, also found utterance in songs of yearning — Friml's "Only a Rose" ("I gi-i-ve you") and Romberg's "Blue Heaven" ("And you and I /And sand kissing a moonlit sky"). Jay Gatsby, a bootlegger, was Cyrano de Bergerac's bootlegger cousin.

The romantic book musicals, based on Continental operetta, and the Broadway spectacles, accentuating show girls and blackouts and slangy repartee, were optimistic. For the most part, they didn't criticize the milieu they reflected. Mild exceptions occurred in the revue form: *The Passing Show* almost always presented a parody of other Broadway shows — Blanche Ring, for instance, as John Barrymore, and Charles Winninger as Lionel Barrymore, performing a 1919 travesty of *The Jest*. In Fred Allen's 1922 edition, a line of chorines chanting taboo words ridiculed the verisimilitude of the language of Eugene O'Neill's stokers in *The Hairy Ape,* that year's Broadway sensation. Never as urbane or as epicurean as the rival *Follies, The Passing Show* at all events fostered over the years several magnetic talents. Among them were comedians Willie and Eugene Howard, who stepped from vaudeville to the Broadway theater in the first *Passing Show*. A fixture of every subsequent production, they were masters of non sequitur.

EUGENE: Who was that lady I saw you with in the street?
WILLIE: That was no street; that was an alley.

The same *Passing Show* introduced eccentric dancer Charlotte Greenwood and featured a song by rehearsal pianist Irving Berlin. Jerome Kern, too, composed a number.

Baritone John Charles Thomas from the 1913 edition later achieved recognition for his concert hall and opera work. Out of that 1913 edition, too, burst Texas Guinan, brassy speakeasy hostess of the jazz age, whose *Variety* ads featured her personal "Marvelous New Treatment for Fat Folks." A picture of Miss Guinan in costume was captioned, "God's Masterpiece and the Most Fascinating Actress in America," and alongside, she testified: "Mr. Shubert, on account of my glorious new figure, made me the star of *The Passing Show* — and, mind you, this very same manager had said I was doomed to oblivion just a short time before when I tipped the scales at 204 pounds." She was endorsing the product of a promoter soon prosecuted by U.S. Post Office officials.

In the 1914 edition, artistic highlight of the series, Sigmund Romberg, the Shuberts' new house composer, prepared the score. Marilynn Miller, an entrancing singer and dancer imported from English vaudeville, also made her debut (she dropped the extra *n* after the Shuberts lost her to Ziegfeld because she was underage), and George White was a featured dancer. Five years later, he began writing and producing the *Scandals* using a fifty-dollar-a-week composer, George Gershwin. The 1914 show, moreover, introduced the modern chorus line, and its source was unexpected: Max Reinhardt and his Deutsches Theatre troupe, the most innovative theatrical offering of the period. Lee Shubert had signed up the visionary Reinhardt — a financial blunder — and the director, attempting to eliminate the invisible wall between performers and audience, created the first "thrust stage." The Shuberts, following his principles, built a Winter Garden runway on which the chorus could sashay through the audience. Legs were bared, midriffs exposed. Chorus ladies, formidable amazons inclined toward military drill and gymnastics or else fulsome soubrettes giggling and frisking, now had freer choreographic potential. They tapped and kicked and executed balletic pirouettes. Undressing the chorine was no doubt instigated by coarse motives, but doing so loosed her from a static and marginal role.

George Gershwin's professional bow (pre–George White) took place in *The Passing Show of 1916* ("The Making of a Girl," no song to remember). The hit of the 1917 revue was Billy Baskette's "Goodbye Broadway, Hello France!" Fred and Adele Astaire appeared for the first time as stars in the 1918 version (their dancing had animated a failed Shubert revue, 1917's *Over the Top,* in which they had secondary roles), and the 1918 show also boasted two interpolated songs, "Smiles" and "I'm Forever Blowing Bubbles." The 1924 annual, last of the cycle, introduced a dancer who received billing as Lucille Le Sueur, later screen star Joan Crawford.

The Passing Show, then, served as a vehicle for the legitimate stage debuts of the Howard brothers, Romberg, Miller, and Gershwin, and in it the Astaires enjoyed their first substantial success. Even by *Follies* standards, this was a not inconsiderable record, but the Shubert revue, when Fred Allen added his name to that distinguished roster, still struggled against a reputation as "second best" to Ziegfeld's. Critical opinion never fazed

J. J. Shubert, though his brother reputedly entertained stray aesthetic sensations. J.J. reminded Allen of a turtle minus a shell walking upright. As the unflattering comparison suggests, relations between the Shuberts and Allen would develop bizarre wrinkles, but for the moment, wariness sufficed. The profit motif was uppermost in J.J.'s thoughts.

During the early summer of 1922, Allen consulted Harold Atteridge, author of libretti and lyrics for the Shubert office. A glance at the annals of 1920s musicals indicates how ubiquitous was Atteridge, now a forgotten figure but the writer of many Al Jolson vehicles, the entire *Passing Show* series, and intermittent *Follies, Artists and Models,* and assorted revels. "Harold was a tireless, all purpose author whom the Shuberts employed until they could invent a machine that could do the same amount of work," observed Allen. Because the writer settled for a retainer fee, he never gained the security that his industry merited, and when Allen visited him at his Riverside Drive apartment, Atteridge was fueling his overworked muse with Prohibition hooch. Stacks of *Tit-Bits, Pearson's Weekly, Punch,* and other humor magazines atop the liquor closet augured well for an idea Allen was about to propose: a funny curtain.

Atteridge confessed that he had been so busy toiling over the Howards' material, he hadn't given attention to other comic odds and ends. Various possibilities were discussed and Allen proposed a running gag. He would tell the audience he had sent his dress shirt with his jokes on the cuffs to the laundry around the corner. Once the next number commenced, he would leave the theater up the main aisle, presumably to pick up his shirt. Coming back a few numbers later, he would discover that he had received the wrong bundle. Other variations would permit him to step in and out of the acts, building toward the climax — the shirt revealed in all its glory, scribbled jokes spilling across the cuffs, the shirtfront and back, and onto the tail.

The idea pleased Atteridge, so Allen showed him a rough sketch for another device, an "Old Joke Cemetery" curtain. Martin Branner, an accomplished comic-strip artist (*Winnie Winkle*) and former vaudevillian, would produce the finished version. Above the "Old Joke Cemetery" rode a jug-eared moon beaming upon headstones and other mortuary monuments, including a statue of Joe Miller. Each stone displayed an archaic joke. The curtain symbolized Allen's systematic investigation of the subject of humor, for he had long before dismissed the possibility of a completely original joke: there were only jokes that went stale faster than others. His expanding collection of books about humor, comic performance, and wit contributed to his act — Allen owned a rare first edition of *Joe Miller's Jokebook* — and frequently he resuscitated quips long consigned to oblivion. From a speech by a contemporary of Edmund Burke, Allen had culled the simile "as ineffective as patting the back of a turtle to please it." An 1899 jokebook supplied a snippet appropriate for bandying insults with a bald orchestra leader: "I see you're still growing — you're nearly through your hair." The comment "It's so hot I feel like taking off my skin and sitting around in my bones" was used by Mark Twain, but Allen located an earlier source from which Twain probably borrowed the line, Lady Holland's memoir of her father, Sydney Smith. Where did Smith run into the joke? It didn't matter; humor worked when it displayed the cachet of an idiosyncratic attitude and delivery. Even the most battered joke sounded new-minted in the telling. If the Howard brothers could pluck a laugh from "Who was that lady I saw you with last night?" Allen could, as he did, set the same exchange in a totally different key.

"Who was that oboe I saw you with last night?"
"That was no oboe; that was my fife."

The jokes on the cemetery curtain, however, were presumably beyond reincarnation: "After running, my breath comes in short pants"; "The church is on fire — holy smoke"; "There was a travelling man (censored)"; "A Prohibitionist lieth here — his ails are over — he is on his bier." Passing under the arched cemetery gate and into the graveyard via its "one-way street," a hearse bore the label "Who's the lady in the hearse? That's no lady — that's my wife."

The theatricality of the effect derived from the audience's gradual discovery of the panorama; the jokes would emerge one by one while the orchestra played "a soft, toe-tapping rustic melody," and audience attention skipped from one joke to another. Then the impact of the visual joke, a necropolis of interred tomfoolery, made itself felt.

> The curtain continued to rise slowly, and by the time the entire cemetery could be seen, the theater seemed to be a huge percolator top holding down hundreds of happy, bubbling shrieks. The curtain just hung there for almost five minutes with nobody on the stage. There were forty-six old jokes lying in state, and no two people in the audience looked in the same direction. As the laughter mounted, men nudged their wives or girl friends to call attention to one particular joke, and strangers were prodding their neighbors and pointing to others. At the peak of the cachinnation the theater was blacked out, a white spotlight swept to the left entrance, and I walked on, carrying a banjo.

The Old Joke Cemetery became a highlight of the Winter Garden production; the joke-covered shirt failed to survive the Atlantic City tryout. A September opening was late for a *Passing Show;* during July and August the cast rehearsed at the Century Theatre in New York. Fred Allen did not rehearse with them. Atteridge and the director devoted their attention to the comedy sketches; as a monologist, his material theoretically polished, Allen watched from the sidelines. At the beginning of the fifth week, when J. J. Shubert, sitting at a table on the cavernous stage, evaluated the revue's contents, Allen was allowed to stand at the table and explain his routines in a low voice. J.J. maintained the phlegm of a boulder. Indeed, a smile would have been a sign of distress. Mr. Shubert's mirth meant the joke was destined for removal.

The show opened Labor Day at Nixon's Apollo Theatre in Atlantic City, and the frenzied logistics of setting the stage and lights and running through the musical cues with conductor Al Goodman did not permit a weekend dress rehearsal. Opening night, the curtain went up at 8:30 and failed to come down for seven hours. Allen sat on a campstool in the wings, and whenever anything went awry, the stage manager sent him into the fray like a football coach with one sound quarterback.

That night the comedian made eighteen appearances; the next morning, when J. J. Shubert read out the revised lineup of two acts and twenty-four scenes, Allen's contributions had been whittled down to three. He now made his first entrance stepping through the curtain after a surprise blackout on a large ensemble number. He wore a frogged black astrakhan coat and a derby and carried a shovel. "You remember me from motion pictures?" he announced. "The man who followed The Four Horsemen?"

Enthusiasm revived in New Haven, that Fred Allen town where the revue traveled next, and the New York opening, September 20, received a cordial critical response. Typical was the phrase "Most lavish revue of the season, moving swiftly despite its bulk." "On a par with the best of the Winter Garden shows," stated the *New York Times* under a headline proclaiming the edition "Full of Vim and Color." The anonymous reviewer observed, "Fred Allen performs the difficult task of coming before the curtain and being amusing all by himself — an unusually hard trick to turn at the Winter Garden." *The Playgoer,* however, took an opposite view, praising Willie and Eugene Howard and George Hassall, but reviving vagrant charges of bad taste. "The fourth comedian of the show, Fred Allen, was, in our opinion, more of a liability than an asset. He was funny sometimes, but his humor is low-grade and inclines toward vulgarity." The same reviewer, however, found beguiling *The Hairy Ape* spoof and the chorus girls as stokers doing unison calisthenics: "A swearing chorus is certainly new on Broadway."

In addition to the Old Joke Cemetery, Allen did a Will Rogers impersonation and a final monologue in which he read a pun-laden colloquial letter from home: "The man next door has bought pigs; we got wind of it this morning. Your father had a terrible fight with him about it, but the man hit your father with a rock in the left ear. It didn't bother your father; he is stone deaf in that ear. The policeman who took him away said he would get his hearing in the morning. The other man, the one who owns the pigs, was arrested for fragrancy. . . ."

Despite benign notices, *The Passing Show,* which usually lasted through the season, folded after ten weeks. Allen ascribed the closing to the tackiness of the production, for, notwithstanding the critics' bedazzlement, J.J. had done the spectacle on the cheap. Perhaps the revue really needed the joke shirt — that is, some unifying principle — since the diversity of the critical responses implies a lack of focus. One critic singled out Willie and Eugene's phonograph-store routine, in which the store had run out of records and Willie, crouching behind the Victrola, imitated Enrico Caruso, Harry Lauder, and Eddie Cantor; another preferred the interlude when Arthur Margetson and Sam Ash on a darkened stage gave a solemn illustrated lecture about fifty-seven varieties of kisses. "Super-excellent dancers," raved *The Playgoer*, describing "the Oriental and decidedly erotic 'Ballets les Conquerants' " that closed the first act; but the *Times* retorted, "Even a confirmed revue attendant might ask a toning-down of the revel that brings down the first-act curtain." The sole area of agreement was the pulchritude of the line. No doubt such reactions as "Scanty Clothing On Pretty Chorus Girls Reminds Spectators of Bathing Beach" provoked the Messrs. Shubert toward their next step in the musical theater, "living curtains" of nude show girls.

Meantime, the show went on the road: J.J. and Lee sought to recoup their investment. Starting in Boston, where Allen's status as hometown hero was reconfirmed, the production did business throughout the cities of the East. (Tickets were $2.50 for the best seat in the house; the second balcony was 50 cents.) A comfortable six-month summer run took place in Chicago, but in October 1923 the company returned to the split weeks, one-night stands, and scarecrow theaters of the Midwest vaudeville circuits. All the familiar vicissitudes revived, more sharply felt than ever since Allen now had put up with them for more than a decade. In Lima, Ohio, the stage was too small for the scenery. "Every time I started to talk in front of the curtain," he recalled, "the stagehands opened the big back doors to bring in the next scene and the gusts of wind would billow the curtain and nearly blow me into the audience."

Once more he inhabited a sealed world where clocks and calendars and creature comforts had no place. "I rarely knew what day it was or what town I was in." J.J. planned to send the cast to California, but not until he had practiced every economy. For the actor, playing in a Shubert road show going west was a modern version of the pioneer wagon train passing through Indian territory; the route doubled on itself as if to hide all traces, and you never knew from hour to hour whether you'd get scalped before sunset. J.J.'s modus operandi involved retaining one or two name actors, firing higher-priced performers, and consolidating three or four or more parts into one. Allen assumed that he himself would survive, but in Williamsport, Pennsylvania, on a Saturday, he received a telegram advising him to report to the Shubert New York office on Monday. Aside from the annoying time element, there was a practical consideration: Allen was the copyright owner of the Old Joke Cemetery curtain. The stage manager refused to part with the curtain, which continued onward. Monday morning, in New York, J.J., busy with affairs of state, could not keep their appointment, so Allen left the producer a note stating that he gave the brothers permission to use the curtain upon payment of a fifty-dollar-a-week royalty. By Wednesday it became plain the Shubert office planned to ignore this offer. Allen consulted a lawyer, and an injunction was served prohibiting the troupe from leaving Wilkes-Barre with the curtain. The stage manager sent a telegram agreeing to ship back the curtain on the night train. The telegram did not mention that he also planned to have a local photographer make a replica. The Old Joke Cemetery was photographed, the original curtain shipped. Light meters were not a specialty of Wilkes-Barre photography, however. The lighting in the theater was so dim that when the photograph was developed the following morning, no one could read the headstones.

Allen's increasingly problematic relations with the Shuberts were not uncommon. Ruthless practitioners of behavioral psychology, the brothers treated their chattels with a mixture of scorn and flattery, depending on the needs of the moment. Performers who crossed them might end up in limbo; on the other hand, comedian Jack Osterman, who in a drunken fury knocked J. J. Shubert through a backstage flat, remained with the touring show since Osterman was required for the finale.

Although Allen's contract had another three years to run, his employers could cancel at the end of any single year, and

after the curtain imbroglio his prospects for performing in another Shubert production looked slender. Accordingly, he had
Mark Leddy book him in Norwich, Connecticut, in order to
break in a new act. Since he was, technically, still a Shubert
hireling, Allen used the pseudonym Benjamin Franklin. It was
not the most inventive of false colors, but offered acceptable
camouflage. Allen claimed only three people knew he was
Benjamin Franklin playing Norwich: himself, Leddy, and the
booker. The last day of the engagement, the Shubert office
phoned and Allen was ordered to return to New York and
join the cast of *Artists and Models*.

The phone call, omniscient, impersonal, above recrimina-
tion, displayed the despotic Shubert flair. Magnanimity was
not a Shubert trait; pragmatism was all. Like Osterman, Allen
was necessary for the show. *Artists and Models* sprang from an
off-Broadway amateur production staged by the Society of
Illustrators in Greenwich Village. Purchased by the Shuberts,
who proceeded to scuttle everything but the title, the musical
was announced at a press conference as "a successful, high-
type, sophisticated revue" in the Folies-Bergère mode. J.J.,
however, fumed over the next day's headline: "Shuberts announce change of policy; to be sophisticated." In the Shubert
lexicon, *sophisticated* meant "nude." The female nudity of
Artists and Models, captured in the show's surviving still photographs, is artificial, with rotary arrangements of show girls
poised against a huge painter's palette, and self-conscious
"classical" nudes in solemn poses (Grecian urn on shoulder,
dreamy gaze, hands clasped behind head), akin to streamlined
car-radiator ornaments. The shock of the performance derived
from movement; the nudes frolicked in the sketches. For the
first time in several seasons, single tickets began to sell as briskly
at the box office as pairs of seats.

Frank Fay starred in *Artists and Models*. His faun's smirk and
bemused timing steeped even the fully dressed sketches in
voyeurism. The star's periodic drinking bouts were a serious
problem, however, and when he disappeared during one of
them, his understudy took over Fay's sketches, while Allen
substituted in a pair of monologues. During his fortnight with
the revue, there could scarcely have been a stronger contrast

of comic styles: Fay was a rake, a fantasist, an Irish chancer; Allen wore a different Irish aspect, shrewd, sardonic, and straitlaced. If Fay imparted a salacious tone to the proceedings, Allen provided a splash of cold water. Physically, intellectually, temperamentally, he did not embellish the risque. Twice a night, after the lights faded on bare bosoms and powdered limbs, he stepped in front of the curtain, "posing as an antidote for sex," as he put it, while women were in the throes of disbelief and men in a morose mood for jokes. It was a deliverance when Fay at last reappeared. Accompanied by his father and a priest, the contrite Fay promised J.J. that he was a changed man. Contracts signed, pledges renewed, the priest returned to his rectory and Fay to his innuendos.

Allen performed for the Shuberts until the expiration of his contract in 1926, and the contract guaranteed twenty weeks of work each year. In *Vogues of 1924,* which starred Odette Myrtil ("The Parisian-London Show Star") and promised "50 Girls, Stars In the Making," Allen headed the supporting cast, a redoubtable one featuring comedian-pantomimist Jimmy Savo in his Broadway debut, and Betty Compton, who later married Mayor Jimmy Walker. For the sixth edition of *The Greenwich Village Follies,* Allen stepped into a show already running, and this, with a few other cast substitutions, permitted the Shuberts to advertise a "new version."

Vogues, not a happy company, had many snags. No one seemed to harmonize: Allen and Savo; the director, J. C. Huffman, and his writers, who were British; Miss Myrtil and Allen, and Miss Myrtil and Savo. She insisted the comedy sketches be given instead to another performer, Charles Judels. Even Lee Shubert had undertaken the show as a competitive gesture. The brothers, bitter offstage rivals, apportioned their domains like the Roman Caesars of the Western and Eastern Empires. Lee governed the real estate holdings and the dramas; J.J.'s dominion was musical comedy. While J.J. was traveling in Europe early in 1924, Lee decided to produce *Vogues* as proof he too could present a successful musical.

Had not Huffman blown up at his writers and stalked out during rehearsal, it is probable that neither Allen nor Savo would have received significant roles. Huffman calmed down and returned, and as a consequence of the incident, Allen was permitted to contribute an opening scene and a series of blackout sketches. (A woman comes across the stage leading a very small dog. Allen asks, "What is it?" and the woman says, "A police dog." "Can't be — it's too small." "That's all right," says the woman. "He's in the secret service.") At the New Haven opening, the styles of the two comedians coalesced. They were a contrast in height (Savo was elfin), in speech, mime, and personality. Following the tryout performances, Judels departed from the cast.

Vogues opened in New York early in 1924 and received complimentary notices that singled out the wit of the revue. Perhaps the "wit" characterization, carrying overtones of British drawing-room repartee, unsettled Broadway audiences; like *The Passing Show,* the musical's box office business failed to meet expectations.

For Miss Myrtil, whose violin playing contributed toward her romantic image, it was the beginning of a trio of Shubert productions. Next came *The Love Song,* and a long run as a fiddling gypsy in *Countess Maritza.* By then she was a seasoned observer of the brothers' shenanigans. Fending off Lee's imperious sexual overtures, she coped at the same time with J.J.'s flinty world view. For example, the business of visiting her mother in France. Since the actress had not been home in several years, she approached J.J. when *Countess Maritza* closed, and requested a three-week vacation.

With a benevolent smile, J.J. told her that of course she could take the holiday. "We'll put in your understudy."

"But she doesn't play the violin," Myrtil protested.

"Well, you're not leaving for two weeks, are you?" said J.J. "She can learn!"

Vogues closed after a fourteen-week run and the road tour in the fall of 1924 was short. To Allen it seemed interminable because of Savo's increasing bumptiousness. The diminutive comedian, who wore a full-length raccoon coat, fur-lined inside and out, appealed to his public as a clown able to sound the upper harmonics of pathos as well as the mocking registers of the pratfall, but for Allen the little man was a chronic nuisance. The New York notices had gone to his head. Since Allen had supplied their material, he tried to improve it, but every change of emphasis made Savo suspicious, convinced his co-star was trying to take advantage of him. Their differences reached the boiling point one night when Allen made an ad-lib remark: "Bring me a mirror. I want to look at my favorite comedian." This enraged Savo. "Step out in the alley," he commanded, "and fight like a gentleman." Allen regarded the incident with resignation: "He had given a piece of his mind to so many people that by the time he got working with me he had only a fragment left."

Back in New York, Allen joined the cast of *The Greenwich Village Follies*. The revue series had begun in a small way in the Village, then moved uptown. John Murray Anderson initiated and presided over the yearly event, which was always marked by taste and intelligence, and among the performers associated with the shows were comedian Joe E. Brown, Doc Rockwell (in the 1929 version), and band leader Ted ("Is everybody happy?") Lewis. The 1925 revue, though, needed help after the shock of a troubled opening, and Fred Allen, Toto, the clown, and Mordkin, a Russian dancer, were brought in. The *Follies* contributed substantially to Allen's career. He provided two monologues, but that winter, for the first time, took part also in a revue's comic sketches. He enjoyed the experience; playing scenes seemed a gregarious change from the life of a monologist, loneliest of performers. The *Follies* finished the season on the road. The *Boston Herald* ("Delights With Fun and Feminine Pulchritude") praised the stage pictures of Oscar Wilde's "The Happy Prince," which opened the second half of the show, and added: "Fred Allen, a monologist with a quantity of really new material, had more than one opportunity, and never failed to find responsive listeners."

In June the *Follies* closed for the summer, but the management in August reassembled a cast for the road tour. Allen didn't expect to get rehired; his salary, by now six hundred dollars a week, was too costly for producers still trying to recoup their New York losses. Consequently, he experimented with a new vaudeville monologue, "The Misconception of Man." The monologue was based on the notion that the human anatomy needed revision. A nose shouldn't be a

case of determinism, jutting out where it has to smell everything; it can go on the top of the head where it can be covered
by a hat. One eye is sufficient for the oval of the face; the
other eye should be placed in the end of the middle finger of
the right hand. With the eye on the middle finger, you can use
your hand as a periscope and see parades marching past when
people in front block your view. Allen's anatomical conceit
has cropped up in subsequent revues, but he was by no means
the only source of the idea. Probably he would have been delighted to learn that Benjamin Franklin — historical Ben —
offered a similar vision in 1779.

> Man, who was destined to drink wine, must be able to
> raise the glass to his mouth. If the elbow had been placed
> nearer the hand (as in figure 3), the part in advance would
> have been too short to bring the glass up to the mouth;
> and if it had been placed nearer the shoulder (as in figure
> 4) that part would have been so long that it would have
> carried the wine far beyond the mouth. But by the actual
> situation (represented in figure 5), we are enabled to drink
> at our ease, the glass going exactly to the mouth.

While Fred tried out "The Misconception of Man," the producers of the *Follies* invited him to return. Going over their
books, they realized that Allen, who was performing in and
writing two monologues and five scenes, saved money they
would otherwise spread over several salaries.

The 1925–26 tour with the *Follies* would prove significant
in other ways, for on this tour Allen's writing began to branch
and develop and assume new forms. From the standpoint of
theatrical performance, however, Allen in the mid-1920s was
at the peak of his invention as a monologist. His monologues
took unexpected musical detours. Throughout the summers
(his off-season), he said, he "always augmented the swimming, baseball and gang diversions by studying one subject";
and so he learned the actual musical rudiments of the banjo he
had acquired in New Zealand, and explored the possibilities of
the clarinet. His motives were professional: "A comedian who
could do a variety of things had more scope for comedy." Or
as Mark Twain put it: "Two things seemed pretty apparent to

me. One was, that in order to be a pilot a man had got to learn more than any one man ought to know; and the other was, that he must learn it all over again in a different way every twenty-four hours."

The clarinet would stand Allen in good stead, becoming analogous to the violin of Jack Benny, although the instrument never saw much service after Allen's theatrical years. Unlikely as it seems, he also studied singing. The summer between tours of the *Follies,* his pal Joe Kelly, who was picking up a few credits at Boston University, talked him into enrolling in a summer course in public speaking conducted by Professor William C. Hoffman. Allen said he attended BU "to keep the ivy company." He would rue his ivy-sitting later, once he became plagued by alumni requests and by a president of the university who persistently tried to get him to do free broadcasts from the campus; but the comedian liked Professor Hoffman. The professor, a theatergoer who had seen the *Follies,* wondered why Allen, on the stage of the Shubert Theatre a few weeks before, was now posing as a college student. A practical joke? Fred explained he didn't want to go around the country making grammatical lapses that reflected on Boston's educational institutions. This amused Hoffman. The course, attended by teachers of rhetoric and public speaking, was no snap, but the professor allowed Allen to audit. "If I get one idea for a routine out of it," he wrote a friend in New York, "I shall feel well repaid. If the class is large there is sure to be a laugh now and then." Hoffman asked the class to pretend it was a Chamber of Commerce for one session, an after-dinner affair the next; and in these public settings may have germinated the comic ideas that were to blossom on the Linit radio show seven years afterward. Teacher and student corresponded over the next thirty years, and in Hoffman's classroom Allen tried out "The Misconception of Man."

Summer reached its close; after rehearsals *The Greenwich Village Follies* began a profitable tour that went as far west as Kansas City and ended in Philadelphia the following spring. Allen's Shubert contract expired. He parted from the brothers with as much relief as when he parted from Savo. Yet before the parting, Allen contributed to their legend.

As the story goes, he was crossing Shubert Alley — a short-cut between Forty-fourth and Forty-fifth streets — when an angry producer came storming out of the Shubert Theatre nearby.

"What's the matter?" Allen inquired. "You look upset."

"Oh, what a miserable son of a bitch," the producer groaned.

"So's his brother, Jake," Allen agreed.

The yarn was possibly apocryphal; Allen never claimed it or alluded to the incident. Anecdotes about authority figures nonetheless spread like prairie fire, and when the joke reached J.J., he barred Allen from using Shubert Alley. The ban meant the performer had to walk around the block. Allen took it as a challenge.

Guarding the alley, Shubert doorman Sam Langford duti-fully enforced the edict. Allen and Langford, the great black prizefighter from Boston, were friends, and their friendship transformed the situation into a game. Whenever Allen saw that Langford was busy, the comedian sprinted across forbidden pavement. Usually he didn't make it, but if he did, he would shout upward at Lee's turret office: "Hey Lee! Tell Jake I did it. I used Shubert Alley!"

Langford always felt sheepish allowing Allen to violate the alley, and apprehensive as Allen passed by. Meanwhile, Allen learned that the Astor family were joint owners of the short-cut. A few nights later, he appeared in the alley and began hopping toward its sentry.

"Now, I don't want no trouble, Fred," Langford said. "You know you're not supposed to be in here."

Allen paused, teetering on one foot. "I'm only using one foot, Sam, so I'm using half the Alley," he said. "Tell Jake it's Astor's half."

He hopped on through, and J.J. lifted the ban within a few weeks.

OLD VAUDEVILLE ACTS exist only in the imagination. For the most part, they perform beyond documenting, a twinkle of nostalgia fading into the cosmos of memory. Yorke and Allen, in the opinion of experts asked to nominate the ideal vaudeville program, deserve a spot on any all-time bill. Allen had met Bert Yorke in 1913, when Bert and his father were doing a baggy-pants song-and-dance routine in Boston's neighborhood theaters. Since then Yorke had graduated to the big time, but every summer, when his path crossed Allen's, Bert suggested they team up together. No longer confined by the shackles of the Shuberts, Allen agreed. The act he and Yorke developed was really two acts and exploited the inherent properties of the medium as dexterously as the painter of an ancient Athenian vase taking advantage of the form and color of the clay.

The Palace Theatre, starting with Frank Fay, booked a popular series of masters of ceremonies, who presented the acts and worked through the shows. It was Allen's notion that two comedians could speed up the pace yet tie the performances together. Assuming the stagehands' tasks, moving props and pianos, the masters of ceremonies would keep the entertainment running without pause from beginning to end, and eliminate the inflexible rhythm of scenic acts alternating with in-one appearances before the curtain. Allen decided to write two acts: Yorke and Allen, the third act on an eight-act bill, and Fink and Smith, next-to-closing. He and Yorke would come on as efficiency experts "sent from the Keith offices by Mr. Albee to investigate and remedy the evils existing in this theater." Among the evils were houseflies wandering into the theater without tickets and the indiscriminate parking of wads of chewing gum. A checkroom for the gum was suggested. A third efficiency problem was the programs. When you've reached your seat, the lights go out and you can't read the names of the performers. Yorke and Allen then volunteered to serve as living programs.

Their bits between acts maintained the momentum of the show, and the Fink-and-Smith act — built around song and dance (they opened to a soft-shoe version of an English music-hall song, "Gravy and Bread," before sliding into a chorus of "Tea for Two") and an acrobatic finale (acrobatics by Yorke, banjo-playing by Allen) — ratified their theatrical skills. A few Fally Markus dates outside New York perfected the act: they opened at the Palace early in October 1926 and were held over before receiving a route, thirty-five weeks on the Keith time. To Henry Kelly, Allen wrote:

> All the hambos were excited when the billing went up that Fink etc. were next to closing and so even if we don't "click," at least I have given them something to talk about and can go home for the rest of the season knowing that they all have some new jokes etc. Sime will probably give you a good idea of the act in this week's *Variety*. I have taken no ads so it should be a legitimate criticism. Hey Ho.

Under "New Acts," *Variety* more than counterbalanced Sime's slam of the Young Fellow Trying to Get Along.

> Allen as a single was strictly for the intelligentsia and as a result led a hectic vaudeville career. His current act is aimed at the collar bone, and those who miss parts of the fly talk will have a chance to laugh at the physical absurdities when Yorke, as a collector, makes frequent appearances demanding various portions of the Allen apparel until he is down to his undies and an umbrella. When the umbrella is collected, they black out.
>
> The bits are punctuated by Allen's running fire of comment, probably the brightest talk ever heard on a vaudeville stage. Allen also contributes half of a comedy double dance and plays a bit on the clarinet. Yorke does an efficient bit of contrast and contributes a solo dance. . . .
>
> As a "single" Allen was too fast and refused to compromise. With his present partner the act contains all the necessary elements for the poets and peasants, and is geography proof. They'll like Yorke and Allen, from half a buck up to $5.50.

The act was not geography-proof. Yorke and Allen needed a big-time setting. In small-time theaters, where audiences had never seen a master of ceremonies, people were baffled. An eight-act program was necessary; the hinterland venues, with four or five acts playing three times a day, couldn't accommodate the dual-masters-of-ceremony concept. Playing Toledo, however, Allen coined an ad-lib destined to be ground by ensuing comedians into the dross of cliché. Gus Salzer, the bald and acerb orchestra leader, disliked the act and expressed his opinion in body language, drooping whenever Yorke and Allen came onstage. Halfway through one show, Allen leaned over the footlights and asked him, "What would you charge to haunt a house?" Less often cited is the Bayonne, New Jersey, bon mot after a cat gave birth in the aisle and the usher scooped up the kittens with a shovel and brought them with the mother to the rear of the house. "I thought my act was a monologue not a catalogue," Allen remarked. At such moments you regret the lack of a tape recorder or camera, but Yorke and Allen continue to engage attention for what survives, the verbal potsherds of a lost yet joyful culture.

8 | Portland

"Oh, Mr. *Al*-len!" James Thurber considered Portland Hoffa's outcry a romantic utterance, as compelling in its own right as a shadowy horn call beckoning Siegfried. "I shall never forget," he wrote her, "Fred's warm greeting to you on the Allen show: 'Portland!' and your answers. In my aging but unclouded memory everything you and Fred said to each other was somehow akin to The Sweetheart Duet from *Maytime*."

"What are the best things on the show?" pondered cultural critic Gilbert Seldes, asked to select the highlight of Fred Allen's radio years. "For myself, if I had to choose, and was held down to a single moment, I would take the accent of surprise and pleasure in Allen's voice as he says, 'Why, Portland!' as Miss Hoffa makes her entrance. Because that, too, has the special Allen quality, the keen delight he has in the miraculous brightness and rightness of everything in the show."

Does it seem strange that sophisticated observers like Thurber and Seldes should identify a comedian-satirist and his addled female foil as the essence of romance? The answer in a postradio era requires going back to the shows and hearing the undercurrent of tenderness expressed in the Portland-Fred repartee through inflection, tone, and delivery. To a certain extent, Allen's technical confidence was characteristic of other ex-vaudevillians who had integrated their wives into their comedy. Jack Benny and Mary Livingstone as real-life husband and wife received a domestic dimension that played against her indeterminate roles as girlfriend and gadfly to Benny's conceited miser. Gracie Allen with George Burns spun a standard "dumb Dora" act into velocities of changing speed and movement, as precise yet as graceful as figure skaters dipping and gliding together. Goodman and Jane Ace captured small-town Midwest America in her malapropisms ("I've been working my head to the bone") and his tart commentary about their mundane neighbors. The originality of the husband-and-wife comedy teams derived from a mutual affection that encouraged risk taking and pushed against stylistic boundaries, and this was as true of Fred and Portland Allen as it was of the Bennys and Burnses. Only death or retirement could part them, and when the teams were broken up, continued as singles or adapted to television, it was impossible to consider the act in terms of a different partner. When the Jack Benny show, for example, shifted to television, his character's consort became Barbara Nichols, but she was a paper-doll presence.

Hobe Morrison, later a *Variety* staffer, was employed for a time ("an elongated lost weekend in my life") by an ad agency that handled the Fred Allen account; he recalled Portland's radio role triggering one of the rare incidents in which Allen worked up a gale-force rage.

The agency vice-president and radio director was a likable, persuasive man and, like most conscientious ad executives, a worrier. It was a joke around the office that Allen's name for him was Mr. Ulcers-with-Suspenders.

When Allen's radio contract ran out, it was always this man's distasteful job, in broaching the subject of renewal, to relay the oil-company sponsor's suggestion that Portland Hoffa be dropped from her featured-comedienne role on the program. Allen invariably refused outright, usually with sarcastic reference to the comedy expertise of oil-company executives. One year, however, the sponsor must have insisted on it and [the advertising executive] reluctantly raised the point again.

Allen was never one to suffer indignities meekly — what self-respecting star ever was? — and this time he blew his stack. [The adman] said later that he'd never seen Allen so angry. The comedian declared that he would discuss dropping Portland from the show only after the oil company president divorced *his* wife:

"You tell him that Portland is my wife, that she makes my life livable, and that her presence on the show is not a matter of negotiation. We're a family and we work as a family. If he doesn't want Mrs. Allen, he doesn't want Mr. Allen. I'm telling you and you tell him — never mention this subject to me again."

Portland was the daughter of Dr. Frederick Hoffa, a jovial optometrist from Jamaica, Long Island. Like John Henry Sullivan, he possessed a talent to amuse. "People would start laughing as soon as he came up the street," according to Portland. The doctor named his two oldest daughters and his only son after the communities in which they were born: Portland, for Portland, Oregon; Lebanon, for Lebanon, Pennsylvania; and the boy, Harlem, for Harlem, New York. When the next infant arrived, he named her Lastone (*en famille* pronounced "Last 'Un"). She was not, however: a fourth daughter, his namesake, was dubbed Doctor Fredericka Hoffa.

Teenaged Lebanon was the first Hoffa to find a Broadway job. "My mother would not allow Lebanon to join the show alone so I was sent along as a chaperone," Portland told an interviewer in the 1930s. "The windup was that we were both signed to dance in a line. I had no desire for show business, but I got the breaks."

Her first name was fated to attract Fred Allen, a student of curious nomenclature, and they met backstage at *The Passing Show of 1922* when he overheard someone else address her. The glimpses of their courtship are oblique yet touching, illuminated by moments like the one George Libby evoked for Portland: "Fred, seeing you off on a Fifth Avenue bus to your relatives on Long Island, with Fred doing an off-to-Buffalo and waving to you as your bus drove away."

During the *Passing Show*'s six-month stay in Chicago, Ethel Shutta and her husband, Walter Batchelor — then assistant stage manager, later Allen's agent and financial manager — made a foursome with Fred and Portland. Walter was an excellent cook and Ethel and Portland did the marketing for their apartment dinners. It may have been the era of *The Front Page* and gang wars in Chicago, but for actors making train jumps from one tank town to another, it was idyllic. "When there were no matinees we spent the days at the beach," said Fred. "On rainy days we went to the movies and later visited one of the excellent restaurants in the Loop, or one of the tea shoppes on the North Side. After the shows at night we investigated different speakeasies and other nocturnal points of interest that Chicago boasted. They were days of laughter and happy times."

By the time Allen went into *The Greenwich Village Follies,* the relationship was serious, but his courtship of Portland stretched out over four years. No one proved a more appreciative audience than she; nevertheless, difficulties loomed. There were religious differences; Portland had been reared in her father's Jewish faith rather than in her mother's Presbyterianism. While she and Allen both understood the precariousness of the actor's life, this roadblock was compounded by his family obligations in Boston. Conservative in his attitudes toward fiscal security — "I had seen enough insecurity at home" — Allen felt reluctant to launch himself on perilous matrimonial tides. All the same, his decision to accompany the successful *Follies* tour of 1925–26 was clinched by the producer's offer to add Portland to the company.

During those five years too, Portland, either with Fred or with Benny and Marty Drohan, who lived at the same hotel, often attended mass in the Actors' Chapel of Saint Malachy's Church on West Forty-ninth Street. The 12:30 P.M. mass was well timed for nocturnal Broadway performers such as Portland, then dancing in *George White's Scandals.* After Yorke and Allen returned from the road for a final week at the Palace, in April 1927, Allen found that Portland had been received into the Catholic church and the pastor, Father Leonard, had given her the confirmation name of Mary. Her conversion was, and remains for her, a pivotal spiritual experience, the still point of the turning world.

"The next thing I knew I had bought the ring, and Father Leonard was marrying Mary Portland and me," Allen related.

A vaudeville friend from Boston, Charlie Lane, was best man, and Kate Starner, a chorine friend of Portland's, maid of honor. Fred had just completed a sketch for Charlie, the lead singer of Lane, Plant, and Timmons, a trio specializing in "fake harmonies" (that is, songs such as "Just a Baby's Prayer at Twilight," which the boys harmonized without benefit of professional arrangement). He was a burly man who had foot problems, and he consequently attended the ceremony wearing white socks with his blue suit.

The 10:00 A.M. nuptial mass began late. Preceding was a funeral mass, which also began late, with the result that the congregation attending the funeral overlapped the wedding. Several people decided to stay. Allen and Lane met at the door of the chapel and prepared to approach the altar, whereupon the nervous groom turned to his best man and, surveying the mourners, whispered, "It's a good thing we're not playing this for percentage."

The ceremony over, the principals went to the Astor Hotel in Times Square, and during the wedding breakfast Charlie insisted they observe what he called "an old Irish custom" — having themselves photographed. So the principals proceeded from the Astor to a sidewalk photographer on Forty-second Street, and the total cost for four pictures — Fred and Portland and Charlie and Kate each received a copy — was a dollar. Then Fred and Portland left for the honeymoon, a split week between Waterbury, Connecticut, and Springfield, Massachusetts, where Yorke and Allen were completing their season.

ALLEN SET TO WORK that summer writing an act for himself and Portland. They rented a cottage with the Drohans at Onset, Cape Cod — Onset had a vaudevillians' colony — and while he concentrated on writing, Portland surprised everyone by the quality of her cooking. Indeed, the culinary motif of their early years lasted throughout the twenty-nine years of their marriage. With Portland's sisters and their husbands, and the Al Hirschfelds, Sid Perelmans, and William Saroyans, they established in the late thirties an informal dining society that assembled at one another's apartments or in favorite Italian and

Chinese restaurants. Allen joked about Portland's cooking —
"her early successes were a salmon loaf and macaroni and
cheese" — but relished its gourmet cunning. "She's such a good
cook," he remarked, "that the last time we went on a picnic
the ants came home with us."

"Portland is going through the cook books alphabetically,"
he wrote from Old Orchard Beach, Maine, a few years later.

> The first day I had apricot jam, aspic, asparagus omelet
> and alligator pears; the second day, bacon, baked apple,
> bluefish and bananas. Today we are up to C and for
> breakfast we had crullers, cutlets and cornflakes. Tomor-
> row she will be into D and I am looking forward to late
> in the summer when she gets down to P and Q and I have
> to live a day on purees and quohaugs. With a bit of luck
> and no ptomaine she should get right through the cook
> book and into the index before we leave here. Then I shall
> return to Radio City and my stomach will probably re-
> port at the Smithsonian Institution.

The act was titled "Disappointments of 1927" and became a
lighthearted coda to Allen's vaudeville years. Its structure revealed a spare yet durable architecture: a telephone stood on a
pedestal at the opening of the curtain, and whenever he announced a celebrity scheduled to appear, the phone rang and a
quick conversation occurred. Mrs. Tiller couldn't appear with
her Tiller Girls; Eva Tanguay was the next disappointment;
and after Allen sang in welcome to Paul Whiteman and his
orchestra, Whiteman and the band sent regrets. That was the
final straw; Allen declared he would do the act alone. Out
came the reliable banjo, clarinet, ventriloquial dummy, and —
a remembrance of things past — juggling equipment. Portland
entered midway through the eighteen-minute act, introduced
by a clarinet solo, "When the Roll Is Called Up Yonder, What
Shall We Dunk in Our Coffee?" and amid dancing and banter,
"Disappointments" finished with Allen's banjo solo.

They played small-time theaters "for three reasons: to keep
working, to give Portland confidence, and to improve the act,"
Allen wrote. While the newlyweds were breaking in the material, Rudy Vallee, following them on the same bill in the

saxophone section of the Yale Collegians, was so impressed
by "Disappointments" that he committed it to memory. There
are discrepancies between his account (in his 1975 memoir, *Let
the Chips Fall . . .*) and Allen's. According to Vallee, he first
saw "Disappointments" at the Palace Theatre in Cleveland (the
theater, says Allen, was in Ansonia, Connecticut) and later used
the act with Allen's permission. Whether or not permission
was granted, Vallee performed "Disappointments" piecemeal
for years. Allen disliked nightclubs and claimed that he had
been to only three in his life; once he went nightclubbing "in
1934 at the behest of Rudy Vallee. During [Vallee's] show Rudy
gave an imitation of me and spoiled my entire evening. Had I
wanted to listen to me I could have stayed home and talked to
myself and saved the cover charge."

Vallee recalled Allen scooping from the footlights an old-
fashioned telephone with mouthpiece and receiver. The script's
easy pacing had a Broadway polish, but the ensuing dialogue
contained a joke from Fred's first performance at the Boston
Public Library:

> What's that, Mrs. Tiller? You won't be with us tonight?
> What's the trouble? Oh, the still exploded! Blew you and
> your husband out into the street? What's that? It's the first
> time you've been out together in ten years? You think
> your husband is suffering from shock? Why, what's he
> doing? Oh, he's running up and down the streets in his
> union suit. Tell him to be very careful, Mrs. Tiller. Sum-
> mer is over, winter draws on.

The "Disappointments" act, interestingly, anticipated Allen's
radio debut: substitute a microphone for a telephone and the
verbal elements survive. But the Keith bookers shunned it
because of the success of Yorke and Allen, an act that never
should have broken up, they maintained. Presently, however,
Allen persuaded a big-time agent to see the routine, and he in
turn convinced Eddie Darling, the booker for the Palace, to
take a look. Portland and Fred opened at the Palace on a program headlined by Fanny Brice and the Gus Edwards Revue,
and *Variety* hailed the dialogue's "witty surprises." "Portland
Hoffa, nice looking girl, does assistant for brief interruptions,
but otherwise, Allen alone sustains an amusing interlude."

As a consequence of the Palace notices, the Allens performed that winter in the eastern big time, then went on the Orpheum circuit, from Chicago to the West Coast, through the summer of 1928. *Billboard*'s "E.H." hastily overtook the act on the road:

> Despite the "disappointment," Allen carries on very well with a snappy line of laugh-winning gags, broken now and then with a bit of song. He is assisted by an unbilled girl, who breaks the single routine twice — the first time to engage in a bit of cross-fire, and the second time to display a nifty set of underpinning. It's too bad he doesn't give her more to do, especially after her second appearance. It might serve to roll the hand up a bit more.

> *"Where do you live, little girl?"*
> *"In Schenectady."*
> *"How did you come to get lost in New York?"*
> *"I didn't come to get lost, I came to go on the radio. I won a contest and ran away from home."*

The evolution of Portland as Fred's collaborator in comedy over the years is one of the fascinating but least noticed aspects of the radio show. Portland during the "Disappointments" act was essentially a decorative adjunct. She had stepped out of the nameless chorus line into the glare of the vaudeville spotlight, yet she still remained anonymous. Both the *Billboard* review and the patter of the act reflect this. Allen asks Portland on her first entrance, "What character do you portray?" She replies: "I'm a chorus girl. I have no character."

It was the era of the "stooge," a butt of the comedian. Shemp Howard was Ted Healy's stooge (and eventually one of the Three Stooges), Dave Chasen was Joe Cook's. Early interviewers picked up on Portland's description of herself as a "wooge," a female stooge, as they were to pick up on her calmly knitting as Allen sweated over comic routines. That the Allens were a model of connubial affection was apparent to the most obtuse observer. According to the journalistic clichés of the day, however, women were assigned to interview Portland about her cooking and furnishings and how she felt about being married to the nation's leading wit. Reporters of both sexes interviewed Allen, but city desks assumed that recipes and hints to housewives were the only news expected from comedians' wives. Because Portland was by temperament warm and "feminine" and domestic, they tended to underplay her professional accomplishments. Between the unidentifiable chorine, though, and Portland's radio debut, a funny thing happened: she acquired a character.

In many ways the character was at first indiscernible — a little girl from Schenectady whose laughs came from the threadbare device of the city's name, a consonantal sneeze. When she and Allen bantered on the first *Linit Bath Club Revue,* in October 1932, she was simply a generic little girl, though now and then she sounded like a preview of the fustian poet Falstaff Openshaw, a character from a decade later. Song titles — circumlocutory song titles — come into their discussion.

> PORT: "Water, You're Not Wanted Around the Front of the House."
> ALLEN: You don't mean "River Stay Way from My Transom" by any chance?

He has trouble spelling Schenectady, and concludes, "Look, I'll get you a one-way ticket to Troy and you can hitch-hike the rest of the way from there." On the next program, however, the little girl returns. A man gave her a lift, she protests, but held the map upside down. Allen thereupon says the words that begin to integrate Portland more closely with the comic action. "Go back on the stage here and tell the stage manager that I said to give you some little part in the show tonight." In the ensuing sketch, Portland is secretary to the president (Allen) of the Drooping Walrus Mustache Wax Company.

The third program, nevertheless, she's still a running gag.

> PORT: I took the money you gave me last week and went home.
> ALLEN: They must have a rubber depot there, the way you keep bouncing back here.

On the next show, Portland for the first time plays herself. The little-girl character will remain a constant of the Linit shows, but now she'll alternate with other possibilities, and Mama and Papa jokes become a comic trademark.

PORT: I can't come tonight. We're moving.
ALLEN: Whose idea was that?
PORT: The landlord's. He proposed to my mother.
ALLEN: He wanted to marry her.
PORT: No, he proposed that we find another place to live.

The Fred Allen Salad Bowl Revue, in August 1933, uses the Chicago World's Fair as setting.

ALLEN: Don't tell me your father came to Chicago in his full-dress suit.
PORT: Yes, he said he thought the moths would like to see the Fair.

The Mama and Papa jokes supply outlines of offstage relationships along with the standard malapropisms. The latter would acquire widespread popularity; early on, when the Portland-Fred exchanges took place after an intermission, she exclaims, "I'm not interluding, am I?" Moreover, Portland's entrances and exits take advantage of the rising and falling modulations of simple phrases — a yodeling "Hello-o," the exclamation "I'll intimate," and her sign-off, "Peek-a-boo."

When the show becomes *Town Hall Tonight,* in 1934, Portland's little-girl character joins the other residents of the small town of Bedlam who march to weekly gatherings in the Hall. No longer is she a generic youngster. She introduces her cousin Willoughby ("Glad to mingle digits with yuh, Mr. Allen," he says) and explains that Willoughby is "more of a wit than a humorist." Allen dryly responds: "He looks about fifty-fifty to me."

Approaching the midthirties, the Portland-Fred duologues become ritualized.

PORT: Mr. Allen.
ALLEN: Yes . . . Who is that?
PORT: Hello.
ALLEN: Well, sir. As I live and try to keep these ten cent

cuff buttons from going off the Gold Standard, if it isn't Portland.

PORT: Yes, I knew you'd be expecting me.

ALLEN: Yes. Into each lute some rift must fall.

There were seemingly endless "Well, sir" variations. "Well, as I try to live and breathe in ragweed season, if it isn't Portland." "Well, as I try to make both ends meet in this tight vest, if it isn't Portland." "Well, as I wince and try to keep my mouth shut with these borrowed teeth, if it isn't Portland." "Well, sir. As I live and try to breathe with the Income Tax Collector's hand on my collar . . ."

Portland never stepped out of character. In June 1935, on the last show of the season, the situations revolve around Allen departing for Hollywood to star in his first feature film, *Thanks a Million;* and that October, when the radio series resumes, Portland remarks to Fred, "Gosh, I wish I could have made the trip to California with you." Here the real-life character seems absorbed by the fictional one, as in *The Jack Benny Show,* where Sayde Marks, Benny's wife, becomes Mary Benny Livingstone.

Perhaps the amateurs on the Allen show — they were introduced at this time, one of radio's earliest amateur contests — helped nudge Portland's generalized little-girl character toward realism. The amateurs, however inept, brought with them the conventions of a world unlike Bedlam. Whatever the reason, Portland, instead of becoming Allen's invention, like Senator Claghorn or Mrs. Pansy Nussbaum of the Allen's Alley years, became, program by program, incomparably herself. Throughout the mock feud with Jack Benny, she commented on the participants as Portland Hoffa, Mrs. Fred Allen, and while the Mama and Papa jokes didn't cease (after each show, Portland always phoned her mother on Long Island for a reaction), Portland's presence assumed an importance on par with Fred's. During the forties, she often cued in the program's guest star, but her commentary also ranged over broader themes, from frozen foods to the United Nations. The March 14, 1948, show found Allen asking her to take over — an inconceivable request during the thirties. On the final show, June 26, 1949, her nonsense touched upon Gregory Peck, socialized medicine, Milton Berle, and Halloween. It is innocent commentary, of course, and topical, but comedic light-years away from misspelling Schenectady. The little-girl, dumb-Dora aspects of the character fade away, and listeners follow the progress of a stereotype into an identity. Fred Allen, like George Burns or Goodman Ace, doesn't fit the popular concept of a romantic figure, but even the opulent Tchaikovsky theme music of *The Lux Radio Theatre* could not match the *Maytime* duets of Fred and Portland. American radio of the period offered few more enduring romances.

9 | Three's a Crowd

Playing Oakland, California, on the Orpheum circuit, the Allens received a timely telegram. The producer Arthur Hammerstein offered Fred a part in a new musical. Hammerstein, uncle of the eminent lyricist Oscar Hammerstein II, had overseen several 1920s musical hits, including *Rose Marie* (557 performances), *Wildflower* (477 performances), and *Tickle Me* (207 performances), and his reputation carried a cachet of discernment and style. *Rose Marie* brought in millions, and in addition to his producing activities, Hammerstein was constructing a sumptuous theater at Broadway and Fifty-fourth Street memorializing his father, impresario Oscar Hammerstein. Arthur's shows, however, were throwbacks to the ponderous make-believe of operetta — *Rose Marie,* set in the Canadian Rockies, *Wildflower,* mingling peasant maids and swains from the Italian *campagna,* and *Tickle Me,* revolving around an American movie troupe on location in Tibet — and *Polly* would prove no exception. For Allen, the offer constituted a chance to perform on Broadway beyond the cheerless proximity of the Shuberts. There might even be a part for Portland. *Polly,* as it happened, did nothing to advance anyone's career, but in retrograde fashion anticipated Allen's sketch-writing in *The Little Show* and *Three's a Crowd.*

Fred and Portland broke the jump to New York at Chicago and at Fort Wayne, where "Disappointments" briefly joined a stage version of the *WLS Showboat,* a radio program broadcast each week from Chicago's Sears Roebuck station. A precursor of *Hee Haw* and *Grand Ol' Opry*, the *Showboat* mesmerized midwestern audiences who flocked to see the in-person actuality of their hillbilly airwave favorites. During three days with the hayseed jamboree, Allen noted the popularity of the otherwise lackluster yokel routines. This derived entirely from radio. An interesting phenomenon, but, headed for Broadway, he did not dwell upon the exotica of Fort Wayne. The Allens continued toward New York: their *Showboat* replacement, a comedian and eccentric hoofer, Bob Hope, made his first critical splash among the gallus-snapping and washboard-thumping.

The blandness of the subtitle, *A Pleasant Musical Comedy*, captures the texture of *Polly*. Reviewers were quick to point out predictable situations recycled so often the original theatrical stockpot had lost its savor. Guy Bolton and George Middleton had collaborated upon the source-comedy, *Polly with a Past*, concocted in 1917 for Ina Claire, and the long run of *Polly with a Past* inspired variations on the same plot in the opulent Ziegfeld musicals *Sally, Sunny,* and *Rosalie*. Like most comedies by British playwrights, *Polly*'s complications relied on class distinctions. A chorus girl agrees to help a patrician Long Islander in his pursuit of a rich young woman. Impersonating a French seductress, Polly is supposed to arouse the heiress's jealousy. The gent discovers he loves Polly more than pelf and after sundry revelations the couple are united at the final curtain. Fred Allen's character, Adelbert Stiles, society reporter for the *Sag Harbor Bee*, did not appear in the original, and in fact was superfluous: Addie came into existence because the show lacked comic relief.

Hammerstein devised *Polly* as a vehicle for June Howard-Tripp, a London musical-comedy star he had seen in a West End revue, *Clowns in Clover*. Known professionally as June because her hyphenated surname was unsuitable for a dancer, she was a demure English rose whose refinement enhanced her charm. Hammerstein thought her singing and toe-dancing warranted American recognition; she could be another Gertrude Lawrence, a second Marilyn Miller. Accordingly, he asked Bolton, Middleton, and Isabel Leighton to update the ingredients that spelled success for Ina Claire; called upon his house composer, Herbert Stothart — he and Hammerstein had published catchy sheet-music melodies in collaboration — and added composer Phil Charig and lyricist Irving Caesar, who had rhymed the durable "dummy lyric" of Vincent Youmans's "Tea for Two." (A dummy lyric, words meant only to fit the music, serves the writer who will supply the final, polished version, and in the case of "Tea for Two," Caesar, to his dismay, found that Youmans considered the dummy lyric ideal.) Mustering proven talents, Arthur Hammerstein felt confident that June's reputation would prosper in America, but 1928 was not 1917, and in rehearsal Allen perceived *Polly*'s creakiness. The names of the characters — Mrs. Van Zile, Roy Van Zile, Prentice Van Zile, Sue, Betty, Polly, Arturo — "sounded like a roll call at a home for passé musical comedy personnel," and the song titles invited parody: "*Comme Ci, Comme Ca,*" "Heel and Toe," "On with the Dance," "Pale Little Bo Peep," "Sing a Song in the Rain." The actors spent their time groping for a thread of credible dialogue in a labyrinth of cliché.

Polly's tryout staggered from Wilmington, Delaware, to Philadelphia, Pittsburgh, and Detroit, as though the objective concerned performance anywhere but Broadway. Since Du Pont money backed the show, every box at the Wilmington premiere was filled by patrons in evening dress. Unfortunately, the rest of the theater was empty. In Philadelphia, the critics considered the script middling, June diffident; and at the end of the first week Hammerstein closed *Polly* for rewrites. The only original players retained were June, Inez Courtney, and Fred Allen. At the start of a fortnight, they would begin rehearsing again with a fresh cast.

Allen's writing, acting, and bouncy comic contrivances in the script made him indispensable, but the juvenile lead, Archie Leach, was fired with the cast. The gall of rejection in his case proved especially bitter, for he had received glowing personal notices — well, a fanfare, anyway, from the *Evening Bulletin.*

Archie Leach as Roy Van Zile, the boyish hero, meets all the requirements for a romantic girl's Prince Charming.

He is more than six feet tall, lean, brown and athletically hard, and his fine cut features, gleaming teeth and curly black hair are well calculated to draw forth feminine admiration. His voice is above average for the male lead in a musical comedy.

June herself was skeptical. "My leading man was tall, dark and handsome," she said years afterward, "but, as far as I could see, he was completely lacking in talent or skill as an actor, singer or dancer. Furthermore, he had a Cockney accent, and his name, Archie Leach, was hardly prepossessing. I liked him personally and he worked hard, but I felt sure he would have to be replaced before our New York opening."

Getting dropped from *Polly* also meant that Archie, under personal contract to Hammerstein, could probably anticipate the nonrenewal of their contractual relationship. Hammerstein had first given Archie a bit part in *Golden Dawn,* a 1927 musical disaster, then moved him into the lead in *Polly,* hoping to save the salary a better-known actor would demand. Now Archie had lost his opportunity for a major part on Broadway. To Fred he confided plans to buy a car, head west, try his luck in Hollywood. Effectuating his scheme would take him three years; Hammerstein, meanwhile, would sell the contract to the Shuberts, who would feature Archie in several shows — principally *Boom Boom,* opposite Jeanette MacDonald, and *A Wonderful Night,* an adaptation of Johann Strauss's *Die Fledermaus.*

In the latter, Archie found himself cast as Eisenstein (or Max, as he became in the new version), a role requiring an operatic voice beyond the range of a Broadway baritone. Hours away from the curtain, Archie's nerve collapsed, but, plodding to the theater, he bumped into Fred, who claimed to have a cure for opening-night panic. They went to the observation tower of the Woolworth Building. It was a drizzling evening and as the two men stood on the observation deck, gazing across the raindark streets and moist lights of New York, the fate of a theatrical production, no longer the only thing that mattered, no longer an intimidating or important human event, dwindled amid that panorama. They would need the long, philosophical vista in the months immediately ahead; for even if

Archie, composure regained, gave his performance, the date was October 31, 1929, a week after Black Thursday, and the commercial stage itself confronted ruin. Archie's ambitions to subdue Hollywood would not prove delusory, however. In November 1931, he and Phil Charig, composer of *Polly,* motored to Los Angeles. *Polly* over and done with, Archie Leach changed his name and developed into the screen's foremost romantic comedian, Cary Grant.

Bolton, Middleton, and Leighton followed Hammerstein's instructions, and the rewritten *Polly* opened as scheduled in Pittsburgh, with a new cast. "For all the difference it made," Allen noted, "we could have stayed in Wilmington." Desperate Uncle Arthur summoned clever nephew Oscar, who was still trailing clouds of glory from the success of *Show Boat,* but the show closed as it did in Philadelphia, with the cast dismissed and rewriting promised. Like Archie's petals of compliment, the favorable reviews fluttered into oblivion: "The story is all laid down at Southampton, Long Island, and there is a lot of folderol about exclusive families etc., none of which interested anybody opening night very much except when Allen came on stage. Then everybody sat forward, with their ears pricked up."

Polly by now virtually served as a comic vehicle. Although the British director didn't understand Allen's humor, it was the only redeeming feature. By now, also, Allen and Inez Courtney had rehearsed seven weeks without pay for two-and-a-half weeks of employment. Altogether, they spent ten payless weeks; Actors' Equity took the position that by performing for nothing the leads were making it possible for some forty Equity members to get work. Then too, Arthur Hammerstein, unlike the Shuberts, commanded personal respect and loyalty. Allen liked him from the start, and throughout the vicissitudes of the tour retained his admiration for the producer's perseverance. (Hammerstein took a $170,000 loss, a sizable sum in 1928 and part of a pattern of reverses that would soon bankrupt him and place his handsome theater in receivership.) But goodwill and enthusiasm could not turn *Polly* into a hit. "Guy [Bolton] was writing night and day, and had been writing this way since the first version of *Polly*," Allen commented. "The trouble was that we had the wrong Guy. We had Bolton — we needed de Maupassant."

In Detroit, despite uncomplaining notices, *Polly* did meager business over the holidays. The first act alone took an hour and a half. Before the New York opening, Hammerstein threw in the towel and placed the tickets with the cut-rate brokers. A smattering of the Manhattan critics, surprisingly charitable, spoke of June in January; but it was the heyday of the wisecracking reviewer, and *Polly* sanctioned open season. "Oh to be in England now that June is here!" quipped Robert Garland in the *Telegram*. Nor were several other notices gratifying: "Spectators had the sensation at times of looking not so much at a person as at a superlatively-designed mechanical doll"; "June runs through an infinite number of living statue poses, holding each just long enough to register, then starting in on the next."

Polly ran only two weeks. June returned to England with her fiancé, Lord Inverclyde of the Cunard steamship Inverclydes. Allen last glimpsed a vestige of the musical on Forty-third Street, where two huge trucks lumbered through traffic, bound for Cain's warehouse, the New Jersey Valhalla of theatrical scenery. On the gate of the second truck, a sign flapped: "*Polly*, Acclaimed by Press and Public."

JANUARY 1929 — and again Allen was jobless. Almost immediately, though, he embarked upon a revue destined to establish a standard in American musical theater: *The Little Show*.

The New York critics in singling out Allen's *Polly* performance had struck a note of good-humored exasperation. Every cast member, the critics observed, fed him lines that got enormous laughs. This was, of course, the upshot of direction that concentrated upon plot actors, giving Allen freedom to add sportive monologues. The critics didn't really object — in sum, they were delighted — but they were also conscious of the workaday obligation of plot-heavy *Polly* to tell a story. Nevertheless, the notices hailed the emergence of a major talent. "This is written in the hope that some other manager will grab Allen and give him a chance in a real show," declared one unsigned tribute. The chance arrived overnight: producer Dwight Deere Wiman sought a comic lead for a new revue — at that point unwritten — and instantly signed Fred Allen.

What amazes an onlooker today is the negligent speed with which *The Little Show* was assembled. *Polly* closed in late January; *The Little Show* opened April 30. The undertaking originated in a series of Sunday-evening vaudevilles presented by an embryonic producer, Tom Weatherly, at the Selwyn Theatre. The Sunday nights stimulated his notion of introducing on Broadway a revue comprised of similar lively material, and he soon found colleagues in Wiman and William A. Brady, Jr. Wiman, heir to the John Deere farm-machinery fortune, had been in the theater some four years and was already known as a modish sophisticate. So solvent was he, reported Howard Dietz, "that he had a wickerwork Rolls-Royce built for him. It was the most expensive-looking car ever to appear in traffic. It was equipped with a bar and this, to Dwight, was its most important equipment. Later he gave it to his daughter Trink, who used it regularly until termites set in. It was made of rare wood, fitting for termites living in a Rolls-Royce."

Although the Rolls suggests conspicuous consumption on the scale of *Earl Carroll's Vanities,* Wiman, later associated with vintage Rodgers-and-Hart musicals of the thirties, evidently had in mind a more elegant variation on the Theatre Guild's *Garrick Gaieties,* second of the Rodgers-and-Hart collaborations, which featured such songs as "Manhattan" and "Mountain Greenery." One day in a speakeasy, Wiman and Weatherly were discussing their prospective show. Howard Dietz, a Metro-Goldwyn-Mayer public-relations executive and sometime lyricist, eavesdropping from the bar, stopped by their table and advised them against it. The four musicals on which he had worked — *Poppy; Dear Sir; Oh, Kay!;* and *Merry-Go-Round* — hadn't earned him a nickel. Wiman invited Dietz to sit down, and before too many rounds of drinks, hired him for one hundred dollars a week and a half percent of the gross.

Although Dietz had invented the trademark of roaring Leo the Lion wreathed by the motto *"Ars Gratia Artis"* ("Art for art's sake"), his heart belonged to lyric writing. A Columbia undergraduate who signed himself "Freckles," he had contributed head-over-heels light verse to Franklin P. Adams's newspaper column "The Conning Tower," and won first prize in a competition for "the college man who wrote the best advertisement for Fatima cigarettes." "Alibi Baby," with music by Arthur Samuels, from W. C. Fields's 1922 musical *Poppy,* marked Dietz's Broadway debut. Louella Gear introduced the lyric, but Dorothy Donnelly, the show's assigned lyricist, refused to permit Dietz's name to appear on either the program or sheet music. Music publisher Max Dreyfus was impressed, however, and so was composer Jerome Kern. A follower of "Freckles," Kern phoned Dietz to ask him if he wanted to write lyrics for a new show. "Is this really the author," Kern said, "of 'I've a Bungalow in Babylon on Great South Bay?' "

"Dear Sir," the new show, failed, and its lasting significance, perhaps, resides in its linking of Dietz and his eventual partner in a song that was not Kern's — "All Lanes Must Have a Turning," contributed by a twenty-four-year-old fledgling lawyer-composer named Arthur Schwartz. The song proved a modest debut in the musical theater, but a debut all the same. Dietz, having added lyrics to Schwartz's melody, returned to his more prestigious partnership with Kern. After all, Schwartz was unknown and, like Oscar Hammerstein II and Cole Porter during their early and fleeting legal apprenticeships, seemed destined to follow the law rather than the captious muse of musical comedy.

Schwartz's father, a thriving lawyer himself, had resolved that Arthur should pursue a legal career notwithstanding the boy's obvious musical aptitudes. An older brother was receiving a musical education and Schwartz *père* thought one musician per family was enough. Arthur's involvement with music, however, rivaled his love of literature. He earned pocket money playing the piano for silent movies at a Brooklyn theater, took formal instruction in harmony, composed marches, and for a time dabbled in journalism. His father remained inflexible. Teaching high-school English on the side, Arthur worked his way through New York University Law School, earned a Phi Beta Kappa key, and passed the bar. The first client of the new lawyer was a businessman who discarded new enterprises as quickly as he changed law firms — and happened to be the father of a would-be lyricist, Lorenz Hart. Through this connection, Schwartz took a job in 1924 as counselor at Brandt Lake, a boys' camp in the Adirondacks. He did not go there for the fresh air or the picturesque views or the trill of the meadowlark, but for the camp shows and a chance to collaborate with Hart, also a counselor. Lyrics to those shows doubtless set a standard for boys' camps never equaled before or since.

Five years older than Schwartz, Hart had been collaborating with another Columbia colleague, Richard Rodgers. Despite well-received contributions to Sigmund Romberg's *Poor Little Ritz Girl,* their teamwork seemed fruitless and they wavered on the verge of abandoning the theater for the more homely pursuits of selling children's clothing (Rodgers) or literary translation (Hart). To imagine masters of popular song such as Hart and Schwartz as counselors in a summer camp for boys stretches credulity; still, Schwartz needed a lyricist, and could scarcely have chosen a better one. "I Know My Girl By Her Perfume," a camp hit, migrated to vaudeville, and "I Love to Lie Awake in Bed," another hit, had a melody Schwartz couldn't dismiss.

I love to lie awake in bed
Right after taps I lift the flaps
Above my head
I let the stars shine on my pillow.
Oh what a light the moonbeams shed.

Summer ended, Schwartz went back to law, and Hart went back to Rodgers. Evidently, the elder Schwartz was prescient, for Arthur prospered as a junior partner, then hung out his own shingle. Still he wanted to write songs, and in 1925 placed his first published piece, "Baltimore, Md., You're the Only Doctor for Me," in *The Grand Street Follies.* An intimate revue, *The New Yorkers,* in 1927, had a Schwartz score and a fifty-performance run. No one save Lorenz Hart seemed to appreciate the songs; Hart advised Schwartz to give up his practice, compose full-time, and seek a durable collaboration. Schwartz decided Dietz fitted the bill. Attending a performance of *Merry-Go-Round,* a revue written by Dietz and Morris Ryskind, verified the composer's conviction. The lyrics were remarkable. Dietz, still seeking a prestigious confrere, nevertheless gently rebuffed Schwartz's proposals. Perhaps it was the boozy atmosphere of Tony Soma's speakeasy, but when Tom Weatherly said he wanted Dietz to meet Schwartz, the former's reticence melted. After two years spent dodging the unheralded Schwartz, the lyricist capitulated to fate.

"Arthur and I got along well," Dietz recalled.

He sympathized with my desire to write revues. They involved short spurts and no plot construction. It was easier for someone who was doing it as a sideline. Sometimes I would suggest a title and even a rhythm with a melody. But more often he would write a tune first. We weren't touchy about criticism. I would say, "The tune stinks." He would say, "The lyric is lousy." We aimed to please each other. We figured that if we succeeded, there were a lot of people like us. Schwartz was a great judge of lyrics. He had an editorial mind and an ear for the fitness of sound.

The first song Dietz and Schwartz completed together, "Hammacher Schlemmer, I Love You," encapsulated the revue's droll, worldly attitude. The title referred to a popular movie theme song of the day, "Woman Disputed, I Love You," and to, of course, the anvil beat of the name of the New York hardware firm. In spite of their nomadic hotel treks, composer and lyricist finished close to a dozen songs within weeks. Allen's costar Clifton Webb was unsatisfied; he wanted a solo number, so Schwartz dusted off "I Love to Lie Awake in Bed" and Dietz retitled the new lyrics "I Guess I'll Have to Change My Plan." From their point of view, the score would be only a partial triumph; their music would receive attention, but the songs destined to outlast *The Little Show* were "Can't We Be Friends?" a contribution of Kay Swift and Paul James (pseudonym of her husband, James Warburg), and "Moanin' Low," composed by Ralph Rainger, a pianist in the pit orchestra. Both were introduced by Libby Holman, third major star to join the cast.

CONSIDER THE THEATRICAL ALCHEMY of Fred Allen, Clifton Webb, and Libby Holman. Three people more unlike can scarcely be conceived, yet onstage they combined the in-

gredients of a sparkling Broadway elixir. However you defined them — classical, romantic, and baroque; superego, ego,
and id; story, dance, and song; wit, elegance, and passion —
they displayed an eloquent and inevitable rightness.

A native of Indianapolis, the thirty-three-year-old Webb was
often mistaken for an Englishman, presumably because only
an Englishman could wear formal attire with such greyhound
impetuosity. The actor at one time owned 137 suits and claimed
to have originated the fashion of red carnations in the lapels of
white dinner jackets. He squired Libby Holman through a
Manhattan of fashionable parties, benefits, and post-midnight
forays to Harlem; and gossip columnists frequently predicted
their engagement and elopement. Webb, an attentive and witty
companion, enjoyed the company of women and fell half in
love with Libby; but his affections were reserved for his own
sex, and his male dressers, Ramona and Kimono, saw to it
that he matched the elegant sartorial standard of his friend Noël
Coward. Clifton's mother, Maebelle, granddaughter of a president of Yale University, doted upon the son on whom she
had bestowed the mama's-boy burden "Webb Parmalee
Hollenbeck." An actor since childhood, he was a painter talented enough to have presented at the age of eighteen a solo
show in New York. The same columnists who hinted at a
Webb-Holman dalliance often alluded to the mother and son
as corporate "Clifton and Maebelle." To be sure, they bick-
ered incessantly, but might have served as textbook illustra-
tions of a Freudian family romance; Clifton's father had been
banished to Indiana when Maebelle displaced him emotionally
with her son. Graduating from dancing school, Webb launched
his career in *Mignon* at the Boston Opera House. While he
lacked an operatic vocal range, he ranked as a dancer with
Vernon Castle, and by the 1920s only the achievements of Fred
Astaire eclipsed his own.

Later Webb went to Hollywood. In the film *Sitting Pretty* he
crowned a fractious infant with a bowl of oatmeal, and the
scene established the debonair song-and-dance worldling among
the screen's comedy stars of the immediate postwar years.
During his own infancy too, he might have been baby-sitter
rather than baby, for the dandy's cultivated imperturbability

came naturally to him. Maebelle liked to talk about recounting a bedtime story to Clifton, when, interrupted, she had to leave the room. Upon her return, the little boy, holding up his index finger, spoke his first word: "Proceed."

Libby Holman, a bisexual, charismatic twenty-five-year-old actress of German-Jewish ancestry, embodied in many respects the kick-over-the-traces, anything-goes hedonism of the twenties. Five feet six inches, with a voluptuous figure, raven hair, and a swarthy complexion, she wasn't beautiful, but she radiated tigerish energy and, despite her shocking expletives, cupid's-bow lips, bobbed hair, and flapper's wiggle, displayed an impressive intellect. Completing her French major in three years at the University of Cincinnati, she was, at nineteen, the youngest female until that time (1923) ever to graduate from the university. Then stagestruck, she moved to New York and a procession of walk-on parts, and stepped from the chorus to sing a sultry tune, Rodgers and Hart's "Ladies of the Box Office," in *The Garrick Gaieties*. The show itself was not the first of the small-scaled, literate revues — that distinction is claimed by *The Grand Street Follies* of 1922, which iconoclastically billed the entertainment as "a lowbrow show for high-grade morons" — but it was one of the most successful. Holman made an impression, and in 1927 appeared in the Ryskind-Dietz *Merry-Go-Round,* where her rendition of a torch song titled "Hogan's Alley" inspired panegyric. The critics dubbed her "a sloe-eyed houri," and her voice, "the wail of a corned beef and cabbage Delilah."

Amid the run of *Merry-Go-Round,* Holman became friendly with Dietz and his first wife, Betty, a connection that helped recommend Libby for the three major Dietz-Schwartz shows in which she eventually starred. Her talent was idiosyncratic; admiration of her sub-basement register with its growls and trombone tones was an acquired taste; she needed sympathetic listeners. A brochure accompanying the release of "Hogan's Alley" on the Brunswick label hailed her as a charmer who "Blues the Vamps and Vamps the Blues," but to the genteel white middle-class audience of the day, Libby's vocal style sounded raw and abrasive. She had based it on the great black singers of the blues (Bessie Smith was her idol);

but conservatory-oriented musicians like Richard Rodgers found Holman's emotive vocalizing unpolished. To Rodgers she couldn't sing on pitch, and her contralto lacked finesse. Another classically trained composer, Ned Rorem, held a different view. Upon her death in 1971, he wrote in his diary: "She was lavish with warmth, and owned the most original of baritone voices, which she gave to us all."

Myopia, a condition that can lend your features an air of unfocused romantic expectancy, conditioned her acting. Dietz, under the misapprehension that Holman had attended law school in Cincinnati at sixteen, declared: "Though she had studied law, she was a frivolous personality who appeared in the nude in her dressing room, and, therefore, had a lot of visitors. Libby was so nearsighted she couldn't see anything more than two inches away from her. She somehow found her way onto the stage, but she could only get off by clutching the curtain as it came in and going off with it."

"*The Little Show* had no outstanding names, at the time it was produced, and it probably made more money than any of the recent musical shows," Allen afterward wrote Mark Leddy. "That happened because no one knew what it was all about, with the result that different things were attempted." Plain, plebeian, and, compared to his costars, ascetic, he immediately set to work writing sketches to augment the additional contributions of Newman Levy, Marya Mannes, and George S. Kaufman. The evening was intended to open with Allen as Prologue, wearing an inverness, getting murdered in front of the curtain. A shot is fired, five daggers discovered in the victim. Prologue, a medieval character, surviving in a twenties revue, illustrates the tenacity of traditional theatrical devices; but the sketch next introduced an up-to-the-minute detective, Silo Vance (after S. S. Van Dine's creation), who summoned the suspects and introduced the players. (The flavor of the introduction to *The Little Show* resembles Allen's many detective sketches during the radio years.)

Holman and Webb, experimenting with ideas of their own, planned a playlet in which Webb as a Harlem "sweetback," or pimp, would dance and mime a situation featuring Holman as his whore. Returning to his squalid room, she would find him in a stupor, a gin bottle beneath the bed, and before rousing him, would conceal cash in her stocking. He would awake, they would execute a feral pas de deux, he would discover the missing cash. This would send him on a rampage, and he would strangle her and exit, horrified by what he had done. Then she would revive, crawl to the door, and hammer against it, all the while producing an ululation of lacerated anguish.

The dramatic situation stirred them, yet despite repeated trips to Harlem, Holman and Webb lacked appropriate music. At rehearsal, however, Dietz heard Ralph Rainger, one of the orchestra's duo-pianists, doodling with a dark-hued blues number. The lyric seemed to write itself; within a half-hour, "Moanin' Low" was complete. The piece derived its musical impact from Holman's dusky timbre. Singing the number through the first time, she repeated the chorus in a lower key, growling and otherwise replicating the sound of musical instruments, while Webb performed a snake-hipped dance. Weatherly and Wiman saw "Moanin' Low" and liked what they saw; but the encounter was too gritty for Broadway, they felt, and only with misgivings did they retain the song destined to stop the show nightly.

The tryout performance of *The Little Show* at Atlantic City augured disaster, and Wiman, in true Scott Fitzgerald fashion, got blotto. By the end of the Atlantic City run, however, the revue was a palpable hit, and on Broadway, the morning after the Music Box Theatre opening, the critics rhapsodized. "Moanin' Low" was ecstatically applauded, as were Jo Mielziner's twinkling contemporary stage designs; even the chorus of twelve, the Chester Hale girls, received acclaim. The revue set a new kind of pattern. "It was a fast show," Cecil Smith has pointed out, "but it also knew the value of slow tempo and quiet tone." In one of the underplayed scenes, two bums sitting on a park bench sing the stock market reports and welcome a street sweeper and policeman, who join in a chorale promising that "money is easier today."

Fred Allen's before-the-curtain monologues (assisted by Portland) transfixed the audience. In "The Man Who Reads All the Ads," he was partnered by Webb. Critic Whitney Bolton described "Mr. Allen gabbling on and on about the way he

had surprised his friends with his knowledge of French practiced on a German waiter, his skill at modern dancing (properly illustrated), his facility at music, all learned in a few easy
lessons in answer to an ad. Meanwhile Mr. Webb interpolated
in repetitious monotone, "We always called him 'Boob.' "

"The Still Alarm," George S. Kaufman's scintillant sketch,
captured the evening's comic honors. Two hypercultivated
gentlemen (Webb and Allen Vincent) are examining blueprints
in a luxurious eleventh-floor hotel suite. The phone rings and
the desk informs them the hotel is on fire. They imperturbably
discuss the approach of the flames. "There is no vulgar display
of terror, rude haste, or selfishness," reported the anonymous
reviewer from the *Times*. The firemen send up calling cards,
and after they arrive, Fred Allen, sporting a Keystone Kop
crepe mustache and ornate helmet, orders ice water. He pauses
to accept a cigar and also takes out a violin, explaining that it
is only on the occasion of a conflagration he has time to practice. Outside, the flames grow ever more ominous, but cool-
ness and good manners prevail. "In fact," the *Times* went on,
"when the floor grows hot and smoke begins to roll through
the windows, good manners have triumphed so completely
that the two hotel guests are seated courteously while the fireman starts to play on his violin 'the little thing' he performed
at the Equitable Holocaust."

Only the highbrow journal *Hound and Horn* condescended
to *The Little Show*'s bright inventions.

New York will patronize Noël Coward, Reinhardt, the
Chauve Souris, Copeau or the Moscow Art Theatre; it
will support talent developed in provincial vaudeville circuits, and produce folk plays from North Carolina or
Oklahoma; and yet it cannot grow anything of its own.
The revue is its characteristic form. *The Little Show* is one
of the best of the recent revues. Clifton Webb, its leading
man, owes his lightness and ease to the fact that he is an
Englishman, and his dancing to his studies in American
tap, most probably to his experience on the vaudeville stage.

Fred Allen reacted by taking out an ad, as he had done so
many times in vaudeville.

BELIEVE IT OR NOT
(Apologies to Ripley)

The Little Show opened April 30, 1929 A.D. Fred Allen, an unknown comedian, awoke on the morning of May 1st to find that *The Little Show* was still at the Music Box Theatre and that he was again in the cast the same as the night before. If the New York Clipper was being published today, Mr. Allen might have received some flattering notices; but since the Clipper has suspended publication we shall never know what its critic thought of *The Little Show*.

Dietz and Schwartz's revue acquired sufficient momentum to exceed the decade and achieve 321 performances. Writing a friend, Herb Jennings, in Norwich, New York, Fred declared: "All goes famous with the Little Sho. Business is fine and pending some Nation Wide disaster we hope to be here well into the winter." The disaster happened in October, but the show lasted through winter all the same.

ON THE LEGENDARY CLOSING NIGHT of *The Little Show*, January 16, 1930, the Music Box was packed with celebrities — Marc Connelly, Beatrice Lillie, Franklin P. Adams, Edna Ferber, Alexander Woollcott, and others — and as the curtain descended for the last time amid tears, thundering applause, and cheering, handfuls of pennies rained down on the stage. Dietz had distributed bags of coppers to his friends; and the performers collected the coins, smiling and bowing with feigned humility.

In February the revue went on the road, opening at Boston's Wilbur Theatre. Elliot Norton remembered a motionless Holman standing in a spotlight beside a piano. "She held twelve hundred people there in the Wilbur Theatre without moving, without a gesture. It was tremendous." The road tour, which ought to have been routine, in Baltimore precipitated Holman's introduction to Zachary Smith Reynolds, heir to the Reynolds tobacco fortune, and this would produce tragic consequences. Although she was involved with a woman at the time, and he was married, Reynolds pursued Libby obsessively. At length he got his way and, following his divorce in

November 1931, Libby married him. Six months later, he died at Reynolda House, his Winston-Salem estate, of a bullet wound after a drunken house party. Libby and Smith's best friend, Albert Walker, were indicted for murder. No one really knows what happened that night; the case, owing to the intervention of the Reynolds family, never came to trial. Libby Holman spent the ensuing forty years shadowed by the ambiguities of a scandal in which guilt, innocence, or the infinite hues between, remained speculative.

When the unsavory Holman-Reynolds affair erupted — agent Walter Batchelor visited Libby on business just before the fateful shooting — Fred Allen reacted charitably, remarking that Libby needed all the friends she could get. In late June 1930, however, with the road tour of *The Little Show* closing, the three principals faced professional hurdles. *The Little Show* had garnered more than a million dollars, but, hoping to establish themselves independent of the stars, the producers did not intend to unveil a new revue with the same cast. They wanted their title to be the main attraction. Thus Dietz and Schwartz confronted the odd situation of competing against themselves: Wiman and Weatherly pushed ahead with contractual plans retaining composer and librettist for *The Second Little Show*. Dietz, mindful of the chemistry of the Allen-Webb-Holman combination, arranged to star them in a new revue for which he would find a producer.

Webb, Maebelle, and Holman that summer sailed to France, and the Allens settled into their two-room apartment in the Warwick Hotel; then Dietz found his impresario in a former vaudeville producer, Max Gordon, and rehearsals commenced in early September. *The Second Little Show,* directed by Monty Woolley and starring Jay C. Flippen, Gloria Grafton, and Al Trahan, opened almost simultaneously. The sequel was not a success; the revue departed from the spare, informal pattern of the original production, although one song, "Sing Something Simple" (by Herman Hupfeld) flashed by in the proper mood. *The Second Little Show,* following a dismal run of sixty-three performances, closed at the Royale Theatre. There would be a third and final *Little Show* in 1931, without Dietz and Schwartz. Beatrice Lillie singing "Mad Dogs and Englishmen" highlighted *The Third Little Show,* but the production duplicated the cumbrous style of its immediate predecessor and once more the public stayed away.

Optimism enlivened the rehearsals of *Three's a Crowd,* as the new revue was christened. Groucho Marx contributed a deft sketch, "The Event," set in a magazine office; Holman was assigned a sort of reprise of "Moanin' Low," titled "Yaller," plus two splendid songs, "Something to Remember You By" and "Body and Soul"; Webb's dance opportunities were abundant; and Allen played the sax and banjo, and in a conquering-hero spoof of Rear Admiral Richard E. Byrd home from the South Pole (with an expedition that included a department store Santa Claus) delivered an uproarious illustrated lecture.

"Something to Remember You By," originally titled "I Have No Words" and composed by Schwartz for a London musical, initially had a quickstep comedy tempo. He intended to use it with rewritten lyrics as a comedy number, but either Dietz or Holman or both (accounts differ) persuaded the composer to treat the melody as a ballad. Sung by Holman to a sailor, whose back alone was visible to the audience — aspiring but unknown actor Fred MacMurray, tenor-saxophone player in the California Collegians, a vaudeville band that also joined in — the plaintive chorus throbbed with loss and longing.

"Body and Soul" presented a knottier problem. Almost a blues, a rare impassioned evocation by the gifted pianist, arranger, and conductor Johnny Green, the song was the score's only interpolation. Green, piano accompanist of Gertrude Lawrence, had composed the tune as special material for her; and she had fetched the unpublished manuscript to England, where she sang "Body and Soul" over the BBC. Bert Ambrose, one of London's most popular bandleaders, heard the broadcast, promoted the piece, and recorded it. Already an English and European hit, the song was a known quantity when Max Gordon secured the American rights, and he lost no time in popularizing it on radio. The reviewer of *The New Yorker* magazine would object that " 'Body and Soul' has had the edge worn off by several hundred saxophones."

Still, if there was comfort in approaching New York with a guaranteed song hit, and if "Body and Soul" came to serve as

Holman's theme, she nearly relinquished it. Three separate writers originally collaborated on the lyrics and she persuaded Dietz to add his own stanzas. None of the orchestrations worked. Opening night at the Erlanger Theatre in Philadelphia, the staging of the number fell apart. Enthroned in a chalice-like black velvet frame, Libby was supposed to be hauled by pulleys toward the stage front, lit by a pencil spot. The effect was meant to celebrate a Venus emerging from the dusk, but the machinery squealed, obliterating the lyrics. The costly pulleys were scrapped. The following night, she sang the song in front of the curtain and received perfunctory applause. At every performance the emotional size of the anticipated hit disintegrated. Should they cut the number? Holman, distraught, rearranged the billing on the show's poster and pinned it to the wall of her dressing room: "Clifton Webb and Fred Allen in *Two's Company*." A worried Dietz journeyed to New York hoping to inveigle Ralph Rainger into reorchestrating the music — he, if anyone, could give it the moody tints, the smoldering intensity of "Moanin' Low." Rainger, reluctant to repeat himself, held out, but finally agreed to tackle "Body and Soul." His solution was again cogent. Bringing the orchestra slowly into the refrain, he allowed the melody to build from a simple piano arrangement while it was sung by Holman and danced by Clifton Webb and Tamara Geva.

Another crisis concerning "Body and Soul" flared just before the opening: the National Broadcasting Company and every Boston radio station banned it. The word *body* in a song title was considered prurient. Max Gordon stuck by the title, but Dietz altered the line "My life, a hell you're making" to the blander "My life, a wreck you're making." The censorship threat today seems ludicrous; however, the production also benefited from the implication that the new show was saucy if not downright lascivious.

On October 15, 1930, *Three's a Crowd* opened at the Selwyn Theatre, preceded on Broadway the previous night by the premiere of George Gershwin's *Girl Crazy*. The back-to-back openings have been described by lyricist Alan Jay Lerner among "the most illustrious of that or any other musical year." For the musical-theater buff, October 1930 was as incredible as the year of the four emperors to a citizen of ancient Rome — a time when everything seemed to be happening at once. There had been only one other period like it in the American musical theater, the remarkable mid-September week in 1925 that saw the successive openings of Youmans's *No, No, Nanette,* Rodgers and Hart's *Dearest Enemy,* Friml's *Vagabond King,* and Kern's *Sunny.*

The moment the curtain ascended on Allen, Webb, and Holman doing "Ain't Gonna Be No Beds," a boulevard-farce triangle of husband, wife, and lover treated as a "boudoir spiritual" in the style of *The Green Pastures,* the show's contemporary spirit was evident: akin to the cartoons of Peter Arno, the verse of Ogden Nash, and the stories of Dorothy Parker. Dietz and Schwartz surpassed even this success with their score for *The Band Wagon* the following June; but *Three's a Crowd* disclosed, better than any show until then, the possibilities of the revue form. "Although no one expects a revue to be a work of art," wrote Brooks Atkinson in the *Times,* "*Three's a Crowd* is a work of art without being any less entertaining as a revue."

The critics acclaimed Holman as "the statue of Libby." Webb, "spindle-shanked, silken and beguiling," danced "Night after Night," a macabre, surrealistic routine in which "he impersonates a young man in a Parisian bar, sick with too much liquor and too many women, but who must dance to the tune the pipers play. About him are strange and dissipated women while bartenders with inflated faces wield immense cocktail shakers. The young man dances until he falls exhausted before the now empty bar." Allen's satires prompted hilarity, particularly his topical jokes ("Times are so hard that the bootleggers in Chicago have laid off two hundred policemen") and his sketch routines, especially one in which he portrayed an Altoona boy who never gets invited to parties, and his Admiral Byrd lecture to a refrain of "snow, everlasting snow." In parka and leggings he intoned:

After a year and a half's hard work in the Antarctic region, we discovered and claimed for the United States not fifty, not one hundred, but five hundred thousand square

miles of brand new snow. . . . The United States now
has enough snow to meet any emergency for the next two
hundred years. Enough snow to settle the unemployment
problem in every city in the country. Four million men
are now out of work. It will take seventeen million men
thirty-one and a half years to remove all the snow and
they won't even make a dent in it.

During this lecture he showed slides of his airplane, Eskimos,
his living quarters, and the South Pole — all blank because of
the everlasting snow.

Three's a Crowd played 272 performances, recovering its initial investment but floundering in the backwash of the worst
season Broadway had ever known. "Business has been so bad,"
Allen wrote Joe Kelly on March 20,

> that this coming Saturday may see me in a position to
> accept a commission in the Army of the Unemployed.
> . . . Last night the manager informed us that when the
> cast, musicians, stagehands, etc had been paid that there
> was hardly anything left for the stars except some possible
> adulation from a few lovers of celestial bodies. Mr. Webb
> expressing great concern flew from his room to acquaint
> the acoustics with the ultimatum that "we might as well
> be out of work as working for nothing." If the business
> during the coming week — when the closing has been ad-
> vertised — picks up we may remain until June sixth, but
> I doubt it.

Largely because Webb negotiated an arrangement to accept
a percentage, *Three's a Crowd* survived the season. "You will
be pleased to learn that business fell off so badly last week,"
Joe Kelly was informed in early May,

> that the three stars of *Three's a Crowd,* who have been
> playing on percentage, received absolutely nothing for their
> week of labor. . . . It seems that Mr. Webb, in making
> the arrangement to continue the show on a percentage ba-
> sis, neglected to state a minimum salary which should act
> as a stop-gap. Business has continued to turn the corner
> for the worse and last week he realized his mistake. I don't

know what will happen, but it burns me up to think of having to spend thirty or forty dollars, on laundry, pressing, help, etc., for the privilege of working eight shows for nothing.

Fred and Portland divided the summer hiatus between a trip abroad and a cottage in Old Orchard Beach, Maine. That fall they embarked with Webb and Holman on a road tour as calamitous as any vaudeville odyssey they had experienced. Allen had been marooned with Japanese acrobats in a Bozeman, Montana, blizzard, falsely accused in El Paso, almost robbed of his comedy curtain in Williamsport, but this was by far the most distressing of his itineraries. The salaries of the principals were cut from fifteen hundred dollars a week to fifty. Audiences shrank, the darkness of the Depression deepened. Telling jokes about Admiral Byrd's solution to the unemployment problem became increasingly difficult when soup kitchen lines shuffled outside the theater and cold winds whipped the ragged coats of the homeless.

RADIO

PORTLAND: Radio sure is funny.
ALLEN: All except the comedy programs.
Our program has been cut off so many
times the last page of the script is a
Band-Aid.

— *Texaco Star Theater*

10 | Don't Trust Midgets

I f you knew what has been going on with this show," Fred wrote Mark Leddy, in December 1931, "you wouldn't be surprised if I took the first open spot you could find in vaudeville." They were still on a percentage arrangement and business was anemic. *Three's a Crowd* opened well in theater-loving Chicago — then played to empty houses. "We have lost every week since opening, and with the assorted salaries and Mr. Webb astride his lavender high horse, there is no telling our end."

By January in Chicago, even the producer abandoned ship:

> Gordon and the Erlanger people [the principal backers], I think I told you, walked out on the show. They will not be responsible for further losses. We are running it ourselves and have booked St. Louis and Kansas City and if it isn't too disastrous we may continue to the Coast. Webb wants to go there to autograph the scenery and leave it in Joan Crawford's backyard, I guess. Louis Lipstone saw the show last night and made us an offer to condense it, if we close and play the picture theaters around here. *Girl Crazy,* which they say is awful, has been packing them in at the picture houses and our show would make a much better offering for them.

The lack of business aggravated backstage tension. "I have stopped talking to Webb, which is fine, and if Bob, the manager, holds out, perhaps we shall come through with flying colors in the form of tattered blazer jackets."

Allen's prognostication, "we couldn't do business in any of the towns coming out here and it's sane to assume that we shan't cause any mobs to form in the theater lobbies at Omaha and Denver," came true in Saint Louis. *Three's a Crowd* back-pedaled to Boston in February for its final booking, a limited engagement at the Colonial Theatre. Webb afterward returned to New York, Holman headed for a Hong Kong honeymoon, MacMurray followed his star toward Hollywood — and a month later Fred Allen reappeared in *Three's a Crowd* at the Metropolitan Theatre, two blocks away from the Colonial.

Thomas McLaughlin and Sue Baxter assumed the Webb-Holman roles, and Allen received top billing, whatever consolation billing may have been in the five-a-day circumstances of the Depression. The Metropolitan was a movie palace; *Three's a Crowd* in a tabloid version lasted under an hour between showings of the film comedy *This Is the Night,* with Lili Damita and Charles Ruggles. Scarcely the ideal setting for an intimate revue, the four-thousand-seat theater was typical of subsequent bookings. In May, from Detroit, Allen wrote Joe Kelly:

> I have been very busy exploring the Great Indoors as the confused guest of the Paramount-Publix Circuit. Every town looks the same to me since they are all about like the quarters you saw in Boston. In Buffalo I saw a sparrow and a cat, for through some oversight there was a window in the dressing room. Here I'm nicely ensconced in a vacuum and yesterday we ate in the dressing room on account of the five shows and today we can't get out because the shows started later and come closer together. . . . I see so little daylight that when we finally get out at night Mrs. Allen and I flap our arms and go up the street towards the hotel, "hooting" in approved owl fashion.

The Allens cheerfully abandoned the Publix movie-vaudeville circuit for Old Orchard Beach. "I shall be back in New York around September first," Allen wrote Leddy. "I have nothing definite. Batchelor has several things on the fire but so have the frankfurt vendors down here which means nothing."

The times called for caution. Vaudeville was expiring, live performance endangered. The heedlessness of a Libby Holman belonged to a callow decade already out of style. Allen felt reluctant to plunge into radio, although he had an exploratory offer from a sponsor, Sheaffer pen. He contemplated the stream of Broadway comedians finding refuge in broadcasting. Should he join the exodus? Aside from relaxing on a Maine beach in the summer of 1932, he hoped to complete three or four sketches like "Disappointments." Wiman had promised him a part in a new revue and no doubt would need material. But Wiman neglected to send a contract, and by September the revue was an evaporating mirage.

HESITANT before a phase of his career alien to any he had experienced, Fred Allen could pause and consider another option: professional authorship.

He still patched and mended vaudeville acts as before, even on Broadway ("Dear Pal Fred: That joke about Lauder is a riot. Hope you will not mind not telling it as it doesn't mean much to you and a lot to me"), but he was expanding, and probing the narrative dimensions of humor. In this he was encouraged by Jack Donahue, a close friend and leading dancer in the *Ziegfeld Follies*. Allen had written Donahue's first vaudeville monologue, and they spent weeks together working on his comedy roles in such book shows as *Two Little Girls in Blue* and *Rosalie*. "Jack always wanted me to stop trying to be an actor and concentrate on writing. I was always afraid to take the risk. As an actor, I could make a living and always have enough money to send home. As a writer, I knew that my relatives couldn't eat my words."

Allen's attitudes about writing were ambivalent. He described his literary tastes as "about three feet five inches of the Five Foot Shelf." Beginning all over again in a new and problematical role daunted him; on the other hand, its long-term prospects were brighter. "A humorist with a column on a newspaper, or one who wrote for syndication, enjoyed a greater security . . . and had a much more satisfying life. . . . "Acting," he concluded, "has never appealed to me."

Having exchanged the pipe of peace, Fred and editor Sime Silverman discussed the prospects of the comedian sending in an occasional *Variety* column. Allen contributed to the annual issues at first, notably "A Small-Timer's Diary" in September 1923. The diary, strongly influenced by the vernacular style of Ring Lardner, draws on personal experience: barren hotel rooms; dangling, unshaded electric bulbs; fickle audiences; the roseate dreams of the performers and sour indifference on the part of the managers. The entries follow the roller-coaster fortunes of a husband-and-wife comedy team at the beginning of the season, from the last day in August through the last day in September. The speaker in the diary is the husband; the couple bumbles from Battle Creek through datelines such as Rattrap and Cannibal, Missouri. In the final entry they dwindle before their comfortless future like Chaplin's Little Tramp walking toward a vast horizon at fade-out: "We open with a tab Monday, 60 net, double. A bird in the hand saves the price of a cage. I'm doing Irish. I never done Irish, but Jolson never seen Alabama. Rehearse tomorrow. The wife says I should join the Elks in case we get stranded."

When Tommy Gray, a popular *Variety* columnist, died in 1926, Silverman asked Allen to take over his column. Editor and contributor, however, held divergent views about the job. To Allen, then touring in *The Greenwich Village Follies*, column writing represented an opportunity to master the techniques of the periodical humorist; to Silverman it was a species of free advertising. Thus Allen was unpaid for "Near Fun," as the column was dubbed (near beer was a Prohibition beverage needled by numberless comedians), and for a time the endeavor went smoothly. "Near Fun" assembled a crazy quilt of random observations and jokes, not too different in concept, though distinct in content, from FPA's "Conning Tower." Allen paid contributors a dollar a joke. At its best, the column was inspired ("Hush little bright line . . . ," for example), and considering the hectic circumstances under which the comedian was forced to write, packing and unpacking a trunk, making jumps between cities, rushing to meet deadlines, the general level was impressive. "Near Fun" was also so miscellaneous that throwaway jokes hedged, say, a news item from Liverpool — jokes such as "left-handed dramatic actor finds it impossible to replace his monocle in his right eye," or the line about the glassblower stricken with hiccoughs who produced three hundred percolator tops before he could stop.

A cloudburst of manna for other comedians, "Near Fun" attracted widespread attention, and theater people whom Allen respected, like John Murray Anderson, added their assurances to Jack Donahue's. Chatting with *Philadelphia Inquirer* critic Linton Martin at a party just before the *Follies* closed on the road, Allen brought up the subject of his writing ambitions. Martin urged Allen to approach Silverman and ask for sixty dollars a week. "If the column is important to *Variety*," Martin said, "Sime will pay you." But from Sime's point of view, it was absurd to pay a contributor whose career benefited from the inestimable advantages of exposure in *Variety*. He told Allen that, according to the prevailing advertising rates, the newspaper was already paying two hundred dollars a week for "Near Fun."

Thus the column ended; but Allen's writing continued. In *The Little Show/Three's a Crowd* period, he worked non-matinee days at Paramount's studio in Astoria, Long Island, and there made his first film, a comedy short subject titled *The Installment Collector,* reminiscent of his adolescent experiences at the piano company. There also he wrote a two-reeler for his Boston fellow-vaudevillian, Jack Haley, and a scenario for comedian Jack Oakie. The turn of the decade found Allen in brisk editorial demand; he contributed to *Judge,* and *College Humor* asked him for two thousand words a month. One evening, before going on in *Three's a Crowd,* he opened a note addressed to the Selwyn Theatre by Wolcott Gibbs, the managing editor of *The New Yorker* magazine.

January 6, 1931

Dear Fred Allen:

Here is our check for "Don't Trust Midgets." It's an excellent piece and we're using it in our issue of January 10.

As a rule we send out author's proof on everything, but
because of the shortness of time in your case it would
have been impossible to make corrections, so I didn't
bother. It was also necessary to drop your piece into a
space occupied by something else, and I had to cut three
lines because of different space. I tried to get you through
Howard Dietz and various other people to consult you
about what to take out, but it's apparently impossible to
reach anybody in the theatre by telephone, so I did it myself. Nothing disastrous, though, I think.

If you have time I hope you'll send us something else.
We'd like very much to have you writing for us regularly.

Despite Gibbs's praise — more than a decade later he still
wanted Allen to write for a summer newspaper on Long
Island — "Don't Trust Midgets" was the author's debut in and
farewell to *The New Yorker*. Later that year he told John "Red"
Pearson, a writer for comic Bert Lahr, "My latest effusion has
been returned by *The New Yorker* with some comment anent
its being too 'broad' for their readers." It does not seem likely
that, involved in the battering demands of his radio work, Allen
tried to place anything in the magazine afterward. A younger
friend, Bill Mullen of Old Orchard, recalled that "Fred was a
perfectionist; he didn't like to do anything he couldn't excel
in," and, given his sensitivity to rejection, he must have felt
discouraged. In any event, "Don't Trust Midgets," a parody
of self-help stories, presents a submerged autobiography beneath its foolery.

Sylvester Prebble, the apple-vendor hero, attains a modest
Depression-era reputation as the first man to open a crate in
the middle of the block instead of taking the corner. The story-
within-a-story chronicles his fall from a former prosperity. In-
specting eggnogs for Liggetts Drugstores is his livelihood, but
vaudeville is his passion. Instead of minding his eggnogs,
Sylvester, gripped by vaudeville mania, spends twenty hours
a day rushing from show to show, and soon gets fired. "If
you're so fond of the theater," he is told, "why don't you live
in it?" Taking this advice, he moves into the rear of the auditorium at the Gargantua Theatre, bringing along a percolator,

provisions, a gunnysack of personal belongings, and "heavy underwear for the summer months when the cooling system would be working."

"I spent a very pleasant year in Z row of the orchestra," Sylvester recalls, but because of a progressive loss of hearing, he shifts closer to the stage, three years in row K and a few years in row A. Then he moves into the pit, posing as a cymbal player, and at length goes onstage, standing next to the actor who is speaking. The audience mistakes him for a master of ceremonies; the performers, for the theater manager. His success leads to an offer from Finger's Midgets: "The act was to remain the same except that I would come out and listen to the dialogue and follow the other actors around." A midget advises him, "Stick to Mr. Finger and you will be a big man." After two payless years Sylvester feels he has served his apprenticeship. He asks for a salary: "I'm the man who spent nearly eight years in the Gargantua Theatre and gave up my future there to come with your act." Mr. Finger is outraged. "Look at me: working with midgets for two years," he cries. "Am I a big man?" Sylvester growls, "Only by comparison," and makes his exit tossing a midget at Finger.

Humor is always in short supply, even around *The New Yorker,* yet other perspectives stretch beyond the droll, surreal foreground (again a bow in the direction of Ring Lardner) of Singer's Midgets, the real troupe prompting the story. Allen's love of vaudeville, his slow, gradual progress, his invasion of the actor's space, and his fitful financial rewards are elements, too. And, in a way, "Don't Trust Midgets" is oddly prophetic about the "molehill men," the vice-presidents of advertising agencies who would harass him during the radio years.

By 1931 he had developed his mature comic-prose style. "An eyeshade, a spittoon and a typewriter are the essentials of his success," Al Hirschfeld commented. Four or five nights a week, sitting in a straight-backed chair at a rickety card table, Allen labored over his writing. Of his many informal photographs, it is striking that so many portray him in the act of composition, collar open, necktie dangling, elastic bands on his sleeves, a wad of tobacco wedged in his cheek while he scrawls diminutive penciled hieroglyphics in the margins of typescript.

"A publishing firm, one Simon and Schuster," he wrote Joe Kelly, in May 1931, "has approached me with intent to foister a dollar book on the Public, belittling the Depression. I have been dickering with them for two weeks, and have submitted assorted jokes, and matter, which would tend to replace the feather, in the risibility tickling at this time."

Nothing came of the project; *Three's a Crowd* required heroic measures, but Allen persisted. "For all his quick wit, his lines didn't cascade forth," Arnold Auerbach remembered. "He wrote the way most people do — thoughtfully, weighing his words, worrying at them. He was highly inventive, of course, but his fertility came chiefly from grim diligence and fierce concentration." The effect of any joke was unpredictable, but Allen meant to control the effect. To Hirschfeld he confided:

> It's mysterious, Al. I know how to make people laugh — and I know approximately when they'll laugh — but I haven't the vaguest idea *why* they laugh. During the Wall Street crash all I had to do to get a wave of laughs through the audience was to mention Goldman Sachs [the Wall Street investment firm]. One night I spotted a friend out front who had lost every cent he owned in the crash. Now, you would imagine that any reference to this disaster would depress him; but nope — all he needed to hear was Goldman Sachs and he was off in a fit of laughter. I can't figure it out.

Like Jack Benny, Fred Allen had the reflexes of a poet rather than a jokesmith. His approach to humor emphasized the resources of language: simile, metaphor, puns, paradoxes, rhetorical devices, reversals of expectation, linguistic transformations. He used traditional devices of exaggeration, comparison, and anecdote, and contrary images were fused into vivid, startling phrases: "The agency men were as quiet as a small boy banging two pussy willows together in a vacuum." "As nervous as a jellyfish on a Ford fender." "Sinatra looks like he's just been evicted from an oxygen tent." On the same subject: "Sinatra signing autographs looks like one pencil writing with another." The famous personification (in a letter to Goodman Ace) "California's a wonderful place to live — if you happen to be an orange." A description of radio announcer Arthur Godfrey, briefly associated with Allen in the early forties, as "the man with the barefoot voice." The imagery of a public-park attendant as "a statue valet who scrubs granite varicose veins." Even traditional exaggeration acquired a fresh twist: "When I was in vaudeville all of the dogs in dog acts knew me. I was always billed so low that dogs kept bumping their noses into my name as they passed the front of the theater."

Steve Allen, Fred's latter-day colleague and namesake, compares this style to the concise captions of *New Yorker* cartoons. Of New York's bantam-sized mayor, Fiorello La Guardia, for instance, Fred said, "He's the only man I know who can milk a cow standing up." The idiosyncratic tone, in Steve Allen's opinion, "is related, and not too distantly, to the humor of the modern, fey, sophisticated cartoon. It makes one think of George Price. Certainly it is a far cry from the general level of radio comedy with which it was contemporaneous." Who but Fred Allen would call a moth "a closet butterfly" or imagine a cross-eyed man "so nervous he bites my fingernails"?

On the rare occasions when he formulated his views about his craft (despite his curiosity about it, he was not given to theory), Allen was crisp and decisive. "Writing monologues," he told an aspiring radio writer who had submitted a script,

> if you start to talk to one final point, and along the way if you drag in extraneous gags and points that further your story interest or heighten the final ending, [then] you have the whole secret of the monologue. Many people start off to go someplace with an idea and, through leaving the central theme to drag in other laughs, they weaken the sum total of the talk and defeat their own ends. . . . Perhaps, later on, if you still stay in radio out there, you can send me some of your routines, and I can look them over for you. As long as you keep working, that is the all-important thing. It is only through constant practice that you can even become a good horseshoe pitcher and if it works with the lowly horseshoe, how much more vital is practice to the spinner of tales.

"Mark Twain would have relished some of Fred Allen's vast exaggerations," Gilbert Seldes speculates.

The extravagances of his puns are like the immeasurable disproportions of Twain's short stories; the unabashed use of corn is typical of George Ade and Eugene Field. Ring Lardner admired him [Allen] intensely. As for the satiric touch, here, for instance, is a report on an outrageous political junket: "The second section of the train bearing the Illinois legislature to New Orleans was stopped . . . by bandits last night. After relieving the bandits of their watches and jewelry, the excursionists proceeded on their journey with increased enthusiasm." Internal evidence will tell the specialist who wrote it; but if it were in Irish spelling, might it not be Finley Peter Dunne? And if it were given as a news item, with appropriate settings, couldn't it come from the Town Hall Newsreel with Fred Allen reading the captions?

Strolling down Allen's Alley, that fixture of his 1940s shows, Fred knocked on doors, and the ethnic types who emerged — voluble vaudevillians — greeted him and told their stories. This was also consonant with humor that bears a close relation to the handiwork of traditional narrative. Social historian Sam Bass Warner notes the similarity between Allen's comic approach and the old metropolitan daily newspaper, with its multitudinous small reports of police news, fires, politics, oddities, and personalities. "For [Allen] the city was populated with stories: each person you passed on the street or read about in the newspaper carried a distinct story . . . which was the person's central being. If you came to know a person well, you would know not only the central life story, but also many of the characteristic stories he created as he traveled along his unique way."

Novelist Edwin O'Connor, the comedian's friend and sometime editor, shared his conviction when he wrote Allen concerning the latter's projected autobiography. It should start with the letter sent him by John Steinbeck urging him to write his autobiography, and then develop along lines suggested by Fred. Fred Allen's story, said O'Connor, would demonstrate "that everybody in the world has his own particular story to tell, that if all these stories were written it would be the complete history of our time, and that here, in this book, is one man's contribution to this history."

Photographs of Fred Allen typing in his study reveal behind him rows of large volumes in sturdy, black bindings. Fifty of these over the years would collect on the shelves, ten feet of some seven hundred radio scripts next to a one-volume collected works of Shakespeare, which took up three-and-a-half inches. The latter was "a corrective, just in case I start thinking a ton of cobblestones is worth as much as a few diamonds." Each of the bound radio scripts had a bookplate showing a jester leaning on the back of a wing chair over a boy daydreaming before an open volume with poised quill: "Ex Libris, Fred Allen." Did he think of them, however — since he was too diffident to claim the laurels of professional authorship — as *books?* Of course, they represent an output of formidable proportions; yet radio, like the stage, is not an armchair experience. Taken properly, however, not in marathon gulps but in leisurely sips, the scripts retain a delectable and manifest flavor. Perhaps the black-bound volumes aren't books as Mr. Glover back at Commerce High School might think of books in his class on salesmanship, but they exhibit the indomitable spirit of humor ballasting a decade of chaos, want, and impending war. They are the autobiographical record of a world made up of the sum of individual stories, not a bewildering realm of corporate identities.

11 | The Man with the Flat Voice

Sunday evening, October 23, 1932: a routine day in radio. That afternoon the Reverend Charles E. Coughlin, the radio priest from Royal Oak, Michigan, broadcast his demagogic views on the social plight of America; later on, Babe Ruth, Jack Dempsey, Lou Gehrig, and eleven other athletic titans, interspersed with the bands of Harvard, the University of Illinois, and the University of California, participated in a forty-five-minute appeal on behalf of the Welfare and Relief Mobilization of 1932; and Ernest Truex, whose initial stage appearance had taken place during the previous century at the age of five in *Little Lord Fauntleroy,* stepped before a microphone for the first time, playing General Robert E. Lee in the drama *Roses and Drums.* Listeners to the debut of Fred Allen's *Linit Bath Club Revue* may be forgiven for not recognizing entertainment history in the making. The country was racked by the Depression, the Hoover-Roosevelt election campaign approached crisis point, a tabletop radio sold for $19.95 ($5 down), and the variety format of the Linit program promised the same admixture as before. How could that mythical figment, the common man — often and anxiously evoked in 1932 — anticipate the aureate promise of a golden age of original comic commentary?

In 1942, Alexander Woollcott, wondering about Fred Allen's radio debut, brought up a guest appearance "in a WOR studio in the fall of 1929, when I was broadcasting two or three times a week for some deluded sponsor and, as you can modestly testify, inviting everyone in God's world to come on the program as guest stars. You shared this rare privilege with Helen Hayes, Father Duffy, George Cohan, Leslie Howard and many another. None of the guests was paid anything, but as the difference between what they got and what I got was slight, the discrepancy seemed to cause no hard feelings." Allen acknowledged his guest turn on the program; he did not mention that three years passed before he felt inclined to venture into radio again.

"Conditions in the theater are always bad over the summer," he wrote in late June to Merrill Clark, a friend from the Midwest. If things got any worse, Fred went on, the Allens could always emulate the natives of Old Orchard Beach, who are "eating candles and using the wicks for dental floss."

Things got worse, and in September Walter Batchelor heard that Linit, a beauty potion manufactured by the Corn Products Company, sought a new program. A cast was assembled, a show fashioned, although the president of Corn Products, a wholehearted subscriber to the doctrine of the divine right of presidents, declined to waste time attending Allen's studio audition. The tycoon demanded to hear the show on a portable phonograph. So nervous was Batchelor that en route to his Corn Products appointment he damaged the phonograph aboard the subway. Not until the audition record began wobbling did he realize it wouldn't go beyond the musical overture plus the opening lines of Allen's initial scene. After several futile attempts, a flustered Batchelor tried still again, and the executive flew into a tantrum and huffed: "Never mind the show. Get me that man with the flat voice!"

For writing and performing in the half-hour Linit program every Sunday evening at 9:00 on the Columbia Broadcasting System, Allen received $1,000 per week, out of which he had to pay his cast. Jolson's contract, by way of comparison, called for $5,000 per radio appearance, and Wynn received the same. Doubtless the bargain price-tag enhanced Fred's appeal to Depression-vexed sponsors. Other comedians were mere

mouthpieces; Allen was the equivalent of a movie theater Bank
Night where patrons won dishes, cash prizes, or due bills —
he gave everyone something extra for the price of admission.
The half-hour show had to be done twice because of the time
difference, with the second performance beginning at 12:00
midnight for West Coast listeners. Beforehand, he submitted
the script to the lugubrious scrutiny of advertising men, and
he rehearsed and timed the scenes, and prepared backup exchanges. At once Allen realized the physical impossibility of
writing and starring in a weekly network entertainment. Al
Hirschfeld recalls the comedian phoning after the first Linit
show: "What am I going to do?" he asked. "I've used up my
whole life." A vaudeville performer based a career upon twelve
minutes of material; radio consumed that material, then demanded more.

Nothing dates faster than huckstering, and by contemporary
standards the Linit commercials exhibit awesome vacuity. Their
unabashed ostentation compels notice; their vaunting formats
swell like the pasteboard dickies on tuxedo-clad butlers in thirties movies. The commercials comment upon hard times with
the ersatz confidence of unimpeded desire. Audiences once accepted these conventions; someday, of course, our own conventions will seem as curious.

(*Fanfare and introduction*)
ROBERTS [Kenneth Roberts, the announcer]: Greetings,
    ladies and gentlemen. The feature which is to follow
    comes as an expression of goodwill and appreciation by
    the makers of Linit, the bathway to a safe, smooth skin.
    THE LINIT BATH CLUB REVUE OF 1932, featuring the
    mirth-provoking Fred Allen and a notable supporting
    cast, comes direct from the sound stage of "The Linit
    Theatre Petite."

The script took pains to establish the illusion of an audience
attending the Theatre Petite's live performance. The versatile
Jack Smart, an eventual mainstay of the Mighty Allen Art
Players and Allen's Alley, who enjoyed a second career as a
professional painter and sculptor, portrayed an usher.

(*Incoming patrons*)

SMART: First aisle to your right, please. Stairway to your left.

FEM VOICE: What a charming little theater.

2ND FEM VOICE: Isn't it, though? . . . So intimate!

SMART: Seats seven and nine, please.

(*Business with seats*)

MAN: May I have a program, please?

SMART: Sorry, sir, there are no programs.

MAN: No programs? I never heard of such a thing!

SMART: I don't believe you'll have need of a printed program, sir, as this Revue is employing a new idea of presentation . . . The show is designed for both a seeing and hearing audience. Those of us here in the theater and those of us in the radio audience.

MAN: So I have heard.

SMART: I think that you will find that everything will be explained from the stage without the inconvenience of a printed program.

MAN: Very well. Thank you.

BARRETT [Sheila Barrett, an impersonator of voices and a featured guest star, here a passing flapper]: I'm just ccrrraaaazzzzzzyyyy about Fred Allen!

(*Orchestra tuning*)

FEM VOICE: Hurry back, dear.

MALE VOICE: I'll be back before the first act.

(*Effect of baton tapping stand*)

(*Silence*)

BARRETT: Oh look! Myrtle . . . that's Lou Katzman conducting . . . He was on the radio for the longest time.

(*Orchestra. Bright snappy overture.* "I Guess I'll Have to Change My Plan," "All-American Girl," "Over the Weekend")

MAN: Ladies and gentlemen . . . May I present Fred Allen?

Others in the cast included Portland; torch singer Helen Morgan; Roy Atwell, specialist in double-talk, gibberish, and verbal blunders ("Master of English as She Is Broken," billed also as "a Spoonerist"); tenor Charles Carlile; Barrett, who impersonated John Barrymore and Zazu Pitts; Mary Lou Dix, designated simply as "actress"; and Ann Leaf at the console of the solo Wurlitzer organ, a pulsating interlude among the violin-dappled romantic confections of Louis Katzman's Orchestra. "Playing an organ solo midway through a comedy show is like planting a pickle in the center of a charlotte russe," Allen afterward wrote; for the sponsor's wife enjoyed organ music and was mesmerized by the notion that a solo organist seated two miles across town could locate the lost chord while performing in time with the orchestra. An announcement prefaced this portion of the show: "The organ music which you hear is being played by Ann Leaf at the console of the Paramount organ in the Paramount Theatre, although miles separate them [Miss Leaf and the orchestra — not, as announced, the organ and the theater]." Sometimes there was repartee implying that a dangerous, unspecified feat hung in the balance: "Are you ready in the Paramount Theatre, Miss Leaf?"

"Ready, Mr. Katzman."

Throughout its twenty-six weeks, *The Linit Bath Club Revue* maintained a simple structure: Sketch, Guest Star, Portland, Atwell's malaprop routine ("Mr. Nallen, my name is Loy Ratwell. No, it's Joy Latwall. No, my name is . . ."). Yet from the start, when Allen stepped to the microphone, clearly — despite the awkward obeisance the show paid its Broadway revue format — something unusual was happening. "Good evening, ladies and gentlemen," Allen said, "I want to welcome you to the opening of our Theatre Petite . . . You'll have to excuse me if I seem a bit nervous. I didn't sleep well. I dreamed I drove downtown in my car, and all night long I kept moving around to different parts of the bed so I wouldn't get a ticket for parking."

The jokes of the stand-up introduction followed the pattern of stand-up jokes everywhere, isolated from what comes before and what comes after, but timing and crisp delivery redeemed them from the banal.

"I read about a man recently who took out a twenty-year

endowment policy and at the end of fifteen years he worried himself to death trying to keep up the payments."

Then Allen voiced his conception of a new radio comedy that in time would detach itself from stage effects.

"We're going to present a revue with a plot running through it." The "plot" came from "the characters employed in, or indigenous to, the assorted locales" — in this case, one of Allen's favorite venues, a courtroom over which he presided. The mood of the court suggested the topsy-turvydom of a W. S. Gilbert sketch rewritten by Groucho Marx.

SMART: I want justice!

ALLEN: Then you'd better get out of here. This is a Court Room.

SMART: Somebody stole my coat.

ALLEN: You don't have to make such a fuss about it. People lose suits in here every day. And sergeant . . .

SERGEANT: Yes, your honor.

ALLEN: You'd better hold my watch until Court is dismissed. I don't like the looks of the prosecuting attorney, either. . . . Who is that emaciated-looking gent in the docket?

SERGEANT: He was left over from last night.

ALLEN: On what case was that?

SERGEANT: Harry Filch, the pickpocket. You fined him ten dollars, but he had only two dollars. What shall I do with him?

ALLEN: A pickpocket, eh? Turn him loose in the crowd until he gets the other eight dollars.

While this may sound antediluvian today, its satirical tone identified it as exceptional among the vociferous humor then cackling across the airwaves. Only Jack Benny would master the medium's comic potential so absolutely, and he would take a different direction. In terms of continuous topical commentary, Allen's conception of "a complete story told each week or a series of episodes and comedy situations" was ideal. Moreover, the topical theme could stretch out and include the attendant details of a radio show. Judge Allen could mention "an orchestra charged with disturbing the piece" and introduce Helen Morgan, the chanteuse celebrated for singing while reposing on a Steinway, with "Ask her to please get down off the piano before she enters the room." The first Linit script ended with an injunction: "APPLAUSE. NICE, HEALTHY AND SELF-RESPECTING." Instead of basking in that applause, Allen, of course, was shaken by temblors of panic. How could he alone fill the Sunday evenings, which suddenly expanded into infinity?

The following week, however, the script, set in the executive suite of the Drooping Walrus Mustache Wax Company ("the wax that's on everyone's lips"), occasioned one of his finest half-hours. The humor, self-reflexive in Allen's funniest style, lampooned the commercialism of radio, and possibly commemorated his recent awkward encounters with advertising executives. As president of Drooping Walrus, he appraised Lou Katzman's first medley:

"That's a fine orchestra, but there are too many violins. Violins won't sell a cent's worth of mustache wax. I want an orchestra with forty cornets. When a cornet player finishes, his mustache is always drooping and wet. We'll make them buy our wax after each program. It will help business."

After another musical number waned, Allen waxed prophetic.

"Call up Columbia," he asked Portland. "That was part of the Linit program. We're trying to sell mustache wax. Tell them if we don't get better service, we won't bother with radio. We'll wait for TV to come in."

The television allusion serves as a reminder that video seemed imminent in 1932; CBS had a regular program schedule for an estimated nine thousand television receivers in metropolitan New York, while NBC had established a station atop the Empire State Building. "The most prevalent explanation for delaying television was engineering difficulties," states William Hawes, a scholar of primitive video, but the Depression was the true overriding factor. "If it had not been for the nation's financial crisis, the public might have had television by 1933, and radio might not have become as prominent as it did."

Fortunately for Fred Allen, the delay would take the better part of the next fifteen years.

Another landmark of the second Linit show was the Drooping Walrus Dramatic Players, forerunners of the Mighty Allen Art Players and, distantly, the inhabitants of Allen's Alley. (By November 30 the troupe had become the Blood and Thunder Dramatic Company.) Their contribution was a playlet attributed to Eugene O'Neill, "Slice Yourself a Piece of Life." The scene opened upon a verbal arabesque, "The Louis XIV Room in the Trask family's farmhouse in Skowhegan, Maine. It is Christmas Eve and Mrs. Trask is discovered rocking the baby to sleep with a rock, in the corner."

An O'Neillian exchange of greetings foreshadowed the action.

"Hairy Christmas, Paw."

"Hairy Christmas, Son."

"Slice Yourself a Piece of Life" ripened into a travesty of nineteenth-century melodrama — a kind of commentary on O'Neill's indebtedness to the theater of his father — incorporating hero, heroine, and villain. The curtain fell upon a Big Free Offer: "Send in three razor blades or ten manhole covers for your trial tubes of Mustache Wax." Allen would discover how guileless his new audience was, when he received before his next program three manhole covers addressed to him, care of CBS.

"AFTER SIX WEEKS everyone was talking about Fred Allen," recalled Roger White, the producer of the Linit revue. "The radio critics were saying 'Who is this Fred Allen?' 'Where did he come from?' "

The cause of the commotion was unmoved, having absorbed the laughter and catcalls of audiences over the years; praise could not turn his head nor detraction make him despondent. In the words of Mark Twain, "it was all as natural and familiar — and so were the shoreward sights — as if there had been no break in my river life." However, three weeks into what Allen clearly perceived as a short-term radio

engagement, he addressed his discontents mainly to Senator
David Walsh's secretary, Joe Kelly.

It seems to be harder for me to assemble my radio programs since Mr. Roosevelt's shadow has been found at
the White House. If this result of the Democratic victory
is noticeable at this early stage you can advise the Senator
that the number of unemployed will be increased by two —
Mrs. Allen and the tireless, from a bellyaching standpoint, Mr. A. . . . The radio work is still tedious and I
don't know how much longer I can keep the thing going
without help. The entire arrangement is so cheap that they
don't want to engage authors or outside help lest it cut
into the melon now being enjoyed by the agents and other
hangers on.

To an old friend, Val Eichen, a retired vaudevillian in East
Hampton, Long Island (Eichen sent Allen weekly comments
on the show's progress), Fred confided:

The programs have been going along swell . . . so far.
Some weeks I get a kick out of them, Val, but after the
two days spent writing them and two days rehearsing and
cutting and consulting with the bosses about what is what,
you don't feel so funny when it gets around nine o'clock
on Friday night. There is always the feeling that you have
to hurry, for every second counts and we try to cram so
much stuff into the half hour that we can't let down for a
second. You should be around some night just before the
broadcast when we are trying to take out forty-five seconds. The guy with the stop-watch and I are cutting out
odd words and reading them so that he can dock exactly
forty-five seconds. By the time you get to the mike you're
afraid to unbend or change a word lest the thing run over.
You know at twenty-nine minutes and thirty seconds
you're cut off the air no matter where you are in a sentence.
    I am always afraid that Atwell will say something that
will have us cut off the air. Last week on the second
broadcast for the Coast, he said, "I can lick my weight in

wild-pratts" and I thought that would be the end, but a few minutes later he came back with "I'll take off my goat and squirt," so it's no wonder that I am sagging at the temples and my step is halting, sir.

Atwell's slippery monologues, however, were straightforward compared to an ever-mounting torrent of treacle: the Linit commercials. The dowagerlike Margaret Santry, whose appearance in a commercial on December 11 rivaled the hauteur of the Marx Brothers' grande dame, Margaret Dumont, had an unforgettable microphone presence. "Women of all countries have their beauty characteristics," she commenced, "but American women lead the world in the highest development of charm, chic and beauty."

Miss Santry had as guests Mrs. Claiborne Pell and Countess Loranda Piccio, and jogged the memory of the radio audience about last season's interviews with the Princess Braganza, the Duchess of Oporto, and the Duchess de Villarosa. Countess Piccio, "married to the Commandant of the Italian Air Forces, an aide-de-camp to Mussolini, has entertained the great Mussolini many times in her villa in Rome." Whether Mussolini found Linit "the bathway to a safe, smooth skin" was not discussed, but the implication of Il Duce's approval hung in the ether. Mrs. Pell said that she had placed a box of Linit in every room of her Newport mansion and she urged friends to follow her example.

The ladies' high-toned chitchat was sandwiched between the halves of a sketch in which Allen once more portrayed a dauntless explorer lecturing upon his "marvelous death-defying film." (The desperation of his writing predicament is reflected by his fallback to the Admiral Byrd routine of *Three's a Crowd*.) This time Captain Allen explored a Depression-stricken tropical isle. The commercial succeeded the following exchange.

NATIVE: The Canoe Factory has shut down. The King even had to lay off two hundred wives.

ALLEN: What's he kicking about? He got rid of two-hundred mothers-in-law.

When the commercial ended, Captain Allen and his party were beleaguered by the clichés of safari.

ALLEN: Curse those tom-toms . . . If they'd only beat one tom, there'd be just half as much noise.

Eventually, Captain Allen, kidnapped by a female gorilla, vanishes with her into jungle depths, and their idyll among the branches concludes only when they are discovered by her husband, a tree surgeon. Margaret Santry and her patrician guests presumably did not linger for the denouement.

Still writing the entire script himself, he wondered again early in December how long he could survive. "The radio program has become the bane of my daily existence," he informed Joe Kelly.

I work all week long, what with arguments, rehearsals, and listening to all the "yes" men [and] I get a lot of Birds-eye Compliments saying how well we are doing without outside help when Cantor and the others have inferior material in spite of the money spent for authors. I hope to last through the contract as there are only six more Sundays after today [the option for the second thirteen weeks was later renewed]. I haven't been to a show, had a drink, seen a picture or done much of anything but write and look for material since you were here last.

Around this time Allen heard of the comic talent of Harry Tugend, an aspiring reviewer for *The Motion Picture Herald* and sometime real estate broker in Greenwich Village. Tugend submitted samples and was engaged, and together he and Allen collaborated upon the radio shows during the ensuing four seasons. Theirs was a cordial partnership (a twig named Fred Allen Tugend would one day appear on Harry's family tree) and they also supplied a barnyard sketch to the *Ziegfeld Follies* in 1934.

The problem of recruiting a dependable collaborator was solved, but Allen brooded over the inequities of their craft: he and Tugend were discovering the shape of a medium along with other writers, often established revue and vaudeville contributors, who had every competitive advantage. To Merrill Clark, he complained:

I hear most of the other programs and, like you, wonder what thoughts are rampant in the minds of the morons who bark the same jokes over the networks week after week. The only way I can figure it out is that the listeners have the same amount of mentality and do not discriminate. Then again, I don't think that all families are rabid radio fans. Most people either like or loathe a program and will only tune in on certain features. You, being more interested in comedy, try to check on everything and naturally the duplication is annoying. . . . We have one of the cheapest hookups on the air and the only way I have been able to make it good is to forget the monetary part and the absence of a budget . . . and work all week myself in an attempt to make each broadcast as good as it is possible to make it.

Fred and Portland moved into a three-room apartment in the Windsor so that she would have more opportunity to practice her culinary talents. The apartment displayed the spartan appointments of the migratory performer. "One room is unfurnished except for my presence and a chair and a table," Allen noted. The burden of the weekly show grew no less oppressive. "There is no sane way of judging the value of a radio program," he wrote Arnold Rattray, publisher of Long Island's weekly *East Hampton Star* and a friend of Val Eichen. "The popularity of it, I mean. If the sales increase, the sponsor is satisfied and the type of product you are trying to sell should determine the class of audience to be attracted."

Merchandising standards defined a world to which Allen was unaccustomed, a maze of dead ends and blind passageways. The censorship of the scripts was not the outspoken gesture of an individual, like the theater manager in South Bend expressing his robust disapproval by hauling down the curtain; it was done by memoranda and committee, a bureaucratic decision, capricious, vapid, and elusive. "I cannot mention banks on the air, so the joke about giving all the banks to Ford is out — 'Ford could put the doors from his second-hand cars on the banks and no one would ever be able to close them again.' " Advertising agencies provoked one of his best-known definitions: "To me, an advertising agency is 85 per cent confusion and 15 per cent commission."

The deadline pressures endured.

It is too much for me, Val. I am all in. This is the nineteenth program, I think, and between routines for Portland and Atwell and the rehearsals and cutting and editing the material written by my co-author, it finally begins to tell. You want to know what became of Jolson and the others. At least they are well paid in defeat. I am lasting longer, but I'll never catch up to any of them from the money end. Still, it isn't bad. I have been living by my own wits for years, and most of the others have to rely on writers and they're at the mercy of whoever provides the material for their assorted ventures.

As the Linit revue neared its conclusion, Allen and Tugend could regard true accomplishment. They had examined a diversity of characters and situations, they were achieving radio pacing and rhythm, the production shone with a professional finish. Allen had written the "Guzzler's Gin" routine about a salesman over-fond of his own product, which Red Skelton came to use as a mainstay of his act. A new spot, "The Most Embarrassing Moment," introduced figures such as Ramrod O. Bumpkin.

"My most embarrassing moment? The night I saw the newsreel of President Roosevelt and his cabinet outside the White House. One of the cabinet members was missing. I called over the usher. 'Where is the Secretary of the Interior?' I asked, and was told, 'He's inside, where he belongs.' Later I realized that I had spoken to the usher without being introduced."

Among the highlights of the series had been Portland's little-girl character, the concoction of Boomtown, an archetypal small town soon to be named Bedlam, and the various community backgrounds, which allowed the writers to involve the cast with a thematic motif. There had been spoofs of Hollywood and *Lysistrata,* and a Sherlock Holmes takeoff featuring Allen as Sholmes, that much-parodied sleuth.

(*Knock on door*)
MAID: Good evening, gentlemen.

(*Shot and shriek*)

SHOLMES: Watson, you bad boy. Where are your manners? Shooting a lady with your hat on.

Their hostess, Lady Whiffletree, serves them tea while their baths are being prepared, and they discuss the Whiffletree Castle murders.

LADY: I've been poisoned!

SHOLMES: Gad, Watson. You've put Linit in the tea and the teaballs in the tub.

LADY: I'll have to drink the bath and you, Mr. Sholmes, will have to sponge off with the tea.

(*Shot and shriek*)

SHOLMES: What was that last shot, Watson?

WATSON: I shot a cat in the hall.

SHOLMES: Good heavens — nine more lives lost!

Ultimately, Watson is arrested for the murder of Geoffrey Smudge, but Sholmes is arrested for the murder of Gaffney Longbottom.

The popularity of Atwell, the "man with a mouthful of porcupines," was a strong factor in the program's success. As an indication of growing acceptance, the billing was changed to *Fred Allen's Bath Club Revue*. The ratings revealed the programs had attracted an audience, and sales of Linit increased; all the same, Allen felt a certain sense of reprieve when he finished the final broadcast and left for an early vacation at Old Orchard Beach. Before he and Portland boarded the Boston train, he had the satisfaction of opening a letter from one of his peers.

April 17, 1933

Dear Fred,

I've been listening to your programs every Sunday and they're swell. Were it not for you, it'd be a pretty dull day. I'm not accustomed to writing mash notes to actors, but I really am grateful to you for the many laughs you've given me.

Ardently yours,
Groucho

"I CAME UP HERE for a vacation," Allen wrote from Old Orchard to Arnold Rattray, "but up to now I have been on the run like a thread in a pair of ten-cent stockings. Have made trips to New York, Boston, and back here, always managing to miss the sun in transit. I would have had a better rest if I had continued working."

He did not abandon hope the Shuberts would produce a new revue, for he still thought of Portland and himself as stage performers. Nothing turned up, and when he prudently tried to arrange a radio show for the fall of 1933, he found no further leads. So, renting a cottage and shipping steamer trunks to Maine (holiday travel still retained vestiges of elaborate Victorian ritual), Allen looked forward to a tranquil summer. He invited Aunt Lizzie and Bob and diverse relatives to visit — and almost immediately was offered the job of replacing Will Rogers, who had decided to leave his program. Rogers was a national icon and the opportunity was tempting, but in the Allen household, domestic obligations took precedence over professional advancement. Fred felt "so involved with plans and invitations," he couldn't accept.

Hellmann's mayonnaise, however, sponsored a half-hour program called *The Musical Grocery Store* on NBC Friday nights at 9:00. The production unsuccessfully attempted to imitate the Linit format, and when the sponsor threatened cancellation, the advertising agency phoned Allen and asked him to take over the contract. In contrast with the Will Rogers show, which had only five weeks to run, the mayonnaise program held out the promise of employment through the end of the year. Mayonnaise was a seasonal item, and *The Best Foods Salad Bowl Revue,* as the show would be titled (Hellmann's was owned by the Best Foods Company), would ordinarily span only the summer months; Allen was informed that if he received the same public reaction he received on the Linit revue, the contract might be extended. Besides, he could put up Lizzie and Bob.

"I have started to negotiate with my actors, but they all want more money," he informed Val Eichen. Atwell alone demanded five hundred a week — half the total budget of the *Linit Bath Club*. Allen liked and respected Atwell, whose occasional toping roused executive hackles, yet the salary seemed excessive. Fortunately, the budget had increased fourfold. "I don't know how my first couple of radio shows will be. The agent is trying to hire people, my fellow writer is working for Bert Lahr, and I imagine that Grofé's orchestra will play variations of the Peer Gynt suite between the comedy lapses, but the way I feel about it, I might as well be in there trying to make the grade."

On August 2 the Allens were in New York in the midst of the worst heat wave the city had endured since 1919. "Roosevelt is certainly getting us back to normal," he wrote Joe Kelly. "We never saw this sort of humidity under the Hoover Banner. I wouldn't say that the program will set new radio standards, but this particular firm has had so much trouble with its shows that the staff is greatly relieved to be able to pass the worry onto someone else."

The *Salad Bowl Revue* with Fred Allen ("Sent to you by the Best Foods Company in the interests of the 446,000 retail grocers throughout the United States and Canada") went on the air August 4 and continued until December 1. Atwell and Portland were back, along with such reliables as dialectician Minerva Pious and dexterous Jack Smart. A vocal group called the Songsmiths appeared with Ferde Grofé's orchestra (Grofé, the former arranger for the Paul Whiteman band, had attracted widespread attention for his setting of Gershwin's *Rhapsody in Blue* and his own *Grand Canyon Suite*), and the announcer was Edmund "Tiny" Ruffner, who, as his nickname ironically suggested, belonged to the fleshly school of radio announcers.

Once again much of the humor was self-reflexive, often joshing the sponsor's product good-naturedly. The first program had a Century-of-Progress theme, with Allen discoursing on the Chicago World's Fair from the deck of a sightseeing bus — a successful device in the Linit series — and an exchange with Portland doing her little-girl character.

"How do you like the Fair?" Allen wanted to know.

"I half like it and I half don't like it," Portland replied. "But I guess I half like it the most."

In the next week's half-hour, the good ship *Bedlam* rescues a man adrift on a raft and clutching a combination salad. "Saved!

Saved! Saved!" he croaks. Why didn't he eat the salad? Because, he responds, "it wouldn't taste right without Best Foods Mayonnaise."

Allen and Tugend introduced a new continuing feature toward the close of the program, "The Etiquette Box." A parody of Emily Post and other arbiters of the social graces, the Box opened with a standardized variation cued like Portland's weekly introduction — "Our Etiquette Department is going at the speed of a turtle's spirit rising on Judgment Day" — and then Allen stated the problem, often as an in-joke for the benefit of associates whose names appeared as contributors. One of them was his friend from Boston vaudeville days Jack Haley (future Tin Man in the MGM *Wizard of Oz*), whom Fred called Jake.

> Mr. Jacob Haley from Hollywood, California. Mr. Haley says, quote, "I have a difficult time eating asparagus. The ends always bend over before I can get them into my mouth and generally the butter sauce misses my napkin and lands in my lap. What should I do?" unquote.
>
> If Mr. Haley will put a teaspoonful of starch in his butter sauce the asparagus will stiffen to the point where the ends can be raised at attention to the mouth. If you too are baffled by a similar problem in etiquette, or table manners, ladies and gentlemen, send me your dilemma and I shall be happy to help you as I have helped Mr. Haley. And don't forget — the best-dressed salad is wearing Best Foods Mayonnaise.

Another satisfied petitioner was "Mr. Harry Emerson from Somerville, Massachusetts."

> Mr. Emerson says, quote, "Every time I serve a salad with Hellmann's Mayonnaise on it, the guests lick off the mayonnaise and leave the rest. What can I do to have them eat all of the salad?" unquote.
>
> This is a common complaint, Mr. Emerson. Hellmann's is so tasty that many hosts open the jars in the privacy of a closet, thus avoiding fatal injuries at the hands of impatient guests who cannot wait until the mayonnaise is placed on the salad. Many a banquet has been ruined

through guests overpowering the chef and eating the mayonnaise out of the jars with their lorgnettes and fingertips. To avoid mayonnaise stampedes and to force your guests to eat all of their salads, simply serve the salads with the mayonnaise underneath and the guests will gladly scamper through the fresh greens to reach this delicious dressing. Some chefs prefer to conceal a Mexican jumping bean in the lettuce. This causes the salad to hop around nimbly, but if the guests are mounted on pogo sticks the salad can be eaten in perfect rhythm.

Should fastidious guests use ten finger-bowls, one for each finger? Every Etiquette Box item was more preposterous than the last, perhaps culminating in the problem confronted by Albert Melnick of Taft, California: "Whenever I eat corn on the cob my derby works down over my eyes and I can't see what I'm doing. I have bitten one thumb off and I'll have to either give up the corn or both of my thumbs." He was cautioned, "A derby is never worn at the dinner table during the summer, Mr. Melnick. The well-dressed man wears a straw hat or beret in the dining room."

On the program of September 1, Allen and Tugend brought forth their first "News Reel," a format that, in the program's next incarnation, would allow them to comment directly on the current events and oddities of the passing scene. During the *Salad Bowl Revue,* this was tied in to a series of sketches in which Allen was a movie mogul in his screening room.

[ANNOUNCER]: TITANIC PICTURES PRESENTS . . . ALL THE NEWS THAT'S FIT TO SEE! Forest Hills, New York — AMERICAN NATIONAL MEN'S CHAMPIONSHIP WON BY FREDERICK J. PERRY OF ENGLAND.

PERRY: I say! It was a hard-fought match, ladies and gentlemen. And I am happy to be able to bring the tennis crown back to London.

(*Cheers*)

ALLEN: Mr. Duncan MacDuncan, the Scotch champion, who did not play at the tournament, gives his reasons.

McD: I'm sorry, folks, I couldn't play here this year. I lost my ball at Wimbledon.

The *Salad Bowl Revue* also occasioned a weekly column that Allen sent to radio editors around the country. "We have kept it going in some twelve key-city papers for the past two months," he wrote on Thanksgiving to Arnold Rattray.

Am enclosing clipping from the Chicago Tribune which has been using it for several weeks. The program finishes December first, but I have auditioned for the Sal Hepatica firm which expects to start a radio campaign after the first of the year. If the deal goes through, I am going to continue to send out the weekly blurb during the time I am not on the air, and then, when I come back I hope to keep it going weekly for as long as I last on radio. I don't know how my fans will stand it, should I start the Sal Hepatica series. If they have been loyal they spent last winter in the bathtub using Linit. Then in August they were called upon to drench their salads with Hellmann's Mayonnaise, and now, if I start for Sal Hepatica they will start off the new year reacting to a laxative. The life of the radio fan is not a bed of fuzz plucked from the pussy willow. . . .

The Country is certainly witnessing strange days what with a Governor condoning lynching [Governor James Rolph, Jr., of California, after an atrocity in San Jose] and Father Coughlin making a ventriloquist of Christ in an effort to strut his frocked exhibitionism.

The duration of a radio performer's career was brief, but Allen also felt partly demoralized by a savage authoritarian strain fomented by the nation's economic adversity. Generally apolitical, he was not a reformer, although his playful wit reminded many a listener of standards of reason half-smothered by political and social events. In the fall of 1933, however, a black rage swept over him reminiscent of Twain's baffled outrage at turn-of-the-century American imperialism. Their careers as platform humorists had in certain respects run parallel. While Allen was not a literary lion, he like Twain had a mass public that confined him — within the limits of the jester's li-

cense — to say only what it allowed him to say. He was now
a celebrity and becoming more so. A celebrity, he would de-
clare, "is a person who works hard all his life to become well
known, then wears dark glasses to avoid being recognized."

"To be a success you have to first get your heart removed,"
he wrote Joe Kelly.

> Then you can ignore the troubles of others and acquire a
> bankroll. If you are inclined to be soft, you are sunk. The
> minute you start to make dough you will find a crowd
> around . . . not your friends as a rule . . . but a fresh set
> of people who feel that because you have worked for years
> to get someplace you owe them something for staying in
> the back rooms of saloons so that they wouldn't be in
> your way while you were trying to get ahead. During the
> past twenty years I have had the misfortune to loan thou-
> sands of dollars and when I blew all of my money in the
> Market not one debtor even offered to return what was
> owed, let alone ask me if I needed anything.

Redirecting his pessimism into personal grievance helped him
to endure it. Nightmare too was intelligible only in terms of
individual experience, one of the countless narratives woven
into the world's warp and weft; but as a devout Catholic he
also felt moral outrage at the obscenity of the lynch mob and
the intolerance of his co-religionist, Father Coughlin — issues
a comedian must eschew. The San Jose horror weighed on
Allen's conscience. Governor Rolph had promised pardons to
everyone implicated. The California lynchings exalted chaos
and darkness in the mass audience he addressed, and the country seemed increasingly hostile to the humane ideals he recalled from his childhood. That same Thanksgiving, he wrote
Val Eichen: "the noose hangs high."

On the other hand, since giving up alcohol earlier that year,
he felt better physically, and expressed a scintilla of the zeal of
a convert to sobriety.

> When we read of Mr. Lee Tracy's recent exhibition in
> Mexico [the actor had been arrested after a drinking bout]
> I think we can overlook my innocent "tequila" moments

there some years ago. Always a pioneer, possibly I am responsible, in a small way, for the rise in popularity of the Mexican liquor composed, as I remember, of two parts of urine taken from a professional glass-eater and one-fourth cactus thorns ground to a fine point, and one-fourth al-cohol taken from a jar in which an appendix has stood for thirty days. My drinking days are over and it is a pleasure to note that my stomach has no memory and is content to slink back to normal and make way for the pleats in my English trousers.

And there were other consolations. No matter what tran-spired in the lunacy of times skewed beyond recognition, Old Orchard Beach remained: a sanctuary where the America of his receding boyhood still lingered, and trolley cars clanged in the mist beside the sea.

12 | Old Orchard

"I shall always remember Old Orchard as a place of magic," Rose Fitzgerald Kennedy said on the threshold of her tenth decade. Turn-of-the-century Boston Irish-Catholic families flocked northward, lured by the same Down East spell. The resort reconciled patrician dignity and shirt-sleeve verve. Bright umbrellas spattered the hard, white sand, and beneath a sky indifferent to the taffy-apple concessionaires and calliopes of a pierhead amusement arcade, hotels and cottages bordered the winking blue agate of the sea. A salesman could cover the entire Maine territory and much of New England by rail, so trains and streetcars put Old Orchard's seven-mile beach within reach of frugal vacationers. (An hour-long ride on the fourteen-mile Portland–Old Orchard electric railway, for example, cost twenty cents.) Fred Allen first visited as a small boy when Aunt Lizzie had her choice of seven or eight day-trips from Boston.

Boston mayor Honey Fitz, his daughter Rose, and their entourage settled in, joining other families of substance, for the summer. Old Orchard in those days retained its nineteenth-century ambience: lawn tennis, kerosene lamps, roller-skating rinks, shooting galleries, bazaars, "flying horses," extravagant health claims for ozone-saturated breezes, decorous flirtations on the piazzas of behemoth Victorian hotels. Each morning the main roads were sprayed to damp the dust, and a town statute prohibited pedestrians dressed in bathing suits on the

central promenade, tree-shaded Old Orchard Street, which
sloped downhill toward the seventeen-hundred-foot Ocean Pier.
By the early thirties, Old Orchard — "The First Beach in the
World" — had acquired a pronounced French-Canadian accent. (The Grand Trunk Railroad provided direct service to
Montreal, and though the Grand Trunk has long since vanished, Old Orchard still boasts the only bilingual exit signs on
the Maine Turnpike.) The amusement district was mushroom-
ing, and in the Pier Casino, where the imbricate rhinestones
of a revolving overhead globe flared and caught fox-trotting
couples in whirling meshes of light and shadow, the saxophones of Guy Lombardo, Duke Ellington, and Tommy Dor-
sey sounded above the wash of the surf. Inspired by Lindbergh, daredevil pilots took off from the beach on abortive
transatlantic flights. In residential Ocean Park, a few miles from
the shrieking roller-coasters and steam calliopes and assorted
clamor of the pier, the Free Will Baptists held Chautauqua-
type lectures and concerts as well as religious services, but most
of the cottages near the Ocean Park border, where the Allens
usually rented, drowsed in the sun. "The seasons opens officially when the first frankfurt has seen its shadow," Allen declared. "There are so many Canadians here, they're putting a
British lion on the merry-go-round and laying off a hyena."

Of the various locales where Fred and Portland summered,
Old Orchard most completely incorporated the comedian's
world view. During the thirties their off-season was, on occasion, curtailed by Fred's Hollywood commitments; in 1937,
because they didn't have time to rent a cottage, they tried a
staid inn at Bay View, Maine. The ceremonials of the expensive resort did not compensate for the loss of Old Orchard's
casual evenings. Of the Bay View House, Fred remarked:

> These places are okay if you have two pairs of pants and
> want to show off your sartorial equipment at mealtime.
> The guests all seem to be trying to outdo each other
> flaunting their finery at the table, and one old tart here —
> I have been checking for 24 meals — has yet to wear the
> same dress twice. I don't know whether she is sleeping

with a tailor in her room or whether she's sticking her finger down the mouths of various moths she runs across and making them cough up garments they have masticated in months gone by.

The summer of 1942, the Allens took a cottage on New York's Fire Island, but Portland found the swimming treacherous. In the immediate postwar years they favored resort hotels like Gurney's at Montauk, and during the late forties and early fifties, when Fred's health was precarious, the Belmont in Harwich on Cape Cod. None became so firmly associated with Allen's personality as Old Orchard Beach, which the couple visited intermittently for nearly two decades. Had not a babble of tourists descended upon him, demanding autographs and otherwise disturbing his peace of mind, he would no doubt have estivated in Maine every year.

Today it may seem odd that one of the most prominent entertainers in America should prefer to summer in a rented beaverboard cottage in "a Maine town so dull the tide went out and never came back." Allen considered this a refreshing prospect. He had no yearning for acclaim. Other celebrities might frolic at a glamorous remove from their public, but the Allen persona was indistinguishable from himself: he was always Fred Allen from Grafton Street in Saint Margaret's parish. Only a scattering of performers joined him in his preference, notably Carmela Ponselle and her sister, the soprano Rosa, who vacationed in the district called Fern Park. Still, Old Orchard, plebeian and vital, recalled the vaudevillians' colonies at Onset and Long Island. Uncle Jim Harkins in the early thirties supervised dance marathons outside the city of Portland; Doc Rockwell's Slipshod Manor was a few hours away in Southport; and the Coney Island attractions around the Pier, however garish, were a rudimentary form of show business not remote from vaudeville's energetic folk art and the fun of amateur nights.

"Let me know how the humor is running back there, Pearson," Fred wrote Red Pearson in June 1933, "as I may be in a position to get you the Whiz Bang rights for the State of Maine if you play your cards. I met Joe Taylor here yesterday. Just as he had a new Dutch act ready, Hitler had to step out and make trouble and Joe is laying off until Hitler blows over."

The clog-dance performers of vaudeville again took a curtain call. "The actors who have worked here for years have played to empty seats so much that they take bows going by a chair factory," wrote Allen. Even today, a commercialized, synthetic Old Orchard Beach enjoys the homespun activities spread before Portland and Fred in 1933. Not long ago, the Chamber of Commerce offered a traditional summer's program:

> *June 19–21:* Escape artist Mario Manzini will wriggle out of a straitjacket while suspended over the square on a flaming rope. *July 4:* Giant fireworks display. *July 6–11:* Ocean Park celebration. *July 25:* Maine State tug-o-war championships. *Aug. 4–6:* Theater festival and Canadian folk music concert. *Aug. 9:* A physique contest for men and women. *Aug. 16:* The state arm-wrestling championship. *Aug. 22:* Major fireworks display.

"There is a jazz band playing at the local drug store," Fred informed Mark Leddy,

> and they rehearse a few cottages from where we live. Right now they are working out a medley containing such numbers as "Put On Your Old Gray Bonnet" and "When we are M A double R I E D" etc. You would enjoy walking into the drug store at night. Just as you get seated to enjoy a soda, these six birds let out a blast from the saxophone section that will curdle the milk in your milkshake.
>
> They are versatile and consistent. Versatile in that they all sing and croon through megaphones that look as though they are cardboard containers that have been varnished. Consistent, since everything they attempt is lousy. The band is called Ralph Armstrong and His Arcadians. The dictionary defines an arcade as "a vaulted passageway or street." If there was really anything in a name then these fellows would certainly be playing in a vaulted passageway or in the street.

Bill Mullen, a young man selling hot dogs on the pier, met Fred and Portland around 1932. As Mullen recalls, publicist Bill McKenney, a friend from boyhood, had rekindled Fred's memories and persuaded him to revisit Old Orchard. Prohibition days, Fred's annual arrival meant that Mullen would meet him in his Model-A Ford and they would proceed to stock up on spirits; but after the spring of 1933, when Allen swore off alcohol, their merriment became more sedate.

"We attended town meetings together," Mullen says, "and Fred took notes with a stubby pencil. He also liked to walk to the Salvation Army meetings — they had cottage camp revivals — and see what was going on. And, of course, he was extremely generous to Saint Margaret's." (The Old Orchard parish bore the same designation as Fred's Dorchester fold.) Mullen, who ushered on Sundays, was in a position to note Allen's liberal benefactions to the church, which in 1933 was undergoing renovations.

The tempo of life flowed in leisurely late-nineteenth-century rhythms: Fred and Bill went to the Portland Exhibition Building to catch a middleweight named Coley Welch, whom Fred held in high regard; there were Sunday dinners between the Mullen and Allen cottages; Aunt Lizzie, Bob and his family, and Portland's sisters came to visit. Mostly, however, eventless days gave Allen an opportunity to read and write and ponder lines for the program: "He's all sail and no anchor." "His hat was so tight he had to butter his ears to put it on." "Quicksand in hourglass — Daylight Savings Time."

Puffing at Webster's Fancy Tails, his cigars of choice, he sat in the shade of a beach umbrella and conducted a multifarious correspondence. Every recipient of an Allen letter followed a different set of epistolary leitmotifs; for Joe Kelly, who also knew Old Orchard, it was the mythology of the inhabitants, the Duffys who owned the pier, the Allen manor "Gulls' Privy," the ins and outs of the Zachow family, the doings of the Pine Point hermit. For Red Pearson it was the Chief (Ed Wynn), the Baron (Jack Pearl), and Lahr (Bert Lahr). The summer of 1938, Fred arrived with a trunkful of detective novels eventually transformed into vociferous radio sketches starring One Long Pan, his parodic version of Earl Derr Biggers's Chinese detective Charlie Chan. That summer, too, he tinkered with other titles for mystery sketches — "The Singing Bone," "The Talking Doorknob," "Her Grace at Bay," "Death Wore a Yellow Girdle."

Old Orchard was close enough to Boston so that Allen could tend to domestic problems such as Aunt Lizzie's operation for cataracts. In the Savin Hill and Grafton Street neighborhoods, he invariably looked up old pals, and imagined the destiny that might have been his without his aunt, the library, and Mark Leddy. To Joe Kelly he wrote:

> Inky Sheehan informs that the Fire Department is the life. "What the hell, I'm all set. Nothing to do but play cards and then I'll get the pension. I got nothing to worry about now." He advised me that Will McDonough has taken Civil Service examinations for the Police Department, Fire Department and the Post Office Department. I don't see how he can hold all of those jobs at one and the same time. If he cannot decide which position appeals to his better self I suggest this means of assistance: Let him imagine that he is a postman delivering a special delivery letter. As he walks down the street he sees a pyromaniac running away from a burning orphanage.
>
> Let his first impulse decide his career.
>
> If he ignores the fleeing author of arson and continues to the house where he delivers the special delivery letter, let him concentrate on the postal job.
>
> If he pursues the incendiary with intent to arrest him, let him look to the Police Department for his future.
>
> If he rushes into the flaming building and attempts to quench the flames, let him take up smoke-eating seriously.
>
> Of course if he forgets to deliver the letter and ignores the whole thing and goes home to futz around his Chevrolet, that will be Will all over.

A counterweight to Hollywood, Old Orchard assumed for Fred a symbolic significance. "Each week I get a show out some way and count one Wednesday off on the way to Old

Orchard." For all its tackiness, the Maine resort preserved an authenticity the film capital lacked. To Allen this was especially evident during those summers he spent on either coast. Hollywood was pretense and ignorance and depersonalization; Old Orchard (whenever tourists granted him privacy), an eden that allowed you to be yourself. Performers in Hollywood "seem to live in a little world that shuts off the rest of the universe and everyone appears to be faking life. The actors and writers live in fear, and nothing, including the houses, seems permanent." On the other hand, Old Orchard, with its tawdry midway, its frequent fireworks diplays, and Chautauqua entertainments, constituted an America he cherished. It spawned eccentricity. The *Old Orchard News,* a broadsheet devoted to the comings and goings of summer residents, displayed unabashed peculiarities like the Pine Point hermit. The newspaper flew the National Recovery Administration eagle over its masthead proclamation, "The Foe of All That Is Evil," and was nominally Democrat, but the columns paid vacillating attention to world and national affairs, and were packed with local curiosities. No province of knowledge was too remote for a headline acknowledgment: "Word 'Spider' May Be a Corruption of 'Spinther' "; "Odd Railroad Expressions"; "Swallows Quicker Than Pigeons to Find Homes." What was *Hollywood Reporter* sizzle beside these Fourth-of-July rockets?

I had been wondering where to place my order for this summer's supply of pinwheels [Joe Kelly had enclosed an ad for a fireworks retailer on the pier]. I generally buy all of the fireworks merely for safety's sake, since one summer Portland went window-shopping with a blowtorch and most of the pyrotechnic dealers resented her curiosity let alone the torch.

I may not take the dip sticks this year, for the grass hoppers were so effective in our window-boxes last July 4th that we feel we should use nothing but the hoppers and perhaps a copious supply of fiery darts. I am also getting a few Roman candles to go with Cardinal O'Connell's new book. All devout Catholics are reading the book by the light of Roman candles so you can see that there

will be plenty of work for all the Catholic ophthalmolo-
gists and perhaps an alarm or two for the fire department.

For Fred and Portland, too, Old Orchard was a place of
magic and some of their happiest moments took place there,
but year by year trouble in paradise mounted. It became increasingly impossible to endure the gawking crowds. Out-of-
work vaudevillians often looked Fred up, as he related in a
letter to Red Pearson.

> Yesterday I was sitting on the veranda when a car drove
> up. I use the word "car" loosely, Mr. Pearson. It was a
> cross between The Iron Horse — you may have seen it in
> an early Fox picture — and a hearse with an outboard
> motor on it. I was just about to tell the driver of this
> phantom vehicle that I didn't sell spare parts when a guy
> looked out and said that he had played on the bill with
> me at South Bend 15 years ago. Charlie [Lane] had given
> him my address, and told this fellow, Charlie Wilson, to
> stop in and see me. Well sir, before he got through telling
> me what pals we were those three days, he had remained
> for dinner, smoked a cigar I was saving, turned on the
> radio to catch 'Amos 'n' Andy' and left some ashes on the
> front steps which I have to sweep.

By 1938 Allen had taken to displaying a "Beware of the
Dog" sign on his Reggio Avenue porch, occasionally hiding
out until intruders left: "This morning an old fart showed up
here with a trained duck for me to see. I was in the men's
lounge and heard Portland say I was out. I had to stay in the
hopper sundry minutes until the duck trainer departed."
The "Beware of the Dog" sign was no deterrent, although
it raised Allen's hopes.

> It is working, I would say, about fifty-fifty. Yesterday a
> small party from Ocean Park foraging for autographs ob-
> served the warning and inquired from across the street as
> to my whereabouts and as to my willingness to part with
> autographs. On this occasion the sign worked. Later in
> the morning a stuttering lad arrived. He ignored the Old
> English proclamation and pattered up the steps to ask about

the collective healths of Harry Von Zell and Peter Van Steeden [the announcer and the orchestra leader, respectively, on *Town Hall Tonight*]. I asked him if he had seen the dog sign and he said that he had, but that since he couldn't read, what he didn't know couldn't very well hurt him.

It appears the dog notice will tend to keep the literate pest at a safe distance, but if we are to forestall the moron and illiterate caller, I am afraid we shall have to install a dog.

The Allens didn't buy a dog — Fred was content to keep the canine realm at bay — but the municipality appointed him an honorary police officer, "in a position to close Beano games, give out parking tickets and arrest people who come to our front portal seeking conversation and autographs." Public relations proved as futile against the onslaught as the dog notice.

Bill Mullen, still a resident of Old Orchard, recalls Fred jogging along the beach in the forties. He was one of the first daily joggers Mullen had ever seen, and probably under doctor's orders. About that time too, Fred appeared on the country club golf course — as a caddy. "He never did anything he couldn't do well," says Mullen, "and since he lacked time for golf, he didn't want to play a duffer's game. Those were the days before electric golf carts. Fred's nephew played in a foursome with Father Bob White from Saint Margaret's, so Fred went along and caddied for them."

The media star turned caddy at the height of his fame is as revealing a recollection as Shirley Jellerson's. She worked in Emmons's Drug Store. Fred and Portland came there almost every night.

It was an old-fashioned drugstore with a soda fountain. Fred and Portland sat at a marble-topped table and ordered a banana split and sometimes he'd start reminiscing about his days in vaudeville. When he got going he'd take the cigar boxes from the counter and demonstrate his juggling routine. It didn't matter who was there; sometimes the store was almost empty, but he didn't need a lot of folks around. Fred just liked to come to Emmons's with Portland and sit around and talk.

The Old Orchard Beach of Fred and Portland Allen has receded in time, distant as Rose Kennedy's porch-rocker colony of grand hotels. A barricade of condominiums now bristles above the Atlantic. The pace of progress at Old Orchard is typified by the Pine Point hermit of yore, a squatter in a tar-paper shack in the swamp behind Seavey's Landing. Fascinated by the hermit's hirsute life-style, Allen visited him in his den: "At high tide, I believe, you can find him twenty feet nearer the road." As a sequel to this visit, the superstar invited him to appear on the program and paid the hermit's fare to New York. But when the man turned up at the studio, the sponsor made an appalling discovery. Delighted by his opportunity to go on the radio, the hermit had gotten himself a haircut and shaved his beard.

13 | Smile, Darn Yer, Smile

During the summer of 1934, Allen began typing correspondence in lower case. Theories for this move range from necessity (he dropped his Corona in a hotel lobby, damaged the shift bar, and never bothered to repair it), to conservation of energy (he wanted to save time), to the fanciful (he had a lurking affection for the poems of e. e. cummings). His radio fan mail was swelling beyond six thousand letters a week and no individual could keep up, but Allen, a two-finger typist under pressure, did his best and dropped the ballast of capitals.

"Doesn't the shift key on your typewriter work?" asked Goodman Ace.

"Yes," Fred replied, "but I've never been able to shift for myself."

To Groucho, he wrote: "This is the new comedy typewriter. You don't have to think. You keep on typing along and the typewriter makes up puns and gags by itself." Oddly enough, Allen typed in lower case, but his handwriting consisted of capital letters, spiky, almost illegible. The visual levity of typographical quips amused him, and on occasions when he did employ lower-case self-consciously, he sounded like cummings's playful distant cousin. Just before a 1939 trip to Boston, for example, he wrote Joe Kelly:

> dear ornithologist . . .
> madam

and
i
are meeting mr. and mrs. sullivan at
the ritz hotel on thursday around six
p.m.
if
you
would
care to join us provender will be supplied
and smalltalk indulged in until such time
as
we have to leave to visit my aunt who basks in
what passes for irish affluence on grafton
street in your locale.
if
you
cannot make it i shall call you at home later
i
close with the familiar canary island salutation,
or rather, the canary island parting cry
"peep-peep."
mr. a.

The epistolary alterations suggest the changes overtaking Allen's life. Mass communication made him willy-nilly a superstar. Now he walked home after a broadcast, headed for his bedroom, stuffed the telephone bells with paper, and slammed the phone into the bureau drawer. Loyal to the barber he had patronized as Freddy James, he found the barber's politics vexatious: "Some Communist wrote a letter to *The Daily Worker* saying that I was the tool of the capitalistic forces since I had lampooned the Party on one of my programs. *The Daily Worker* printed the letter and upset my barber and he gave me a lousy haircut, so you can see these are trying days for radio favorites." Listeners began naming offspring for Fred. "At this writing there are six babies around the country bearing the name of Allen in my honor, and it is going to be hell when I retire from public life and change my name back to Sullivan, explaining to my many prodigies that their cognomens were hitched not to a star but to a wagon, the wheels of which finally fell off."

After Thanksgiving the *Salad Bowl Revue* ceased as scheduled. *Fred Allen's Sal Hepatica Revue,* Wednesday nights from 9:30 to 10:00 P.M., went on the air January 3, 1934, via WEAF of the National Broadcasting Company. The program originated in the spacious art-deco surroundings of Radio City's Studio 8-H, the site of the Toscanini NBC symphony concerts, a setting widely considered the ultimate word in crystalline sound. (Though streamlined, the studio actually had slipshod acoustics.) Allen could not bring over Roy Atwell as a regular performer lest he give listeners the impression the show wasn't fresh. (Then too, Sal Hepatica, a mineral-salt laxative, may have been apprehensive about Atwell's arias to their product.) But other standbys were back: Jack Smart, Eileen Douglas, Minerva Pious, ratchet-voiced Lionel Stander.

Notwithstanding Atwell's departure, the show retained much of its previous flavor during the next three months: "Well sir, as I live and try to keep my raccoon coat from running up the steps when I pass the Yale Club, if it isn't Portland." The second program revived the ever-dependable Captain Allen, this time leaving for the East Pole and slinging gruff nautical commands at his crew. "Man your larynx, sailor! Scrub the fo'c'sle! Clear the decks! Save the tinsel!" The Etiquette Box gave way to "The Question Box" in order to provide latitude for comic comment.

Here's a letter from Thomas Farmer of Los Angeles. "I'm the best-dressed man in Los Angeles and the first man in California to wear a flower to bed in the lapel of my pajama coat. How can I keep my spats clean? Every time I get home after chasing a fire engine, my spats are always covered by mud. Yours for spotless spats."

Spat is a nasty word, Mr. Farmer. It doesn't look well on the end of your leg. However . . . I am inventing a cellophane spat-fender which hangs down the front of the trouser cuff and prevents spattering. But until my spat-fender is on the market you might try wearing your spats under your stockings. This will keep them clean and you can fool your chiropodist. Watch his face when he removes your dinner-door spats.

On March 21, 1934, the troupe broadcast the first hour-length program, sponsored by Ipana toothpaste and Sal Hepatica. The format, at first known as *The Hour of Smiles* but retitled *Town Hall Tonight* by July 11, profoundly influenced the shape and movement of the show. Ad agency intrigue frothed offstage. The Bristol-Myers Company, sponsor of the *Sal Hepatica Revue,* also sponsored a preceding musical half-hour on behalf of Ipana. The program was not prospering. An interoffice memo proposed that Allen's agency grab the previous half-hour from a competing firm and consolidate an hour of entertainment. Could they sell two products on the same show? Was brand identification possible? The fell deed was done in short order, a catchphrase concocted: "Ipana for the smile of beauty — Sal Hepatica for the smile of health."

The show's approach, aimed at a mythic small-town America, opened with the musical theme "Smile, Darn Yer, Smile," performed at first by Lennie Hayton's and later by Peter Van Steeden's Ipana Troubadours, fading after sixteen bars for announcer Tiny Ruffner's circus-barker introduction. Through the fabric of a marching band filtered crowd cheers.

> TINY: Up the street to the Town Hall goes Fred Allen and his weekly parade . . . Lennie Hayton and His Ipana Troubadours play a sparkling tune . . . Fred is up there ahead, waving and beckoning to us. Let's join him! There's excitement in the air and the whole town's going!
> (*Music up and fades for*)
> TINY: MOVIE STARS!
> MAN: The censors are here to see you, Miss East.
> GIRL: I can't cut nothin' out now, Joe. It's Town Hall Tonight!
> TINY: PUBLIC OFFICIALS!
> MAN: You'd better get back to the jail, warden. Two-Gun Feinberg is loose.
> WARDEN: I can't tie him up, son. It's Town Hall Tonight!
> TINY: JUDGES!
> MAN: I ain't guilty, judgey. I was doin' about ten miles an hour.

JUDGE: Case dismissed! Say, I'm going to do 50 right now.
   It's Town Hall Tonight!
(*Music up to finish*)

Allen's workload had doubled in three months. Writing an hour-long show with Harry Tugend and performing in it week after week presented a daunting responsibility. Yet the hour-long format survived until June 28, 1942: eight years of seven-day weeks, thirty-nine weeks a year. No other comedy program of the period met these demands; even Jack Benny basked in comparative repose in the medium's prime spot, the Sunday-at-seven half-hour, and if inspiration flagged, he could always assume the comic persona he had invented for himself and his team of writers. Allen began each week afresh. The schedule was onerous, yet severe as it was, it also filled a fundamental need in him for structure, order, and precision.

"He works harder than a ditch-digger because he can't find a shovel to lean his mind on," an awed interviewer commented. Allen's second broadcast finished at 1:00 A.M., and after mingling among his fans, he left the studio with Harry Tugend and (later in the decade) "the boys," Arnold Auerbach and Herman Wouk. They retreated to an all-night delicatessen on Sixth Avenue, ordered food — the aroma of dill pickles and hot coffee wreathed the jokes — and discussed the components of the next week's program. Usually Allen reached bed around four in the morning.

Thursday, he rose at 11:00 and, bypassing the expensive health club across the street, went to a neighborhood YMCA and boxed three rounds with Joey LaGrey, the armory champion of New York. Alternatively, Fred played two games of handball doubles, jogged on the indoor track, or tossed the medicine ball exactly 100 times; his set at the Y consisted of cops and post-office workers and cabbies. Thursday afternoon, he consulted the guest star for the coming week, and they went over their notes. Sometimes a special promotion took place: recording, for example, the "voice" of the papier-mâché Fred Allen that stood outside the Bristol-Myers exhibit at the Chicago World's Fair, to Allen's shame, bellowing jokes. ("My likeness can be heard a mile away," he lamented.) Thursday night, no matter how advanced the hour or lengthy the work, he completed the first draft of the guest spot. Strolling on the East Side with his friend and producer Arnold Peyser in later years, they fell into a conversation about those first drafts and writing. "You have to do it every day," Fred observed. "I have a theory there's a subtle rhythm between the hand and the mind, and when you interrupt that rhythm it becomes increasingly difficult to get started again. When that happens I write letters, or anything at all."

Friday, he responded to fan mail. Uncle Jim Harkins took care of the routine letters, but Allen always found himself with more priority requests than he could handle. He felt ambivalent about the audience to which he owed his success, and which at the same time exerted a tyrannical sway over its favorites. The letterhead designed for him by Al Hirschfeld showed a frock-coated Fred Allen trapped between the pages of *Joe Miller's Jokebook,* shouting "Help! Lemme Out!" The letterhead summed up radio stardom.

At the moment I am writing a Mrs. Hannington of Brookline to permit her daughter to stay here and pursue her career in radio. I am making arrangements with a hospital to continue narcotics treatments for a gentleman from Boston. I just paid for six weeks of treatments and the fellow has been out one week and feels "very nervous." He thinks two more weeks will straighten him out. Last night a friend of mine came to the broadcast after he had eaten some seafood or someone had given him a Mickey. He was deathly sick and at 11:55 P.M. I left him on a toilet seat while I rushed upstairs to regale California with my labored wit. All through the hour, bulletins came from the first-aid quarters as to my friend's condition, and at 1 A.M. when I finished he was so weak I had to ask Uncle Jim to accompany him to a distant point in Jersey in a cab. Mr. John O. Hewitt, who hasn't had his rent since 1935, is after me again, and Mr. Fred Lareine, a gentleman with no legs, came in his wheelchair last night to advise me that the Veterans of Foreign Wars are holding up his pension money and his landlord is holding up a final notice.

Arnold Auerbach remarked with surprise that Allen, who so obviously relished the company of plain people, was also subject to flashes of misanthropy. Passing Radio City Music Hall one day, and a huge lobby photograph of Charles Laughton as the Hunchback of Notre Dame, Allen said, "Doesn't scare me, I see hundreds of 'em in the studio audience every week." Individuals were one thing, crowds another; he would go to extraordinary lengths to aid a panhandler down on his luck, but he despised the mindless arrogance of audiences. When Joe Louis, the heavyweight boxing champion, made a guest appearance on the show, a Houston, Texas, couple dispatched a telegram:

AS LISTENERS AND ADMIRERS OF YOUR PROGRAM TONIGHT HEARD JOE LEWIS [sic] A NEGRO ADDRESS YOU AS FRED. WE BEYOND THE MASON AND DIXON LINE DON'T TOLERATE OR LIKE IT AND WE OF THE SOUTH WILL APPRECIATE IT IF YOU WILL REFRAIN FROM ALLOWING NEGROES TO CALL YOU FRED OVER THE RADIO.

"These are the kinds of morons I have to put up with," Allen informed Joe Kelly. And to another friend, he said, "They're in life's dead storage, the parking lot of humanity."

Fan mail was important all the same: it represented obligations incurred through direct personal contact. He had supported the household on Grafton Street, and now the livelihoods of others depended on him and he was painfully aware of what might happen in the Depression when you lost your job.

Friday night, he and Portland enjoyed a brief interval of leisure, a movie or a restaurant. Saturday, Allen plunged into work on the program again. He reintroduced the News Reel, a spry cavalcade of topical absurdity. While its items initially ran to such subjects as an interview with the founder of the Society for the Abolition of Profanity on Golf Courses, the segment constituted mass entertainment's pioneering satire on the manners and mores of the day. The Passé News became the Bedlam News ("Sees Nothing, Shows All!") and grew increasingly pertinent over the years. It was the golden era of the newsreel, grainy panoramas of Hitler's goose-stepping

legions alternating with the Atlantic City beauty pageant.
Newsreels transformed headlines into pictures; the Town Hall
newsreel caught the medium's breathless pace and swift montage effects. At the same time, however, the installment remained resolutely a segment of radio, describing events in terms
of sound.

There was another general writing conference Saturday, and
Saturday night involved rewriting and tailoring certain sketches.
Allen did these longhand to avoid disturbing neighbors in the
hotel. "I make up a lot of phoney trials with leads taken from
Case and Comment, a lawyer's magazine," he said. His brother-
in-law, Arthur Hershkovitz, a lawyer, brought over the magazine along with miscellaneous legal journals. The hillbilly trial
sequences on later programs ("I'd like to dedicate the next
hog call to my husband") were, for enthusiasts such as
author H. Allen Smith, a high point of Allen's humor.

After mass on Sunday, he combed the papers for viable items,
then spent the remainder of the day and night integrating elements of the script. Sylvester "Pat" Weaver, the show's producer between 1935 and 1937, came to the Windsor Hotel with
the "continuity" section of the program that he had written —
the introduction, lead-ins, commercials, and ending. Portland's sister Lastone, who served as secretary, finished typing
the first draft around four in the morning, and the script was
left with the doorman to relay to a Western Union messenger.
Late Monday morning a groggy Allen rose and visited his so-
cialist barber and walked to Radio City. Mimeographed copies
were ready for the first studio rehearsal, a two-hour session
from one in the afternoon till three. Since a zestful exchange
on the page could fall flat on the air, every line was timed and
polished. Following rehearsal, Allen, with his director and
writers, spent three hours on the script, then returned home
to make a final version of some fifty pages of dialogue. This
was mimeographed on Tuesday: one copy went to the sponsor, a second to the advertising agency of Benton and Bowles,
a third to NBC's Continuity Acceptance Department.

With the script out of his hands, and with sponsor, ad agency,
and network in control, opportunities for bureaucratic cross
fire were abundant. No wonder he often alluded to meddle-

some bureaucrats — the Vice President in Charge of Kleenex, the Vice President in Charge of Doorknobs — and defined a conference as "a gathering of important people who singly can do nothing, but together can decide that nothing can be done."

"They will not let us refer in fun to a mythical town on Long Island as 'Dirty Neck' because it might offend Little Neck or Great Neck," Allen told a radio editor. To Joe Kelly he could be more explicit: "Those bastards are still interfering with the Town Hall. They just called up to say that Mr. B. — one of the 'heads' — had changed the whole thing around for tomorrow. After I worked until four this morning to get it in shape. The old hall isn't as peaceful as it sounds on the air."

Mr. B. soon developed into a bête noire.

A week or so ago word was whispered around the offices, "Mr. Bowles is back." To you, a man harassed in sleeping and waking hours by unholy spectres of Master Curley [James M. Curley, the Irish-American boss of Boston] rising at unexpected times and places, the cry "Mr. Bowles is back" means nothing. Mr Bowles is one of the heads of the advertising agency. A man, Mr. K., who has had his finger on the pulse of the Great American Radio Listener since God knows when. He is the man that discovered that the radio audience had the mind of a 14-year-old boy until the 14-year-old boy missed it and demanded and received his mind back.

Mr. Bowles is the man who, after you have worked all week to concoct a mess of drivel that will barely skim through the loudspeakers without leaving a stench in a radio owner's parlor, rushes in at 4 P.M. on Wednesday afternoon and tears the entire show apart, leaving nothing but punctuation marks for you to put some new words between and have it ready to convulse 30 million listeners from coast to coast by 9 P.M. Eastern Standard Time.

Well . . . Mr. Bowles is back after a hard summer of resting first one cheek and then the other of his well-groomed pratt on the mahogany deck of his boat. He lit into the old Town Hall with a will, sir. As a result I have had to eliminate the educational feature and spend countless hours in research so that I can produce a travelogue weekly. He also has removed the finish of the program, and one night insisted that The Question Box, a feature loved by 27 million listeners . . . showed the wind turning. In other words, he has kept me in hot water until my testicles have begat a permanent red glow like the bottom ember in those fake wooden fireplaces the gas company sends its customers around November first.

If the script escaped surgery, rehearsals began at 10:00 on Wednesday morning, the actors in a separate studio from the musicians and the announcers. The dress rehearsal took place at 1:00 and each section was dovetailed. Sometimes the performance would run ten to fourteen minutes too long; a seven-minute spread was allowed for applause and ad libs. At 9:00 P.M., the fifty-three-minute show went on the air. The repeat show began the cycle once more.

The success of *Town Hall Tonight* exceeded that of both the *Linit* and the *Salad Bowl* revues. The stage techniques of the earlier programs appealed to sophisticated audiences, but Allen, perfecting a radio style, was now creating an entertainment both populist and patrician. Allusions to such characters as Pop Mullen, "popular owner of the lunch wagon 'Belle of the Alley,' who is letting down his tailboard to be used as a cocktail bar," and to Bedlam's grocer, Hodge White, made them tangible presences. Unlike the characters of Allen's Alley, Pop Mullen and Hodge White were reported upon rather than enacted. And Hodge (born Charles) was no fiction. A moon-faced, affable bachelor-grocer from Dorchester, Massachusetts, he represented one of the sturdy links to Allen's boyhood. He and Fred had known each other since Aunt Lizzie moved the family from Allston.

Lunch wagons, motorized and without personification, would outlast the thirties, but the neighborhood grocery store that Hodge founded was already vanishing. Only twenty-two feet wide and flanked by a vacant store and a garage with a sign announcing, "Flats Fixed, 35," the aromatic interior was crammed with a medley of goods, from cans of Bistix crackers to (in the midthirties) trays of 1890s hatpins. An ancient cast-iron stove stood among a clump of chairs. Hodge, born in nearby Andrew Square, and his bookkeeper-assistant "Mame" Carr, greeted customers on a first-name basis, and if times were lean, "carried" them. "This store is like a part of me," Hodge said; it was virtually a Dorchester Avenue club, the neighborhood's nucleus. Johnny Sullivan had learned to juggle using Hodge's eggs and vegetables. Hodge remembered him hauling Raymond Young's cart as assistant in the portable Punch-and-Judy show Raymond lugged around Dorchester, and like the rest of Fred's neighborhood crowd, the grocer called Allen "the ackter." "Why, I can see him right now, placing three tomatoes in [Will] McDonough's hands, turning him around three times and yelling 'Bet you can't hit me,' and McDonough would let fly and the tomatoes would land everywhere except on Johnny." A half-dozen photographs of Fred decorated the walls, including a shot of the mountainous Italian boxer Primo Carnera holding Allen aloft. "The ackter" had signed it, "To Hodge — See what I did to Primo." Wednesday nights, Hodge hung up his straw hat and apron, and he and Mame listened to *Town Hall Tonight*. Applause, music, laughter, and Fred's voice filled the store.

> Hodge White says the customers will have to be more careful this week because he is displaying a new shipment of California cucumbers and he doesn't want the customers thumping them to see how ripe they are, even if they do mistake them for watermelons.

Or:

> Hodge White, the first grocer to put hives in his store for homeless Vitamin Bees, says that you boys hanging around the meat counter have got to quit fooling with the hamburger machine. Somebody put the machine in reverse Monday night and it's been backfiring hamburgers around the store all week. Hodge says fun is fun, boys, but meat is high enough without having to scrape it from the ceiling.

Although Hodge instantly passed into contemporary American folklore, he never sought to exploit his celebrity as the country's archetypal grocer. It never occurred to him to do so. He aroused affectionate memories of the individual values of the small tradesman of an earlier time, and like that small tradesman he preferred simple diversions. As long as he could listen to Fred on Wednesday nights, he was satisfied. From time to time fans or reporters visited and Hodge submitted to interviews, but fame's keenest pleasure stirred once a week when he closed the store and tuned in the program, a wraith of a smile manifest on his ordinarily solemn features.

The amateurs, a fixture of the broadcast starting January 2, 1935, also evoked the past, and introducing them, Allen must have recalled dinky Boston theaters, Sam Cohen and his antics, and Johnny Sullivan holding a handkerchief above the contestants' heads. "I first went on at an amateur night," he told the radio audience. "We used to come on the stage wearing a big smile and walk off wearing a tired tomato or an eggplant rampant." The amateurs, however, were not his idea.

"There has been much banter for and against the amateurs, but nothing that is said will influence the advertising agency," he confided to a friend.

> They wanted me to put them on and I have been auditioning people and trying to get a good variety each week so that the unfoaled talent wouldn't be too bad. Some of the amateurs have more guts than I have, and it will only be a question of weeks before some dirty-necked comedian will show me up at the mike. I don't see the people until Wednesday night so all of the banter has to come out of my mind at a moment's notice. I have decided that when the night comes that I can't think faster than one of the amateur acts I should quit anyway, and meanwhile I shall go on saying what comes into my head in an effort to make spontaneous fun.

Had Cohen been exceptionally long-lived, he might have caught fortune's wheel of amateur-show popularity on the upswing. This time the fad intensified into a national mania. Filling Sam's role was Major Edward Bowes, whose trademark was indeed the wheel of fortune and whose catchphrase, "Around and around she goes, and where she stops nobody knows," echoed across the land. The amateurs on *Town Hall Tonight* antedated *Major Bowes' Original Amateur Hour* on coast-to-coast broadcasting by a few months, but the major (Army Intelligence, 1917–18) had been conducting an amateur show on WHN, New York, throughout 1934, and the popularity of the Town Hall contestants may have been the catalyst for his subsequent Chase-and-Sanborn hour, which began in March over NBC. Major Bowes instantly shot into the heavens of entertainment like Santa Claus astride a meteor. The Town Hall amateurs nourished professional aspirations — among them were actress Ann Sheridan, comic Garry Moore, and Frank Sinatra (who later sang with the Hoboken Four introduced by Bowes) — and the first-prize winner received fifty dollars, a silver cup, and a week's engagement at the Roxy Theatre. Major Bowes cast a wider, popular net. By fall, he occupied first place on the rating charts, the *Original Amateur Hour* was receiving ten thousand applications a week, and listeners, voting by phone and mail, swamped the network offices each week.

There was an element of desperation in all this; the success of Major Bowes reflected not only the dream of stardom but the havoc of hard times. The mirage of a better life beckoned amateurs, who streamed toward New York, migrants from juke joints and mortgaged farms and bankrupt businesses. "In one month of 1935 alone, *Newsweek* estimated that 1,200 amateurs had applied for emergency food and shelter," social historian John Dunning states.

> Bowes, anticipating a share of blame for the city's welfare problems, had established a rule that only residents of New York or its boroughs were eligible to participate on the show. But this did little to stem the oncoming tide. Once a person was committed to the dream of fame and fortune, establishing New York residence was easy. And so they came, players of jugs and washboards, tap dancers, foot shufflers, piano players, mimics, tellers of old jokes, duos and trios and quartets and more. There were harpists and yodelers and chime-ringers and harmonica players. The harmonica may have its virtues, but we seldom heard them on *Major Bowes*. There were flutists and ukelele pickers,

fiddlers who wanted more than anything in the world to
be violinists.

Allen, in any event, was disinclined to take the amateurs as
earnestly as did the major, who stashed a bodyguard in the
wings lest unruly losers turn on their benefactor. The Bowes
show with its sententious tone and "honor city" (a city along
the network selected by the host for a Chamber-of-Commerce
encomium) was fertile material for parody and yielded Fred
many a lighthearted sketch; Major Bowes himself was an
Allen fan from the first Linit program onward. Never an essential part of *Town Hall Tonight,* the amateurs gave way on
December 9, 1936, to a format titled "Varieties." "We have
abandoned the rigid amateur requirement maintained in our
new talent shows for the past two years," it was announced.
"We feel that most of the talented amateur artists in the New
York area have had an opportunity to appear on our *Town
Hall* contests, and starting this week we are auditioning and
will present acts not necessarily amateur."

Under that rubric, the evening of December 30, 1936, a ten-
year-old violinist named Stewart Canin from Edgemere, Long
Island, played Rimsky-Korsakov's "Flight of the Bumblebee"
and thereby ignited a feud on the classic order of Montague
and Capulet, intense as the dispute between New England clam
chowder and the Manhattan brand.

14 | The Punch-and-Benny Show

At least three ear-witness versions record Fred Allen's ad-lib following Master Canin's performance. Frank Buxton and Bill Owen in *The Big Broadcast* give, "A certain alleged violinist should hang his head in shame," which sounds pithy enough for the show's strict time slot; then there is Allen's recollection, "If Mr. Benny had heard this tyke's rendition of 'The Bee' he should hang his head in symphonic shame and pluck the horsehairs out of his bow and return them to the tail of the stallion from which they had been taken"; while the target of the quip, listening to the show in Hollywood, said he burst out laughing at:

"How old are you?"
"Ten."
"Ten years old and you play 'The Bee' so well — Jack Benny ought to be ashamed of himself."

The show-business feud between the comedians sprang from Allen's habit of inserting the names of friends and colleagues into his scripts, a hidden signature like the emblems of old-master painters. "He probably said that, knowing that I was listening to the show," Benny went on, "just to make me laugh." Allen envisioned his broadcast in terms of individuals with whom he communicated (Jack Haley, Hodge White, Jack Benny), as though the program substituted for a private letter. Al Hirschfeld, for example, enjoyed novel sound effects, so

Allen made sure that the program's sound-effects expert, Agnew Horine, traversed an extensive sonic repertoire during the episodes of "One Long Pan, Oriental Detective." (The sounds were cued to the sketch's repeated exclamation, "A lewolower!") This time, Benny responded.

> So, on my next show [Sunday, January 3, 1937] at the very tag of the show — what we call the tag — I said to Mary [Livingstone] — and this was merely to make Fred laugh — "Take this: I'm going to dictate a message to Fred Allen. 'Dear Fred: I am *not* ashamed of myself. When I was ten years old I could play the "Bee" too' " Well — the next week Fred had some stooges on who were supposed to have known me in Waukegan, Illinois, to prove that I couldn't play the "Bee." Then I brought people on from Waukegan who said I could — Before we knew it we were into the darndest feud you ever saw — which was very funny — and the strange part of it is, I can safely say, it was from six to eight months with this feud before we even called each other on the phone about it.

Benny's recollection almost twenty years later appears mistaken. The feud wasn't planned, and unquestionably time elapsed before he and Allen discussed it, but they must have been in touch earlier than six to eight months, since the climax of their mock rivalry was a face-to-face broadcast encounter in New York's Pierre Hotel on March 14. Jell-O, sponsoring the Benny program, could on that occasion claim one of the largest listening audiences of radio history.

The immediate show-business antecedents of the simulated feud went back to 1927 when announcer Nils T. Granlund and singer Harry Richman jousted on WHN, trading insults as a running gag. Orchestra leader Ben Bernie and columnist Walter Winchell based a pseudo-feud on this precedent. The device proved useful long before Winchell's day: in 1909, Gray and Graham, a vaudeville act, and the Four Musical Cates wrangled for months in the columns of *Variety* over which team owned the world's largest saxophone. The genuine antagonisms that fueled the Freddy James–Harry LaToy ripostes also gave the antagonists opportunity to advertise. For advertising was the point of the game: a radio "feud," say Abel Green and Joe Laurie, Jr., achieved the purposes "of reaffirming public interest in one another's programs, and spotlighting perhaps newfound listeners (potential customers) on another show's product."

The comedy of the feud was basically comedy of derision rooted in American frontier traditions of exaggeration, swagger, and the deadpan tall tale. The technique was not remote from Mark Twain's description of a riverboat pilot blown up on a steamboat on three different occasions and each time falling through the roof of the same log cabin onshore. The third time the owner moved away because he "was a nervous, sedentary, student-sort of a man, trying to cipher out the Development business, and Survival of the Fittest, and one thing or another, and he said he would rather move than be always being interrupted and bothered so." The exaggerations of the Benny-Allen feud are often as imaginative: spleen proliferates like a Wagnerian motif, from a murmuring brooklet of resentment among the woodwinds into an epic cataract of envy among the brasses. On the other hand, the limitations of the comedy of insult, its essentially primitive character, disclose neither Benny nor Allen at his zenith. All in all, however, we can be grateful for its highlights. Circumstances brought into conjunction the sovereign radio comedians of their era, combining their separate styles into good-natured dialectic.

They had ties of affection and (by way of contrast to most comedians) admired each other's inventiveness. "Practically all the comedy shows owe their structure to Benny's conceptions," Allen remarked. "The Benny show was like a 'One Man's Family' in slapstick. He was the first comedian in radio to realize you could get big laughs by ridiculing yourself instead of your stooges." According to Benny, "Fred Allen was probably the only comedian I could have had a successful feud with."

Benny's vaudeville career resembled Allen's; born the same year, both started about the same time — in 1912, Benny, a seventeen-year-old violin prodigy, was expelled from high school and afterward toured the circuits with an older pianist named Cora Salisbury. After one season she retired, he found another partner, and five years later they played the Palace in a musical parody. The wartime U.S. Navy assumed the catalytic role in Benny's development that Australia played in Allen's. Before joining the navy, Benny was essentially a fiddler, but during his service days he worked out a routine with the novelty ragtime composer Zez Confrey and began experimenting with camp-show monologues. Returning to civilian life, the performer (born Benjamin Kubelsky) became Ben Benny, a comedian whose violin served him as a prop like the dummy or the vestiges of juggling in Allen's act. (Later the billing was changed to Jack Benny in order to avoid confusion with maestro Ben Bernie.)

Low-keyed and self-reflexive, Benny's comedy style also displayed an affinity with Allen's. Just as the latter sat, legs dangling over the stage apron, and bantered with the audience, Benny used the theater environment itself as a prop. At the curtain's rise he was discovered, back to the audience, playing violinist's scales. The notes stopped; he turned around and in a flash of surprise announced, "Oh, I guess I'm on," and performed a number. "Instead of doing 'jokes,' " states Benny's biographer, Irving Fein, "he tried to build his humor around events of the day so that it sounded ad libbed and current. He'd talk about new one-way streets, flappers, his troubles trying to get a date and keep a girl, about 'cheap' things he did which were taken from Scotsman stories that were then in vogue." This involved risk. Benny was patently Jewish, and stereotypes of the penny-pinching Scot overlapped stereotypes of the money-grubbing Jew. So urbanely did he handle ethnicity, however, that the failings (cowardice, miserliness, braggadocio) of the fussbudget Jack Benny character turned into signs of specific identity rather than generalizations about a social or racial group. Listeners never identified Benny as a "Jewish" comedian any more than they identified Allen as "Irish"; each of their troupes had a Jewish or Irish ethnic type (Schlepperman on the Benny show, Ajax Cassidy on Allen's Alley), while the star comedians themselves were all but deracinated members of the white middle class. The corrosive racial slurs of vaudeville, epitomizing the frictions of upwardly-mobile-immigrant city life, were integrated into a different social pattern — the mammoth web of information and entertainment of a communications network. Dialect comedians like Jack Pearl became an anomaly in radio. Of course, ethnic anachronisms defied the process, notably *Amos 'n' Andy,* but as John Crosby observed in 1951, theirs "was not a Negro world." It was "a world of blackface — a fantasy world . . . like something out of Walt Disney." (An alternate critical perspective is given by television reviewer Les Brown. Within a racial group, he argues, stereotypes often strengthen the individual's bond with the group, but "on television with its vast and heterogeneous audience, the honest kidding of ethnic types becomes something else, tending to validate the stereotype as a true representative of a whole people, and in that way contributing to prejudice.") Allen and Benny, least prejudiced of comedians, offered public images of studied neutrality, although their programs teemed with comic stereotypes. In this sense they adapted to the impartial realm of communications, while never quite abandoning vaudeville's singularity. Benny's hyperbolic love of money became an incongruous commentary on American materialism. The penurious man, after all, is a medieval comic butt and universal figure; Benny rescued him from the ghetto and restored his universality.

Critic Gary Giddins, an admirer, states that Benny "may be the only great comedian in history who isn't associated with a single witticism. He got his biggest laughs with two exclamations — 'Now cut that out!' and 'Well!' — and impeccably timed silences." He was the master of the eloquent pause, counterpoise to Allen, master of the extemporaneous retort. Quotation books are liberally salted with Allenisms (often without attribution), but Jack Benny's supreme fiction was himself. "You wouldn't dare talk to me like that if my writers were here!" he exploded after Allen had festooned the air with wit. It was not true, however, that, in Allen's deadly phrase, "he couldn't ad lib a belch at a Hungarian banquet." Benny was a respectable ad-lib performer, no mere mouthpiece for a stable of jokesmiths. The jokes didn't matter as much, though, because he was creating a persona as memorable as Micawber, as zany as Zuleika Dobson.

A writer named Harry Conn conceived the Jell-O program, in Giddins's words, as "situation comedy based on the lives of the performers, complete with sophisticated sound effects. Instead of revue skits and strings of jokes, each show would be a variation on a constant theme: life with Jack Benny." The star maintained a staff of comedy writers, and Fred Allen recommended one of the best, a young man named Ed Beloin. Having a staff kept the program's squirrel-cage wheel of plot spinning week after week, and Benny's budget permitted him to hire outside talent. Thus his program developed along separate lines from *Town Hall Tonight,* where Allen wrote, edited, and commented upon topical absurdities. The private life of the Allens seldom intruded upon their routines, not even in fictional guise, and the radio character of Fred Allen (despite One Long Pan, the Down East characterizations, or the Benny ripostes) was indivisible from the historical Allen. He and Benny were alike in two fundamental professional respects: each saw radio as a medium for the free play of the imagination, and each was an original.

Benny's reaction to an unruly matinee audience during his vaudeville days could as easily have been Allen's. Violin tucked beneath one arm, Benny emerged from the wings. His opening music ebbed away, and he said as he advanced toward the footlights, "Hello, folks." The audience, spoiling for riot, roared and booed, and a tomato splashed on the boards. Benny continued walking until he reached the other side of the stage. "Good-bye, folks," he said, and made his exit from that theater forever.

He preceded Allen into radio by a year, introduced over the microphone by Ed Sullivan and responding, "Ladies and gentlemen, this is Jack Benny talking. There will be a slight pause while you say, 'Who cares?' " During the early thirties his program alternated with four or five others, including Allen's, in the ratings of popular comedy shows; but by 1937, the Year of the Great Feud, he was firmly ensconced, the most popular comedy star of radio, a position he would preserve (now and then overtaken by Allen) until the advent of television. Therefore, Benny had less to gain from a mock feud than his colleague; but they never regarded the ruse as a professional rivalry. Benny, too, was a student of humor, and the most appreciative of audiences.

Tickled by the concept, they deployed it, theme and variation, throughout the years to come. Allen indeed wrote one of his most brilliant scripts tracing the errant career of Gypsy Jack, the vagabond fiddler, to mark Benny's guest appearance on the final program in June 1949. By then the insult jokes defined them so completely that the comedians continued to toss the incidental barb back and forth; but the heyday of the feud occurred during the first three months of 1937. No Sunday or Wednesday passed without an additional flourish.

In January, Benny sent a telegram announcing he could perform the "Bee" at the age of ten; and he claimed he had a picture to prove it. Allen thereupon commented that "l'affaire Benny" constituted "a new low in composite photographic skullduggery" and interviewed the alleged photographer, who confessed that the picture had been taken in the Bide-a-Wee Pawnshop where little Jascha Benny had hocked his violin. Furthermore, Benny had posed for the picture, holding the violin the wrong way.

Benny took his cause to the cast of his own show, but found them unsympathetic to his clothespin-on-the-nose Allen imitation. Next, Allen welcomed a group of "experts" that included an actuarial statistician. After hearing the data on Benny, the latter announced, "This man will live to be 104 years and six months of age." Allen then called upon a companion expert, Dr. Gustave Strad, celebrated music authority.

"You have heard the playing of Jack Benny?"

"Yes," said Dr. Strad, "and he will never play the 'Bee' until he is 105."

And so it went — Stewart Canin returning to play a solo, Allen challenging Benny to better Stewart's performance, Benny accepting the challenge and discovering that he had mislaid his violin. At length, Benny, recovering his fiddle, delivered a quavery rendition of the "Bee." Allen said, "I have never heard such wailing and squalling since the time two ghosts got their toes caught in my Ouija board." On Benny's next program, which originated in New York, Stewart Canin was his guest. "What did you want to see me about, Mr. Benny?" Stewart asked. "If it's about the violin, I don't give lessons." The adult Stewart would in fact become a professor of music at Oberlin College.

Town Hall Tonight suddenly burgeoned with musical jokes. "LONDON, ENGLAND," the News Reel intoned — "Toscanini hurries back to America to play 'Bee'!" References to the piece punctuated the Mighty Allen Art Players performance of "Colonel Claghorne's Bet, or She Was Only the Hat Check Girl but She Refused a Tip on the Derby." Allen protested Master Canin's treatment at the hands of Benny: "Of all the cowards. The last time he got into an argument with the Dionne Quintuplets he invited them outside one by one."

Is it any wonder that the climactic face-off at the Hotel Pierre gripped the attention of the nation? "The audience was in a mood of anticipation. Jack and I were given ovations. During the first part of the program people were laughing at straight lines, they couldn't wait for the jokes." Under the circumstances, the showdown risked inevitable anticlimax, yet somehow proved cathartic. Contemporary audiences may find it difficult to imagine that two comedians in New York commanded such rapt attention; contemporary comedy appeals to special constituencies rather than radio's mass listenership. "The dialogue," Allen said, "frankly didn't live up to the pandemonium." At the close the stars stepped into the hallway to settle their quarrel via fisticuffs, but returned arm-in-arm reminiscing about their shabby days in vaudeville. On that note, where actuality began, the hot-war phase of the feud ended; they would keep the Punch-and-Benny show operative, however, through one preposterous scene after another, including a pants-dropping descent into burlesque buffoonery. This highly uncharacteristic episode was first concocted by Benny's writers out of frustration at their inability to top Allen's improvisations. Guest star of an Allen program, Benny, taunted beyond endurance, dropped his pants and revealed underwear blazoned "LSMFT" — initials standing for the slogan of his then-sponsor: "Lucky Strike Means Fine Tobacco." Over the shrieks of the audience, he proclaimed, "My underwear can out ad-lib you." Turnabout was necessary, and on a subsequent program when they were parodying *Queen for a Day* (a daytime show in which women received prizes on the basis of mawkishly revealing what they would most like to have), Benny won a free pants-pressing and saw to it that Allen's trousers were removed onstage. "For fifteen years I've been waiting to catch you like this," Benny shouted. Allen, possessed by laughter, for once could not ad-lib. "You haven't seen the end of me,"

Benny continued. Their feud was a caper among the frontier humor of the Colonel Crockett almanacs of a prior century.

"You're so mean, Benny, you'd put a tack in the electric chair!"

"Oh yeah? Until you were born, nobody knew what a cramp looked like."

"Benny, you ought to get out of your body and rent it to someone who can use it." Animated by an "anything you can do, I can do better" rhetoric, their exchanges eliminated frontier brutality but preserved frontier bluster in a thoroughly modern manner.

> In days of old when Rembrandt created a canvas, he was done with it. When Whistler painted his mother, his job was done. His mother did not then have to make personal appearances on radio or go to theater lobbies to strum up goodwill. Now, take my situation: when you make a picture with Benny you have to go around in an attempt to get rid of it. You speak to the Good Humor men you meet and ask them to say a good word to their customers. Unlike Van Gogh, Corot, or any of the great artists of tradition who were finished with a picture when they were done, the movies finish a picture and then start on it. I believe it is called "marketing the product."

The date was Wednesday, December 18, 1940, the place the Paramount Theatre in New York, and costarring with Jack Benny in the comedy *Love Thy Neighbor,* Fred Allen was on a promotion tour. He did not like the picture, his third feature effort; he did not like the inanities of the promotion tour; but he was, to his gratification, back east. With a modicum of luck he would never have to set foot again in California.

Between 1935 and 1952, Allen made six Hollywood films. If his reputation rested on them, he would have been forgotten before the last forlorn reel. His top movie remains a toss-up between his debut, *Thanks a Million,* and the episodic *We're Not Married* (1952). The former, starring singer Dick Powell, is a topical comedy (with a script largely by Nunnally Johnson) about a crooner elected a state governor; in the best sequence of *We're Not Married* (again, with a script largely by

Nunnally Johnson), Allen and Ginger Rogers portray professional lovebirds who, despite their off-mike distaste for each
other, conduct a "breakfast chat" radio program from their
home. Allen's collaboration with Johnson flourished on both a
personal and professional basis. ("So far as your stuff was concerned," Johnson wrote him, "with Ginger, you couldn't have
asked for finer, more sincere laughs. The marriage sequence
got the picture off to a really wonderful start.") Worst of the
screen efforts was, possibly, *Love Thy Neighbor*. All six productions, pale, decent, and forgettable, maintained a uniform
level of mediocrity. Allen's films enlisted potent talents —
Jimmy Durante, William Bendix, Johnson — but seldom delivered the excitement promised by the cast.

Comparison with Jack Benny again proves instructive. Essentially a radio star like Allen, his film career was fitful, but
Benny in one glorious moment disclosed the scope of his cinematic potential. While Allen's pictures were directed by such
journeymen as Roy Del Ruth and Richard Wallace, Benny in
To Be or Not to Be had Ernst Lubitsch supervising the project
from start to finish. An equivalent Allenesque moment might —
tantalizingly — have occurred: Alfred Hitchcock, early in 1943,
planned to direct a movie starring Fred Allen, but Allen objected to a plot twist by scenarist Sally Benson, and the project
was shelved.

To Be or Not to Be grated on critical sensibilities as a tasteless
spoof about a troupe of Shakespearean ham actors outwitting
Nazis in Poland. The film's distribution in 1942, when real
Nazis swept across Europe and Russia, signaled commercial disaster. Critical opinion has since swung tentatively in the other
direction (including the response to a slapstick remake by Mel
Brooks). While some commentators still find the mixture of
farce and melodrama unpalatable, others consider Lubitsch au-
dacious and original. Similarly, Jack Benny's performance is
viewed with admiration; he portrays "that great, great Polish
actor, Joseph Tura," one half of a husband-and-wife team
known as "the Polish Lunts" (the wife played by Carole
Lombard).

Film historian James Harvey, for example, considers it dar-
ing on Lubitsch's part to show Benny acting Hamlet:

Cast of *The Little Show* on the boardwalk at Atlantic City during
the 1929 tryout. *Front row, center, from left to right:* Clifton Webb
(*holding Scottie*), Libby Holman, Fred, and Portland.

"The Still Alarm" sketch by George S. Kaufman, hit of *The Little
Show*. Hoseman Allen and a fellow fireman listen to the elegant
Clifton Webb and Allen Vincent (*far right*) discussing the approach
of the flames.

Webb, Holman, and Allen in *Three's a Crowd* displaying the insou-
ciant spirit of the cartoons of Peter Arno, the verse of Ogden Nash,
and the quips of Dorothy Parker. (*Courtesy of Culver Pictures*)

"Everything you and Fred said to each other," remarked James Thurber about Portland and Fred Allen, "was somehow akin to The Sweetheart Duet from *Maytime*."

Fred invading the Southern California territory of his dearest
enemy.

No one was ever a better audience for an ad-lib than Jack Benny,
here reduced by an unexpected sally to helpless laughter.

Mugging for the camera, old stage colleagues Cary Grant and Fred Allen meet again in Hollywood as an unidentified middleman looks on apprehensively.

Before it bears the stamp of the master, Allen (*in bow tie*) and his staff go over the week's radio script. Shirt-sleeved at Allen's side, his collaborator Herman Wouk.

A galaxy of 1940s radio personalities prepares an army show during the Second World War. *Clockwise from left:* unidentified sergeant, Jimmy Durante, Fred, bandleader Kay Kyser, unidentified, Bob Hope, unidentified, Jack Benny (*hidden by hat*), and Archie Gardner (*Duffy's Tavern*).

Fred and an unidentified piano accompanist savor the songs and banter of Maurice Chevalier (*left*), forever the boulevardier in a perennial Paris of sidewalk cafés and chestnuts in blossom.

Even seaside with Portland at Old Orchard Beach, the treadmill of writing a weekly hour-long radio script and keeping up with correspondence never ceased.

Working seven days a week, often throughout the night, Fred Allen sustained a unique level of radio comedy. Over his shoulder on his study's shelves are the black-bound volumes of scripts that comprise his lifework.

A pause. He comes in from the back of the stage, and walks slowly and portentously, holding an open book in front of him as if reading, to the footlights. A *long* silence — reproaching the audience even before he speaks to it. It's an extraordinary vision: an *aggrieved* Hamlet. He closes the book — with limp wrists — and looks up, pettish and wounded, in almost a trance of irritable self-love. By the time he begins the speech — whereupon the scene dissolves to his wife's dressing room — he's already said everything. (He performs the same scene, with lovely and subtle variations, twice more in the movie.)

Nothing as cinematic as this, nothing geared to the rhythm of the visual image, occurs in a Fred Allen movie. Benny throughout his career yearned to become an actor, a light leading man. "They always cast me as the Jack Benny character I portrayed in vaudeville and radio, and that isn't me." Allen, conversely, was the vehicle of his own dialogue; he didn't cherish ambitions to express another aspect of himself, his acting experience was gained in revue sketches, and he seemed to attract directors who had a preconceived notion of what to do with him. They cast him as a tinhorn or confidence man, and assumed they ought to tailor his personality to sardonic wisecracks. His directors reveal their uncertainty through devices in which they try to make his scenes approximate the radio broadcasts. *It's in the Bag* (1945), for instance, finds director Richard Wallace keeping the camera immobile, Allen in constant and frantic motion. Carried over intact from radio is an episode in which Allen, coveting an antique chair, interviews Minerva Pious as Pansy Nussbaum. The two-shot sequence, valuable documentation of a scene that might have been on Allen's Alley, also demonstrates the impossibility of reproducing radio comedy in a visual medium. *It's in the Bag* may well be the perfect film to look at with closed eyes. The sound of Mrs. Nussbaum's voice implies a woman of physical stature, one of P. G. Wodehouse's dowager-dragons perhaps; instead, the diminutive woman answering the knock on the door is doll-like, a reminder that the presence of Mrs. Nussbaum lies entirely in her voice. And no matter whom Allen was supposed to delineate, he remained resolutely himself. In thirties and forties Hollywood this was, of course, no defect, but the movie image distanced Allen's singularity. Radio placed him inside the fantasies of his audience, yet a movie centering about his inimitable vocal delivery was useless. He did not photograph well, and his attitude toward the camera was shy and vigilant.

Benny typified the midwesterner who emigrates to California and discovers hedonistic abundance; Allen was a carpet-bagger from the East, banished and restive until the moment he shook off the burden of sunshine and returned to civilization once more. The last of the name comedians to remain broadcasting out of New York, he loathed California, land of the nutburger and the drive-in mortuary. "To me it all looks like Waterbury on a rainy Sunday, there are but few places to go, and . . . the outstanding social event of the week is the fight at the Hollywood Legion on Friday."

At first, he was hopeful about films. Before he and Portland went west for *Thanks a Million* in the summer of 1935, he thought of moviemaking as he once thought of radio — another string to his bow in case he found himself jobless. (He was then second and third in the ratings, and so popular that during his absence from the show he sent a weekly telegram, read over the air.) Mack Sennett, originator of the Keystone Kops and the patriarch of movie comedy, believed Allen could succeed in Hollywood. Recalling a 1931 Allen screen test Paramount executives "found only mildly funny," Sennett wrote Allen that "their decision broke my heart, as I knew you then to be the great comedian which the world now acclaims you."

Cowriter Harry Tugend (ultimately a studio executive) was the decisive factor, and convinced Allen that he ought to reconsider picture making. The first rushes were encouraging: "I have been sending a weekly wire to the program and working on the picture dialogue which has really prohibited my vacation from starting. Portland is getting all of the rest, and she thinks it is fine. She goes around with Mrs. Jack Haley and Mrs. Jack Benny, and since the Bennys have a swimming pool, Portland is in her glory and the pool most of the time."

Opening in New York at mid-November, *Thanks a Million*

received gratifying notices. The scenario, inspired by such political caricatures as *Of Thee I Sing,* manipulated topical allusion cleverly, including most of Allen's scenes and "The Alphabet Song," the Yacht Club Boys' musical send-up of New
Deal acronyms. "When you stop to consider, as Fred Allen
does in the picture, that a jazz bandleader was actually elected
lieutenant-governor of the state of Washington," Leo Mishkin
wrote in the *New York Telegram,* the plot did not seem far-
fetched (entertainers and public office were then deemed in-
compatible). Richard Watts of the *Herald-Tribune* said, "The
photoplay shows you how a populace, bored with the futile
dullness of a routine machine politician, elects a successful entertainer, who has been nominated as a merry whim of the
bosses, head of the state, virtually by acclamation." Allen played
the manager of a stranded theatrical troupe; Powell, the crooner
and governor-elect; Ann Dvorak and Patsy Kelly, the female
leads; and then there were specialty routines such as Rubinoff
and his fiddle and spluttering by veteran character actors Raymond Walburn and Allan Dinehart. "The real hero of the
campaign, as well as of the photoplay," said Andre Sennwald
in the *Times,* "is Mr. Allen, whose cinema debut can be set
down as a happy success."

A fortnight before the premiere, Allen was interviewed by
a *Times* reporter, who was somewhat taken aback by his tobacco chewing. ("Mr. Allen shifted his quid again and fired
pointblank out the open window of his hotel room. [Hurried
note to the hotel management: It was quite all right; there was
a terrace.] 'Would he like to play Hamlet?' 'No,' he said, 'I
leave that to the actors. They've been playing the first three
letters of it so long they shouldn't have any trouble getting up
the second three.' ") Despite the hazards of making the movie —
he had developed sciatica after several takes of a scene in which
he and Patsy Kelly hop out of a bus in the rain and fall into a
trough of flour paste — Allen told the anonymous interviewer
that he looked forward to appearing in and writing film scripts.

Disillusionment with Hollywood, however, had already set
in; and his hopes for an alternate career were withering. "The
people here seem to live in a little world that shuts off the rest

of the universe and everyone appears to be faking life," he wrote from Hollywood after the starting date of *Thanks a Million* had been put back four times.

> The actors and writers live in fear, and nothing, including the houses, seems permanent. One or two bad pictures washes up an actor, writer, director, and about everyone else associated with them, and for that reason the people in the picture business scurry from office to home and vice versa with hunted looks. If you are lazy or incompetent and have any sort of a contract that assures security for a given period it may be heaven, but for a steady diet, it is too much for me.

Subsequent California visits reinforced this judgment. There was the problem of originating the radio broadcasts at the same time. In late 1937, Allen spent two months doing both and getting along on three and four hours of sleep. "Working at the studio, I had to be up at six and six-thirty, and when I returned at night I still had a radio script to write which kept me up until one and two," he told Joe Kelly.

> In order to present the program in Hollywood we had to transport some twenty people out there, musicians, actors, office help, writers, etc., and when the whole thing was paid for, all I had was the use of the hall and a chance to let my many fans hear from me. I will have to call you in order to work out a way that will enable me to either stop working altogether or fix it so that I can "ease off" as we say in Maine. . . . I am not a small-time Confucius. I am not Poor Richard. I am merely a resident of Dorchester, doomed by some evil fairy around Moseley Street to roam the earth until such a time as my penance has been paid.

He didn't like the process of filmmaking, Hollywood's feverish preoccupation with status, or the jingoism of the Los Angeles Hearst press.

> Comedy pictures should get money for a long time to come, but I can't grind out this stuff [radio scripts] and

worry about a picture, too. All of the material they have given me to do in pictures is written along formula lines. If I ever did get a crack at something that suited me I might be okay, but I don't care much for that medium. The whole thing is so synthetic from the first conference down to the preview, that I don't go for it. It is true that good comedies can be made working on empty sets with tired grips around and, after ten takes, nothing to inspire the actor, but I would have to have a little more experience in pictures before I could be of much use to anyone.

The Allens eschewed the limousine offered by the studio; they rented a car with a chauffeur, however, since Fred didn't drive. During negotiations, Allen took the black chauffeur aside and said, "With what I'm paying in rental, you could be making payments on a car. Why don't I just give the money to you?" The chauffeur agreed, and turned up at the wheel of a jaunty, cream-colored Ford in which Fred and Portland sped to receptions thronged by Rolls-Royces. Informed by an agent that the Allens ought to lease a Beverly Hills mansion so Fred could live up to his role as a star, he answered, "Get a small place for Portland and me, and don't let on you know us."

"Jack Benny leaves tomorrow for Honolulu," he reported in July 1936. "He wants us to use his house and swimming pool while he is away, but it must cost a fortune to run it, and when he stops working there is quite an expense with nothing coming in. If this picture comes out lousy I will never come out here again. The sun is out all the time, but I like to see a cloud once in a while."

The six films won't bear analysis. Movie buffs will note that the source of *It's in the Bag* was *Dwenadset Stulow*, a story by the Soviet satirists Ilf and Petrov, that ecdysiast Gypsy Rose Lee performs in *Sally, Irene and Mary* under her real name, Louise Hovick (script by Harry Tugend, starring Tony Martin and Alice Faye), and that in "The Ransom of Red Chief" episode (directed by Howard Hawks) from Allen's final picture, *O. Henry's Full House,* he replaced his old revue associate Clifton Webb, originally cast as one of the swindlers outwitted by

an eight-year-old. The anthology format reflects producer Darryl
Zanuck's enthusiasm for the British picture *Quartet,* based on
Somerset Maugham's short stories; O. Henry, moreover, ranked
high in Allen's esteem. Yet he and Oscar Levant, lugubrious
in flashy checked suits, look embarrassed by their roles.
Whenever and wherever the "Ransom" sequence succeeds is
not due to the stars, one critic has pointed out, but to the
story, and "the parents' quiet acceptance of their son's enorm-
ities." Even as trivia, the second story in *Full House,* "The
Cop and the Anthem," which pairs Charles Laughton and a
Marilyn Monroe on the verge of stardom, has more pizzazz.

The bounty of the Hollywood visits was not onscreen
comedy but a stream of anti-California witticisms. If-you-
happen-to-be-an-orange, of course, and its variation, "At the
age of fifty everybody in California starts looking like an avo-
cado"; the definitions of Hollywood Bowl ("Carnegie Hall on
the half-shell"), Hollywood Boulevard ("Main Street in slacks"),
and Hollywood itself ("a place where people from Iowa mistake each other for stars," and where there ought to be "portable swimming pools for people who live in trailers" and bottles of rain in the museums); the comment about the egotistical
performer who wore sunglasses while attending mass ("He's
afraid God might recognize him and ask him for an autograph"), the star who drove past with his mistress ("He's traveling *a la tarte*"), the Hollywood pecking order ("An associate
producer is the only guy in Hollywood who will associate with
a producer"), and the fantasy environment ("Hollywood love
scene: big moment in a movie when a male star who is wearing a toupee, false teeth and a rented tuxedo, embraces glamor
girl in wig, artificial eyelashes, false fingernails and bustle, and
says, 'Darling, we must come to ourselves' ").

Of photographers who specialized in hackneyed portraits of
movie queens descending from Pullmans, Allen said, "After
all, there are only two ways to get off a train: You can do it
the normal way, or you can back off because you love California so." It summarized his point of view about the West
Coast and its charms.

So, too, did a routine that he copied into a 750-joke logbook
during his vaudeville days:

PRODUCER: Can you dance?
APPLICANT: No.
PRODUCER: Sing?
APPLICANT: No.
PRODUCER: Act?
APPLICANT: No.
PRODUCER: Welcome to Hollywood!

15 | People You Didn't Expect to Meet

The odd relationship between Fred Allen and Rear Admiral Richard E. Byrd, bouncing back and forth in a Ping-Pong game between real life and tomfoolery, reached an August 1934 climax when Allen broadcast a special show to the admiral's base at Little America. Sponsored by the state of Maine, the goodwill program was heard by the expedition amid temperatures of minus sixty-four degrees Fahrenheit. Notwithstanding the involvement of his friend Bill McKenney, Fred felt reluctant to serve as master of ceremonies: he was buried by obligations and, more to the point, "Bob and the girls [aunts Lizzie and Mary] arrive tomorrow or the next day." McKenney at length persuaded Fred to write a skit "with intent to get under the Admiral's raccoon underwear and scratch his risibilities," as Allen put it. The show proved successful, Allen claimed it was heard over refrigerators coast to coast, and seven years later Byrd himself appeared as a program guest.

Having declined the chance to replace Will Rogers in 1933, Allen received a permanent offer from the McNaught Syndicate when Rogers perished in a 1935 plane crash with pioneer aviator Wiley Post. "I turned down the Will Rogers syndication thing again two weeks ago. . . . I feel that it is better to do smaller things competently than it is to have so many irons in the fire that you have to use a brassie on the green." Privately, he felt that Rogers, who said he never met a man he didn't like, had been too accommodating toward politicians. "If I ever saw fit to make the remarks about our officials that Rogers has spouted into the microphone, I would find myself learning to play bridge with Gaston Means [a swindler involved in the Lindbergh kidnapping case and in Washington scandal]."

The Admiral Byrd and Will Rogers incidents particularize the spokesman's role Allen had come to assume. The topical nature of his material thrust him into commentary, and in the manner of the English poet laureate he was expected to produce the proper occasional utterance on demand. He occupied a national stage larger than any in his native city, but Aunt Lizzie implied that he ought to give serious consideration to his future; he had done enough for levity, now it was time to think of permanence. Fred listened to her admonitions to depart frivolous New York and settle nearby, although both knew it was too late. "I have just returned from Boston," he would write Groucho Marx. "It is the only thing to do if you find yourself up there." For the rest of his life, Allen found himself returning. In May 1935, he announced:

> I have been to Boston with disastrous results. I contracted lumbago on the train or from my aunt [the source turned out to be an abscessed tooth] and I have been in bed for the past ten days. . . . I can't stand up straight and I am almost crooked enough to run for public office. I hope to get my spine in ramrod formation for the broadcast tomorrow night, since I presented a grotesque appearance last week. I was slumped over listening to Tiny tell people what Sal Hepatica would do for them, while I, an employee, crawled around the studio like a wisp of drunken ivy.

Boston in his letters began to sound like the radio small town of Bedlam. For Joe Kelly, Fred struck the fustian circus-barker pose of *Town Hall Tonight.*

> I am not the type of man who enters a metropolis in ferret-like fashion, to slink around its outskirts playing my predatory profession under the mantle of darkness. I am

not the sort who, groundhog fashion, sticks his head out
of the Boston end of the East Boston tunnel on the first
warm day for the questionable pleasure of seeing my
shadow and returning to my lair. I am not the type of
man given to tip-toeing around the Public Garden, after
the first frost, awaiting an opportunity to slip my pet toads
into the Frog Pond so that they may live at the city's expense over the winter.

[On] the contrary, when I visit a city, bands meet me
at the station. They are but bands of relatives, to be sure,
but bands nevertheless. Abattoirs start full-blast, slaughtering fatted calves. Children rush from their toys and
games to tag along following me as I march through the
middle of stately thoroughfares with steady tread. Dogs
howl, cats meow, camels at the zoo give off a rare odor
which is often blamed on me for no apparent reason.
Chameleons change their colors. Birds start south, knowing that my reception will chill the entire city. Laws are
hurriedly passed, the key of the city is hidden in its
municipal vault, mendicants rush to my side to match
tatters . . . and chaos is king, sir.

These are the things that happen when I come to Boston, and until such time as you look out of your window
to find the peace of Mason Street profaned by oaths and
catcalls of a motley throng fleeing North Stationwards,
you will know that I am missing. The day you do see the
entire population of the capital of Massachusetts rushing
to the North Station, then you will know that I am arriving at either the Back Bay or the South Station.

It you have seen a man there who looks like . . . Fred
Allen . . . give him my sincerest sympathy.

As the fall radio season of 1936 opened, Allen, with
twenty million listeners, was probably the country's most
popular Bostonian since the heyday of Ralph Waldo Emerson.
(Lanky college freshman John F. Kennedy, who would become Allen's successor in this role, had just entered Harvard.)
He finally acknowledged radio as his primary medium, for he
skipped a chance to join the cast of an ill-fated edition of Zieg-

feld's *Follies*. Popular acceptance, as always, meant security, the chance to keep working; but his mood after the eruption of the Spanish Civil War that July was as pessimistic as it was during the weeks he first began broadcasting. Indeed, many of the same darkling portents persisted.

> Read that Father Coughlin arrived in Boston surrounded by guards with rifles and tear-gas bombs. Apparently, he isn't going to be crucified without a struggle, and from recent indications I would say the good old rampant do-minie's mind is turned around to match his collar. . . . Morons and optimists can still cram the streets laughing and oblivious to the dangers ahead, but the capitalist has his troubles. I have stopped eating Spanish omelets. Some Loyalist chef is apt to put a firecracker in with the eggs and blow my teeth out, and I can't sing Ipana's praises with my bare gums showing.

Once more he supported the Democratic ticket of Franklin D. Roosevelt and John N. Garner, although actors of that period seldom revealed their partisan sympathies. Early in October, Alf Landon, the Republican candidate, canceled a Wednesday-night half-hour supposed to usurp *Town Hall,* and Allen had

> to run around and assemble a half-hour of fun in a hurry. Frank, as you may surmise, will receive my vote for this bit of Republican treachery. If Alf won't keep his word with the broadcasting company, he surely won't consider the taxpayer when he gets into office. . . . I think that Frank will win, and while I am a capitalist at heart, I feel Frank has good intentions and will attempt to stem con-ditions, whereas Alf would probably open sunflower lines for the folks once he got into power.

Following Frank's landslide, however, Allen faced a crisis: Harry Tugend had responded to the siren call of Hollywood and once more Fred wrote the program himself.

> I risked the ire of Cardinal O'Connell through penning an Irish classic — the word used loosely here — the first week,

and last night I blossomed out as the author of a Scotch sketch. If I can only get the various nationalities weaned away from the program there will be fewer people to please each week, and with only a little responsibility I won't have to care whether the programs are any good.

A few weeks later he considered a submission by Arnold Auerbach and Herman Wouk, young Columbia graduates, and decided they might have the ability to take Harry's place.

THE NEOPHYTE SCRIPT-WRITERS, active in the college magazines *Jester* and *Spectator,* and the *Varsity* shows, were not unacquainted with comedy. A protégé of philosopher Irwin Edman, Wouk wanted to write, and in 1936 that meant anywhere. When they joined *Town Hall Tonight,* their employer was Dave Freedman, Eddie Cantor's chief writer, known to his subjects as "the Tsar of All the Gags." He maintained vast joke files, timed the duration of his laughs, supplied the needs of a half-dozen weekly shows, and was probably the highest-paid writer in the field. Eventually, Freedman and Cantor had a falling out; Freedman sued, claiming that he had originated Cantor's program format, but before the case reached trial, the writer died of a heart attack at the age of thirty-eight. Allen had planned to testify on his behalf, and many colleagues, rightly or wrongly, blamed Cantor for provoking the attack.

Both Auerbach (in his memoir *Funny Men Don't Laugh*) and Wouk (in his novel *Inside, Outside*) present portraits of Freedman. He was generous, abrasive, extravagant, profane, erudite, procrastinating, Falstaffian yet completely Jewish in his life-style and idiom, and Auerbach felt an emotional bond with the writer that was lacking in his compartmentalized professional relationship with Allen. The extroverted Freedman made Auerbach part of a family; the introverted Allen made him part of a radio broadcast. Fred was decent, conscientious, sympathetic, and complex, and his art originated in the intellect. "Fred Allen was a champion," Auerbach wrote.

No performer or writer has ever duplicated his combination of style, viewpoint and wit. Wouk and I were lucky to be with him in his prime. Our contributions to his career were small, but we were there. The year Babe Ruth hit his 60 homers, even the bat boy must have felt a sense of participation.

Of the two [Allen and Freedman], I respected Fred more. As a boss, he was surely the more considerate and generous; yet it was [Freedman] whom I loved.

Auerbach viewed Freedman as a surrogate father; Wouk, however, found Allen inspiriting. "He was a role model and still is," Wouk recalls. "Fred was one of the most honorable men I ever met. He was the best comic writer radio ever developed, and here we were handing in what must have seemed to him mediocre material. I was twenty-one years old and making two hundred dollars a week, a remarkable salary for the Depression. Not once did he tell us our contribution wasn't good enough."

For Auerbach this was off-putting; Allen would laugh inordinately during the script conferences, but the heartier the laugh, the less inclined he was to use the joke on the program. Gradually Wouk and Auerbach recognized the boss was nudging them along, letting them absorb the rhythms and inflections of the program without destroying their confidence. The routine was entirely different from their novitiate with Freedman. He hired apprentice gagmen merely to cull jokes from his files. A certain number of jokes on a fixed theme added up to a Freedman show, but *Town Hall* required plot development, characterization, and style.

Gathering experience, Wouk and Auerbach wrote the program's newsreels; the show-within-a-show of the Mighty Allen Art Players in assorted settings, from British manor houses to Ozark shanties; and a feature called "People You Didn't Expect to Meet." For the most part, these were guests — everyday people, not actors — with unusual occupations (the segment thus foreshadowed the television game show *What's My Line* of Allen's last years). The occupations, like beekeeper or puzzle wizard, were usually not too exotic, and the guests participated in a scripted interview with Allen. John T. Fitzgerald, the head of a bartender's college, was asked, for instance, "How do you get a wet quarter off a wet bar?" and imparted a trade secret: "Press it with your thumb and slide it to a dry place."

Allen's new collaborators interviewed the guests in advance. "People" required preparation; the guests were not held up to ridicule, and the tone was relatively straightforward. When Mayor La Guardia, for example, barred organ-grinders from the streets of New York, a hurdy-gurdy player named Alfred Fiorella was recruited for an appearance. Because Fiorella couldn't read, Uncle Jim went to Brooklyn and coached him in rote responses. The interview ran overtime during the dress rehearsal. Script trimming had to fall elsewhere, and the organ-grinder recited his lines verbatim.

Wouk and Auerbach look back on this period affectionately. Both were spellbound by the theater. Influenced by Noël Coward's *Tonight at 8:30,* Wouk was writing three one-act plays; Auerbach would eventually devise Broadway hit revues such as *Call Me Mister, Inside U.S.A.,* and *Bless You All.* The late thirties were a time for them of heady opportunities, of inventing their own scripts and situations, of festive trips to Hollywood on the *Super Chief* with members of the cast and crew (Allen, sequestered in his roomette and typing next week's script, emerged only for meals), of flowers and royal palms at the Garden of Allah and the klieg-lit hullabaloo of evening movie premieres. "We never had a contract," says Wouk. " 'Do you want to try it again for another year?' Fred would say, and that was that." Auerbach later felt a throb of guilt because he was thriving in drear times — "Governments crumbled and Fascism flourished; war grew closer every week. And every week Herman and I, unseeing witnesses to history, conscientiously ticked off another 'topical' sketch" — yet their far-from-blinkered newsreels transcended trivial amusement. The Fred Allen broadcast did not distract listeners from the state of the world; instead, the program assumed comedy's traditional task of putting the world in proportion. The scimitar-flash of Allen's wit glittered onstage and off, and Auerbach and Wouk, striding along beside him, took part in a star's progress through the streets of New York — through panhandlers' gantlet, the hysteria and hostility of autograph hounds and celebrity-worshipers. A photographer captured them once: Wouk and

Auerbach flanking Allen, who wears a derby and a chester-field; they are obviously in a hurry, but all three are laughing, and their laughter beats against the shadows of skyscrapers.

"Fred's wit showed a youngster like myself the importance of a single word in constructing comedy," Wouk remembers.

> Once we were discussing what happened to Lee Tracy in Mexico. [The actor after a bibulous night had greeted the sunrise over the parapet of his terrace by answering a call of nature. The Mexican general whose tunic was spattered on the terrace below summoned his guard and jailed Tracy.] At the time, the film *The General Died at Dawn* was pop-ular, so I remarked to Fred, "The General Dodged at Dawn," and just like that, Fred shot back, "No, Herman: The General *Dried* at Dawn" — a word's difference, but what a difference.

The style of the scripts reflected Allen; his imprint, as in the Tugend days, gave the program its particularity. "God knows where we will all be by 1945," he mused. "If I keep doing this work I'll be in some sanatorium and the madam will no doubt snatch a job as bouncer at a convent, or something." The am-ateurs were succeeded by the "College Contest" winner, who would appear, extol the merits of his or her school (a Major Bowes "honor city" touch), and offer an interlude of song, comedy, or dramatic sketch. Wouk and Auerbach adapted to the house style and Auerbach likened the experience to a young apprentice doing touch-up in Rubens's workshop. A succes-sion of buoyant talents succeeded them, notably Nat Hiken, later known for Phil Silvers's Sergeant Bilko television series.

In time, Allen employed four writers, though he still did the bulk of each script. The gifted humorist Frank Sullivan — *The New Yorker*'s cliché expert, "the Sage of Saratoga Springs," and a friend of Fred's — couldn't get the hang of it, however, when Allen hired him in 1938. "He never had a line on the program," Auerbach says. "Show business was such a differ-ent métier, the punch lines and everything else — it just didn't work." In 1941 Wouk entered Columbia's Navy V-7 program for deck officers, and Auerbach went to Hollywood briefly before his army service. Years afterward, in the lobby of a

Broadway theater where *The Caine Mutiny Court-Martial* was having its premiere, Allen greeted Wouk with the words, "It's a long way from One Long Pan, Herman"; but since a writer's experiences shape him in countless subconscious guises, it was perhaps not as long as it seemed.

Radio is aimed at the imagination. For five years, Auerbach and Wouk wrote thirty-nine programs a year heeding Allen's dictum: the listener should be able to picture a fly crawling up the Empire State Building. The gleeful highlight of their tenure, however, had nothing to do with such gossamer nuances of fancy. A golden eagle named Mr. Ramshaw dive-bombed the studio audience in the 1940–41 season and triggered more sustained pandemonium than the wildest contrivances of a Marx Brothers farce. Everything began placidly enough, when Allen read a *New Yorker* item about Ramshaw and his trainer, an English falconer, Captain Charles Knight, and decided they might make an interesting pair you didn't expect to meet. The eagle proved cooperative, so docile that in rehearsal he was awarded an extra dramatic morsel.

CAPTAIN: I think Ramshaw would prefer to fly without the script.
ALLEN: He'll ad lib, eh? Well, I'm not telling Ramshaw how to run his business, Captain. It's up to you.
CAPTAIN: Very well. I shall have Mr. Ramshaw fly around the stage and land back on that bandstand. Ready Ramshaw? Go!
(*Bird flies around stage and lands*)

The preflight interview emphasized Mr. Ramshaw's rapacity. Captain Knight uttered such lines as "I've seen two young Golden Eagles kill each other in a fight with the mother looking on calmly all the time," and "The eagle flies around, looking for game. When it spies a victim it swoops down suddenly and sinks its talons into it."

Allen's prefatory comments during the actual show included an apprehensive ad-lib about Uncle Jim.

ALLEN: Mr. Ramshaw is looking around, Captain, he isn't getting hungry by any chance, is he?

CAPTAIN: I don't think so, Fred.

ALLEN: Uncle Jim is pigeon-toed. He's wearing his Sunday-in-Muncie, Indiana, shoes. If Mr. Ramshaw is near-sighted he might defoot Uncle James.

Circling an empty studio, the eagle executed commands smartly, but that night he no sooner got aloft than the glint of the orchestral instruments dazzled his homing instinct. Wings spread, Ramshaw wheeled across the audience. Amid the shrieking and the guffaws and uproar of twelve hundred people, Captain Knight shouted instruction. Presently, frightened by the lights and clamor, the eagle perched on a high stage column near the ceiling. As Allen put it in *Treadmill to Oblivion*: "The imbroglio caused him to forget even the cruder points of etiquette. Mr. Ramshaw gave visual evidence that he was obviously not a housebroken eagle." He almost scored a direct hit on John A. Howe, a Fordham undergraduate who earlier in the program had presented Allen with a plaque. "If you have never seen a ghost's beret you could have viewed one on Mr. Rockefeller's carpet during our sterling performance," Allen responded to a subsequent memo from an outraged NBC executive. Tapes of the broadcast don't capture the rampant backstage chaos. Captain Knight carried a pocketful of chicken heads for just such emergencies. According to Allen's recounting of the incident for Joe Kelly, the Captain stood off-mike, waving his gruesome tidbit and shouting, "Come down, you bloody bawstard." In perhaps the most unenviable position of all was vocalist Wynn Murray. As Captain Knight with his chicken heads attempted to entice the eagle off his eyrie, she sang a ditty titled "When Love Beckoned on 52nd Street."

The show, unraveling, tried to retrieve the precisely measured equilibrium of its high-spirited billing, "3600 seconds of fun and frolic." Announcer Harry Von Zell proclaimed the virtues of Ipana, but Allen, moderator for a new feature, "Mr. and Mrs. Average Man's Round Table" (a downscale version of a popular professorial discussion panel, *The University of Chicago Round Table*), never reached the evening's topic. Introducing a guest associated with the manufacture of saxophone reeds, Allen had to heed a fresh feint by Mr. Ramshaw. "The eagle is a bird of prey," he said, "and I think we'd better start praying." He began to sound as desperate as a unicyclist back-pedaling on a slackening wire. "All we need is Mr. Ramshaw to make his own station break. . . . It looks as though he might go with the lease. . . . We've just phoned to book a steeplejack next week. . . . Mr. Rockefeller is hardly building ad-lib exits around here."

By and by, Captain Knight sent out for a steak, and thus beguiled, Ramshaw returned to his trainer's wrist. The broadcast was a shambles, although the Mighty Allen Art Players managed to perform a strangely clairvoyant sketch, "The Tub of Silver," spoofing an NBC giveaway show called *Pot o' Gold*. Through an elaborate framework that made it arguably a game rather than a giveaway, *Pot o' Gold* between 1939 and 1941 eluded the networks' veto of lotteries. The formula included a telephone book, a roulette wheel, and Horace Heidt and His Musical Knights performing snatches of melody. (Heidt's was possibly the first and last musical organization hired to accompany a roulette wheel.) Ben Grauer, the host, phoned telephone numbers selected via the bouncing ball. People who weren't home received $100, and for answering they might win $1,000. The streamlining of this top-heavy quasi-lottery would soon take place.

"The Tub of Silver" featured a blustering southern colonel. Declared a winner of the contest, he rejected the prize because it wasn't in Confederate money; Allen would return to lampoon this character-type. Meantime, one of his listeners was more impressed by the parody than the errant eagle.

November 23, 1940

Dear Fred,

The last time I saw you, you were standing in front of the box office at the ball park — in a sport shirt, bifocals and a two days' growth (apparently you don't take the Burma Road)!

Wednesday night I happened to be at home and when I heard your steel-rasped voice emerging from the Capehart (the $1100 model, not the $600 model), it was too, too divine. I especially liked the interview with the eagle, but what k-k-killed me (as Frisco would have it) was the ten-minute skit deriding radio commercials. It should have been done years ago and proves beyond a shadow of a doubt you are America's Voltaire, England's Ring Lardner, and Spain's Heinrich Heine.

> Admiringly yours,
> Groucho

IF CAPTAIN KNIGHT'S Mr. Ramshaw, an eagle you didn't expect to meet, panicked audiences, Fred Allen had other kinds of audiences dependent upon him: down-and-outers and the needy. Although he threatened to resign from the species if he could get back his initiation fee, and claimed that life was "a biological misadventure terminated on the shoulders of six strangers whose only objective is to make a hole in one with you," he practiced a rare humanitarianism. His correspondence with Washington bureaucrat and Boston politician Joe Kelly (who had intermittent access to what passed for Depression patronage) is rife with passages in which Allen himself either constitutes a one-man charitable enterprise or calls upon Kelly's assistance.

> Much as I hate to do so, I have been asked to inquire whether there is ought that can be done for a Mr. Charles D. Finn. Mr. Finn formerly operated a hat store in the Little Building, and what with students going bareheaded and non-Catholics never tipping their hats when passing their churches and wearing their hats practically a lifetime, Mr. Finn was forced to abandon his activities. Lean times have come upon him and of late he has been a foreman on the WPA where his record is good, and since he is a widower with two children, his present plight is really a dilemma. Christ knows that I am not acquainted with Mr. Finn, but Bill Thompson and another gentleman from Boston asked me if I would ask you if there was anything that might be done on Brother Finn's behalf. From what I gather while I am not looking for jokes, there is another [WPA] project about to break in our vicinity and I imagine that is what Mr. Finn has in mind.

To Kelly, Fred sent evidence "that ten dollars will still go a long way under this administration."

Mr. Burton Halbert's an old juggler who is now over seventy and doubled up with arthritis, which makes him over a hundred and forty. He read that I was formerly a juggler and he has bombarded me with joke books and assorted poems. To repay him for annoying me, I sent him [cash] to buy Sloan's Liniment, and apparently he went haywire and outfitted himself from cornplasters to having his scalp Duco-finished.

Enclosed was Burton Halbert's letter:

Went to Los Angeles last Tuesday and stretched that ten-spot all over the city thusly. A much-needed pair of shoes. Pair of pants and belt. Two BVD's. Two shirts. Medicine. Cornplasters, etc. "Millionaire for a Day" wasn't in it the way I threw money around Los Angeles, and I'll bet the merchants thought that Uncle Sam had paid the soldier boys another bonus! I sure thank you for kindness, and if and when you visit L.A. I invite you to as many home-cooked meals at my home as you and Portland can *stand* of 'em.

Testimony concerning Allen's philanthropy is so plentiful that detailed examination risks the redundant or the insipid. He financed students through college, paid medical expenses, bailed out foundering lives, and never in a self-regarding style. Invariably, he took the sting out of the situation.

Poor Charlie [Lane] has been living from hand to mouth so long that his right arm should be well-developed.

Just returned from Boston tonight and found your letter with the enclosed money orders. You have screwed up all my bookkeeping and thrown an apewrench (this is bigger than the well-known monkey wrench) into a system I have used for many years. I told you long ago to forget the loan. Now that you have double-crossed me I have to make an entry on one of the clean white credit sheets that I have kept blank since LaToy first borrowed carfare from me one night in the Daisy Restaurant on Howard Street.

Sent Cap Smith money for suit, socks, shirts and haberdashery so that he will be able to see his friends on relief.

Allen had always been a conspicuous soft touch. His radio-announcer cousin Ed Herlihy recalls that the comedian's charities became more systematic during the radio years. At the end of the program, the orchestra played continuing choruses of the theme until the "Off the Air" sign flashed. Then the musicians hit a discord and Allen addressed the studio audience. "If you've enjoyed our little show, the next time you pass a Texaco station, for God's sake go in and keep the guy company — he's lonesome." The audience dispersed; but frequently ten or twenty people lingered, waiting for the West Coast broadcast. Allen would wander down the aisle, pausing to chat with these fans, often ex-vaudevillians who had appeared with him on bills in Oshkosh and Oswego. Some, down on their luck, went backstage and visited his dressing room (which doubled as Toscanini's greenroom), where Uncle Jim screened visitors. "What is it, Uncle Jim?" Fred would ask. "Clamping the dentures?" And Uncle Jim would nod, confirming that the visitor was putting the bite on for a loan. It was always, he said, a constructive kind of giving. He remembered a fellow who came backstage to see Fred.

"Mr. Allen —" the visitor began, and Fred said, "It wasn't Mister when we played on the same bill in Topeka thirty years ago."

"Oh, I'm all washed up in show business," the ex-vaudevillian said. "They're gonna put a slug in the lock of that fleabag I'm staying in, and if I don't come up with thirty bucks, I'll be carrying the banner."

"Well," said Fred, "what can you do?" and the fellow said, "I'm handy around a gas station." Fred gave him a hundred dollars to get started, and took his phone number; and for a whole year, once a week, he called the gas station and said, "This is Fred Allen. Is my friend So-and-

So there?" He did it just to give him standing among strangers.

Time magazine guessed that when Allen was clearing two thousand dollars a week, in 1947, he allocated to charity at least five hundred dollars of that sum. No one really knows the precise extent of his benefactions; whenever he walked down the street he carried neatly divided packets of one-dollar, five-dollar, and higher-denomination bills, and he was adept at palming them into waiting hands. The host of grifters Allen sustained on the streets of New York received as much attention as friends, acquaintances, or correspondents; but a subtle difference of attitude obtained. Professional spongers, of course, did not suffer quiet desperation. Allen treated them as even-handedly as the others; still, their roles were dissimilar, for they served as members of a supporting cast.

The panhandlers generated their own script. A regular recipient who subsisted entirely on Allen's handouts spurned the money one day, because, he said, he needed a raise. His expenses had increased: he had moved into his girlfriend's apartment and the landlord had doubled the rent. Allen paid. Once he and Al Hirschfeld passed a ragged street violinist outside Carnegie Hall and, pressing a bill into his cup, Allen asked if he needed work. "Talk to my agent," the violinist replied.

Every Sunday, Allen met an old hobo near the Dorset Hotel. When the tramp failed to appear one Sunday, his benefactor was agitated; indeed, Portland had seldom seen Fred so distressed, and not until he scoured the neighborhood and discovered the old man had mistaken the date did Allen relax and leave the handout in an envelope. Still another moocher, known as The Whistler, stationed himself where he could catch Allen emerging from mass at Saint Malachy's on Forty-ninth Street. This coign of vantage also abutted a Broadway ticket office, and eventually The Whistler received a job in the office. "Hello, Fred," he would say, emerging, and Allen would respond, "Hello, Whistler," and slip him two dollars. The Whistler was uncommonly resourceful: on his birthday, he took the day off but arranged to have an associate collect the money. Allen started to walk away, then returned. "By the way, I'm going to the West Coast for eight weeks," he said. "Here's sixteen dollars for The Whistler and tell him I'll see him when I get back."

The cast now and then acted less like an entourage than a mob. Sometimes Allen in a hurry tried to outwit them, using different exit routes from the studio; he could not understand why his ruses never succeeded. Whenever he rounded a corner, he found panhandlers flocking ahead. At length an informant disclosed there was a lookout stationed in the mezzanine who, for a piece of the action, alerted the others. Eluding pursuit one evening, Allen vanished into the night, and the thwarted crowd responded by kicking down the door.

Why did he underwrite them? Compassion is the first, obvious, and undoubtedly correct explanation. But Fred Allen's generosity exceeded ordinary limits; it incorporated hard-core derelicts as well as the needy, and his good works literally manifested the tenets preached by all world religions. Seymour and Rhoda Lee Fisher, however, researchers who have made the only long-range study to date of the personality of the professional comedian, offer a psychological hypothesis. According to their data, comedians as children are "overloaded with responsibility and called upon to be adult beyond their years. To an unusual degree they were expected to care for themselves and to act as caretakers for their brothers and sisters. A large proportion began to earn money in their teens and actually provided partial support for their parents." Overtaxed professional comedians, at work while their privileged contemporaries are allowed to grow up, "are made to feel that virtue is a function of sustaining others." Comedians in childhood, the Fishers maintain, are dedicated to absurdity because they are treated absurdly — although they are children, they cannot betray dependency or childlike traits. A major motif in their lives is "a feeling of having been burdened beyond reason. He or she becomes a public figure who feels constantly motivated to soothe and cheer others with humor, but who simultaneously tells them in a thousand ways that the world is a ridiculous place."

Whether or not the Fishers are correct, altruism by any other name remains altruism. And Arnold Auerbach comes closest, perhaps, to identifying the attribute that gave Allen's altruism its particularity.

> Charity has become a high-powered industry, with hard-sell executives, advertising campaigns and computer systems, stressing the sweet theme of tax deductibility. But in those unsophisticated days, the individual moocher had to act for himself. The needy, lacking a front office, a middleman and an IBM machine, put the bite on directly. Donations went straight from wallet to palm.

In brief, nothing fundamental has changed about charity itself; what has faded from the contemporary scene is the exchange — "Hello, Fred," "Hello, Whistler."

VALENTINE'S DAY 1942, Aunt Lizzie died. She was eighty-four and had fractured her hip at the beginning of February. Mike, her bedridden husband, had long since died, but in her widowhood she still occupied the same second floor in the Grafton Street three-decker, which, thanks to Fred, she owned. On the first floor lived Daniel O'Connell and his mother. "Funny thing, I used to have his dummy, Jake," O'Connell said.

> Don't know what became of it. Fred always sent me a hundred dollars for Christmas; I was the kid downstairs and I think he always thought of me that way. He loved my mother. From time to time, he'd get Aunt Liz to go away on trips. When he did, my mother took care of Liz's husband. My mother weighed only eighty pounds, but she could lift that man and help him move around when she had to.
>
> Fred never forgot that. The day they buried Aunt Liz, Fred came out of Saint Margaret's Church with Portland. He saw my mother at the church and walked over to her. He embraced her, and then, without saying a word, took her by the arm and walked her over to the limousine the family was using at the funeral. My mother rode to the cemetery that day with the family.

16 | Allen's Alley

Early in the 1930s, columnist O. O. McIntyre chided Fred Allen for his parsimony. Allen was accustomed to the vagaries of columnists, since he often substituted for them while they were on vacation, and a few, like Neal O'Hara in Boston or the radio critic Alton Cook, were close friends. Furthermore, the comedian was inured to fantasies such as a report in the *Boston Record-American* that described his study as dominated by a baleful portrait of England's King George III that alarmed the cleaning women. In spite of such harebrained experiences, Allen, writing Arnold Rattray when McIntyre's piece appeared, could not stifle an epistolary groan.

> I eat at a drug store in the morning. An orange is an orange in a drug store, and since all I have is orange juice and coffee, I can get bad coffee in a drug store easier than I can get it at home and I don't have to dry the cup and saucer, nor the little orange juice glass, when I leave the drug luncheonette. I defy Mr. McIntyre to prove that I eat dinner at a drug store and I defy him to catch me quaffing bicarbonate regardless of where I eat.
>
> I run an apartment without servants. All I do in the apartment is go to bed and work on radio programs. I do not need a servant to help me get into bed since I do not drink, and . . . a servant cannot help me write the radio

shows. I have hired many writers and even they couldn't help me a great deal so we must acknowledge that, regardless of Mr. McIntyre's attitude, a servant for collaboration is unnecessary. I'll be god-damned if I am going to hire a servant to please Mr. McIntyre, and then just have the lackey sitting around the apartment watching me go to bed, get out of bed and write radio scripts. . . .

My enormous pay is also a figment of Mr. McIntyre's unsteady conjecture. Ten people share the weekly stipend. There is agent's commission and countless obligations, some inherent, others transient, that augur ill for my financial stability in later life. What is left I share with two state and one federal income tax departments, and what remains is small recompense for an eighteen-hour day and the multiple headaches that go with the daily routine of the radio comedian.

Instead of publicly disputing McIntyre, Allen enjoyed revenge of an exquisite order: he borrowed a McIntyre journalistic device — walking down an alley, knocking on doors, and talking to the people who answered — and converted it into the most popular segment in the program's history.

"Allen's Alley" began on December 6, 1942, but Allen had been contemplating the concept for several years. His allotted time slot, now the *Texaco Star Theatre,* faced revamping; with the onset of the war, the government frowned upon commentary, however mild or playful, about current events. ("You may never have thought of your car as a military machine, and yet it is exactly that," began a commercial on *Texaco Star Theatre.* "For whether your car takes you to a war job, to civilian defense duties, or merely to market, it's helping you do your share toward Victory.") As a matter of fact, Allen had conducted a 1939 gag interview with Dr. Gaffney Flubb, a physicist, the same week the atom-smashing techniques of a very real physicist, Dr. Enrico Fermi, were confirmed by his Columbia colleagues. On the broadcast, Allen pumped Dr. Flubb for the practical purpose of his fission research. The doctor replied defensively, "Well, you never know when someone may come in and want half an atom."

Obviously, the government couldn't let comedians stumble across state secrets, so McIntyre's door-knocking device was fortuitous. "Allen's Alley" was the result, as usual, of experiment and diagnosis. At the beginning, there were two major figures: Minerva Pious, the superb dialectician who had been a mainstay of the Mighty Allen Art Players, and Allen Reed, the voice of Falstaff Openshaw, "the shoddy Swinburne," "the vagabond Voltaire," a moth-eaten poet from Hallmark greeting cards out of John Barrymore. The best-known characterization on the program during the early forties, Falstaff specialized in Mother poems, and his copious supply disclosed Allen's genius for theme and variations. Upon entering, Falstaff would mention the lyrics he had been composing lately — "Those Aren't Spots on the Sugar, Mother, You're Putting Your Dice in Your Tea," "Elegy in a Size Twelve Shoe," "Said the Horsehair to the Violin String, 'May I Be Your Beau?' " — a catalogue that might culminate in a proclamation like "the greatest love song ever written for a movie."

> *Hopalong Cassidy, I love you*
> *I swear by the western moon,*
> *Hopalong Cassidy, you'll be mine,*
> *I'll share your saddle in June.*
> *We'll be hitched in the old corral,*
> *You're my Hopalong, I'm your Sal,*
> *In a year, or two, we'll be three,*
> *Hopalong, you and your horse, and me.*
> *Hopalong, Hopalong, please be true,*
> *Giddyup Hopalong Cassidy, I love you.*

The 1943 Alley underwent several alterations before Allen retired from the air from July to December. The inaugural subject concerned opinions about FDR's recipe for coffee — the president had recommended reusing the grounds — and John Doe, who lived in the first house on the Alley, observed, "The President's coffee tasted like something you'd get if you milked a rubber reindeer."

For three years characters came and went, although Mrs. Pansy Nussbaum scored an immediate hit and Openshaw ended every segment on a note of iambic absurdity. After the first season, John Doe was liquidated. Apparently Allen thought him too generalized, and in his place he substituted an equally bland but more specific figure, Mr. Hollister. Doe suffered an unlamented fate.

> ALLEN: Where's John Doe, the man who used to live here?
> HOLLISTER: He got drowned in his Victory Garden.
> ALLEN: How could anyone get drowned in a Victory Garden?
> HOLLISTER: He had leaks in his watercress.

Among the ragtag residents of Allen's Alley at this juncture were Samson Souse, a drunk; the indistinct Miss Tallulah Traub; and Mrs. Prawn, an uncomely lady on the order of a Gilbert-and-Sullivan contralto. When Openshaw departed in 1945, his bardic chores were assumed by McGee and McGee, a team of songwriters. (Their repertoire consisted of such songs as "It's Watermelon Time in Waterbury, Baby, So I Can't Elope With You.") Significant additions, however, were a dimwit named Socrates Mulligan and Senator Bloat, a porcine politico. Charlie Cantor, playing Mulligan, had graduated from criminal parts on *The Shadow* and *Dick Tracy,* and was a virtuoso of vocal imbecility. "He could do a half-dozen different comic clods, in all ranges," declared Auerbach, "from the 'high dope' [a Walter Mitty-ish little nonentity] to the 'low dope,' a slack-jawed boob, who started every sentence with 'duh.' " Cantor moved from the Alley to *Duffy's Tavern,* a successful show set in a Third Avenue shebeen, where he portrayed a witless customer named Clifton Finnegan. Senator Bloat, portrayed by the dependable Jack Smart, provided latitude for political humor within the constraints of the war years.

In 1945, the Alley acquired the cast by which it is best remembered. Nationwide radio had entered its twilit phase, servicemen were returning, and the glow of peace and affluence undoubtedly contributed to the nostalgia that enfolds listener recollection of the 1945–1947 cast. Six minutes into the first program, announcer Kenny Delmar as Senator Beauregard Claghorn, the stentorian southern version of Bloat, had tossed off two phrases repeated everywhere for months: "That's a joke, son!" and the afterthought, "That is." ("Somebody, ah say, somebody's knockin' on mah door! Who is it? Ah'm from the South, the deep South, that is. Ah'm from so far down South that mah family is treadin' water in the Gulf Stream!") The senator drank only from Dixie cups, sported Kentucky derbies, and never drove through the Lincoln Tunnel. Delmar, a Bostonian of Greek descent, was no radio stranger to high public office. He had panicked millions during Orson Welles's celebrated 1938 Mercury Theatre "War of the Worlds" Halloween broadcast in which he played the Secretary of the Interior issuing emergency instructions on how to cope with invading Martians. CBS censors demoted the character, originally written as President Roosevelt by Howard Koch and John Houseman, to a cabinet member. Complying with their dictates, Delmar nevertheless read the Secretary of the Interior in Roosevelt's voice. Thus listeners who tuned in late assumed they were hearing the president's attempts to quell the panic.

The Claghorn character ("his vest knows how the rind of a watermelon feels") derived from Delmar's impression of a Texas rancher who once gave him a ride in a Model-T Ford. Minerva Pious heard the travesty, brought it to Allen's attention, and he selected Claghorn as a replacement for Bloat. (Jack Smart had departed for Hollywood.) At the close of his first month on the show — now sponsored by Tenderleaf tea on Sunday nights — Claghorn was a runaway fad, the inspiration for toys and gimcracks (compasses that only pointed south) and records ("I Love You, That Is" and "That's a Joke, Son").

Also new that season was Maine native Parker Fennelly as Titus Moody, the New England farmer with a delivery as dry as a biscuit. ("Howdy, bub.") He used his laconic style to express madcap exaggeration. How did he like radio, for instance? "I don't hold with furniture that talks," he said. Shrewd, homespun Titus personified that exemplary American specimen, the backwoods philosopher. Fennelly had played the type to perfection with his partner Arthur Allen in early radio's *The Stebbins Boys of Bucksport Point* and a Mutual network show called *Snow Village Sketches,* set in New Hampshire. A playwright as well as a character actor, Fennelly wrote *Cuckoos on the Hearth,* which still enjoys popularity among little-theater groups, and the bittersweet comedy romance *Yesterday's Lilacs.*

George M. Cohan produced the latter, but Cohan also rewrote and broadened Fennelly's delicate thematic variations on a longing for a lost love. As *Fulton of Oak Falls,* starring Cohan, it opened on Broadway in 1937, received dour reviews, and closed after thirty-seven performances.

Completing the roster, Peter Donald as Ajax Cassidy ("We-e-ell, how do ye do?") did a stage Irishman preserved from the quagmire of total stereotype by the manic velocity of Donald's performance. With this quartet "Allen's Alley" acquired a stylized tempo, making swift comic points in a caricaturist's shorthand.

> ALLEN: Well, here we are, back in Allen's Alley, Portland.
> I wonder if the Senator's home. Let's knock.
> (*Knock on door*)
> (*Door opens*)
> CLAGHORN: Somebody — ah say — somebody pounded mah plywood!
> ALLEN: Yes, I —
> CLAGHORN: Claghorn's the name! Senator Claghorn, that is.
> ALLEN: Well, tell me Senator, how do you feel about the President's idea to advance American music?
> CLAGHORN: Little ole Harry knows music, son. Down Independence way they call him Hoagy Truman.
> ALLEN: Fine.
> CLAGHORN: The South has the best musicians. Phil Harris. Robert E. Leopold Stokowski. Guy Lum-Bilbo.

The Senator's specialty, telescoping the names of real senators like Mississippi senator Theodore Bilbo with band leaders like Guy Lombardo, resulted in a geyser of puns. Mrs. Nussbaum, often the next stop (placement varied), related the issue of the week to her husband, Pierre, although her problem wasn't Pierre but entanglement in Yiddish-American idioms. Pierre, who remained offstage, was a schlemiel more than a tad henpecked, and he fled from domesticity to the dubious asylum of the racetrack, "Epstein Downs" and "Hia-Levy."

ALLEN: Ah, Mrs. Nussbaum, what is your reaction to American music?

MIN: Thanks to American music, I am meeting my husband, Pierre.

ALLEN: Pierre likes music?

MIN: Life to Pierre is a song. He is courting me with singing.

ALLEN: When he proposed —?

MIN: Pierre is singing "Let Me Call You Sweetheart."

ALLEN: When you were on your honeymoon —?

MIN: We are arriving at Grossinger's. Pierre is singing "Down the Old Lox Road."

ALLEN: When you started housekeeping —?

MIN: Pierre is singing "You Are My Sunshine" with a patter chorus.

The transition, "Let's see what Titus Moody is up to," along with the requisite "Howdy, bub," preceded his reflections on American music.

TITUS: My granny used to play the zither.

ALLEN: Was your grandmother good?

TITUS: When Granny'd play "Can She Bake a Cherry Pie, Billy Boy" —

ALLEN: Uh-huh.

TITUS: You could smell cookin' coming out of the zither.

ALLEN: Gosh.

TITUS: Toward the end, Granny played her zither standin' up.

ALLEN: Showing off?

TITUS: No, her lap got tender.

The fourth and final stop on the Alley introduced Ajax Cassidy: "What's all the to-do? Who's wanting a brawl? Oh it's you. How do ye do?" Ajax, it developed, had organized a choral society at Kerrigan's Kozy Korner.

AJAX: Before we start to sing, each man has ten or twelve glasses of beer.

ALLEN: Good.

AJAX: Then he has four or five nips of grog.

ALLEN: I see.

AJAX: Then if it's a bitter cold night, as it generally is, he may have a hot buttered rum.

ALLEN: But I thought your Choral Guild met to sing.

AJAX: We do, me boy, but confidentially —

ALLEN: Yes.

AJAX: It isn't the singing we enjoy.

ALLEN: No?

AJAX: It's the preparation! Goodbye to ye, Boy.

"The Alley," ventured *Time*, "is a fairly serious attempt to take four large U.S. social groups, personify them — and play them for laughs." Considered in less elevated terms, the Alley was substantially a throwback to vaudeville stereotype rather than an innovative venture into comic sociology. The narrative expressed Allen's pleasure in storytelling and the ageless techniques of theater: first, the introduction of recognizable characters, then a scene showing them responding to a current news item. Fred predicted that Titus Moody would outlast the others: "Titus will be getting better when the other characters have dried up and blown away." The only one of the four who meets E. M. Forster's definition of a "round" character — someone who reveals more than one facet of personality — Titus could, with a bit of tinkering, easily fit into a realistic setting. The others are "flat," identified by tag lines of speech and a single aspect of behavior. Allen never solved the problem of writing Senator Claghorn and Ajax Cassidy as figures capable of development. Irish-American groups were persistently repudiating Ajax's blarney about Kerrigan's Kozy Korner saloon just as blacks earlier had protested *Amos 'n' Andy*. (Claghorn received such broad brushwork that the South never rose against him.) Mrs. Nussbaum's vocal tag was Yiddish-American dialect while her character tag was Pierre. Despite the genius of Minerva Pious, the boundaries of the character were immovable. The difference between the representation of Jewish characters in the Alley and in a Woody Allen film, say, is the difference between the 1940s and the 1980s.

Even during the forties, however, the Alley's stereotypes

bothered many listeners. "Allen's approach to some social issues is not made more digestible because of Allen's spicing," grumbled the radio critic of *The New Republic,* "but as long as he keeps up the kind of fun he launched over NBC Sundays at 8:30, I'll continue to listen anyway." In essence, the Alley anthologized devices that Allen had been using for years. The meaningful background — a southern mansion, an urban tenement, a New England farmhouse, and an Irish hovel — harked back to the *Linit Bath Club* era; the ethnicity would have gratified audiences on the Keith-Albee circuit; and Allen as interlocutor–straight man reduced to exclamations such as "Gosh!" "And then —?" and "Uh-huh" paced the action. That pace, however, was extraordinary. Drama critic Elliot Norton in a discussion of comedians of the period suggested how Allen differed from the others — through a satirical approach, and a disdain for the customary repetitive question-and-answer technique of vaudeville comics.

> The reason for the repetition is a cynical disbelief on the part of actors in the quick-wittedness of the audiences. In every audience, the comedians have always argued, there are dimwits, people who won't get the joke unless you ask the question twice and even point it so that the dullards may, first of all, understand the question, and second, get some hint of the answer. Allen disregarded all this. When he or one of his creatures, as for instance Senator Claghorn (all of whose dialogue Fred writes) is going fast, you just listen and get it. Or you can turn to something else.

By the 1948 season, nevertheless, the Claghorn and Cassidy figures had grown monotonous. They were replaced, briefly, by Sergei Strogonoff, the music critic of *Pravda,* whose tag line was "You bore me," and Humphrey Titter, another version of Openshaw. Mrs. Nussbaum in all her verbal finery and Titus Moody, appraising the world's folly like a farmer watching a thunderhead over his cornfield, stayed with the troupe.

The newsreels of *Town Hall Tonight* preserved the absurdity of the topical scene; the Alley sequences represented return to a simplistic past, a vaudeville Valhalla, and may have captivated older listeners for that very reason. Allen knew what worked in comedy, but the postwar world was changing so rapidly that classic procedures somehow didn't mirror change-less human behavior as clearly as before. Just the same, at the end of 1947, the Fred Allen show basked in the affections of the audience and the Alley stretched into radio's future in-definite.

Allen himself took a wary view of this success. "He knows that his radio popularity will not last forever," reported his friend H. Allen Smith. "He wants to be a humorist in print when it's all over." The end came more swiftly than anyone imagined, however. By the spring of 1948, the program had tumbled to thirty-eighth in listenership, a casualty of the greed it trounced from week to week.

17 | Stop the Music

Mindless, philistine, and stale, *Stop the Music* on the American Broadcasting Company's radio network was everything *The Fred Allen Show* was not. The musical game appealed to a basic human proclivity — getting something for nothing — and added a mixture of suspense, popular melody, and audience participation. The genre flourished while the Federal Communications Commission debated the legality of giveaways: to a postwar audience starved for consumer goods, the $20,000 and $30,000 cash prizes staggered credence. *Stop the Music* would thrive for five years and wane with the expansion of television, yet for a period the program articulated the bland materialism of the late forties. It was the present in competition with the past.

The program idea conceived by bandleader Harry Salter, radio executive Louis G. Cowan, and several colleagues struck ABC officials as a bonanza before it went on the air, and they sold time to sponsors in one of the most hotly contended slots of radio, Sunday nights from 8:00 to 9:00, against the half-hours of Fred Allen and ventriloquist Edgar Bergen and his dummy Charlie McCarthy. The contest format was uncomplicated. Harry Salter's orchestra played a current tune, sometimes with vocalists Kay Armen and Dick Brown humming the key passages. Meanwhile, the host, Bert Parks, phoned numbers at random across the country. Once his connection went through, a telephone sounded and Parks chortled, "Stop the music!" The contestant then had an opportunity to identify songs, collect a cornucopia of prizes, and become eligible to identify the "Mystery Melody," a harder challenge with a jumbo jackpot. "We do not identify listeners in advance," insisted producer-director Mark Goodson, whereupon reporters interviewed winners Kenneth Crosbie, a beer salesman from Bluffton, Indiana, and Reginald Turner of Winston-Salem, North Carolina, and both testified that, due to the program's time requirements, they had waited more than an hour, surrounded by helpful families, before naming the Mystery Melody.

On his first program for a new sponsor, the Ford Dealers of America, Allen parried in frolicsome style the threat from *Stop the Music*. The second half of the program featured a lampoon, "Cease the Melody," with Henry Morgan as a burbling Parks ("What's that . . . your radio is on, but your hearing device is off?"), addled contestants identifying the patriotic anthem "America" as a ballad ("The Tree in the Meadow"), and a handsome catalogue-list of prizes: "a genuine TV set; a saloon and bartender to go with it; 4000 yards of dental floss, practically new; the gangplank of the *Queen Mary;* two floors of the Empire State Building; 800 pounds of putty for every member of the family; twelve miles of railroad track, and a roundhouse completely furnished; a shovel, plus twenty unhampered minutes in the basement at Fort Knox."

The program opened, by way of contrast, on a serious announcement: Allen promised to bond his audience with an insurance company. He assured listeners he would redeem (up to $5,000) prizes they missed by tuning in *The Fred Allen Show* rather than *Stop the Music*. This was a tactical misstep. The announcement, a latter-day restatement of the ingenious ploys Allen practiced in vaudeville, received massive publicity, but the scheme backfired. Obviously, the audience had to hear *Stop the Music* in order to know what it was losing; and radio critics quickly pointed out that fighting giveaways with giveaway offers undermined the aims of protest. The insurance offer spawned fraudulent claims and Allen canceled the bond after a few weeks.

John Crosby reported the only dispute in which the claimant may have had a case. In Ravenna, Ohio, a seventy-six-

year-old farmer named MacDonald admitted to police that he
had shot and killed a sixty-eight-year-old farmhand after a
wrangle over whether the pair should listen to a giveaway
program or to Jack Benny. The giveaway fan held the field
until his disgruntled employer returned with a gun. Presumably old MacDonald then settled down for a therapeutic laugh.
Allen remarked to Crosby, "Things have come to a pass indeed when a man in Ohio has to shoot his way to the radio to
get at Jack Benny."

Allen's shafts at *Stop the Music* bristled with righteous anger,
and for several weeks he lost his gaiety. Chaffing absurd human and social behavior, he held a long-term jester's license,
but his jibes against a specific and popular rival smacked of
frustration. The best approach to the situation might have been
to ignore it, or, like Edgar Bergen, to organize a strategic re-
treat. Bergen in January 1949 withdrew for a year from radio,
returned on CBS, and shortly thereafter regained his popularity. Allen, however, chose to recognize and challenge the existence of the noxious giveaway, and as a result, seventeen years
of creative accomplishment crumbled in weeks. Now the lac-
erating, Swiftian indignation so often ascribed to Fred Allen
sprang to his lips, yet a stronger indignation was lost on commercial success. The zesty old *Town Hall* narratives belonged
not so much to an electronic environment but to a small-town
world where phantasmal band music floated across a village
green. *Stop the Music,* said Harriet Van Horne of the *World
Telegram,* "tumbled Fred Allen from the plush pew reserved
for Hooper's Top 10 to a camp stool in back of *Lum 'n Abner.*"

RESENTMENT did not rankle long; soon Allen regained his
form. *Stop the Music* had administered the coup de grace, yet
the final months of *The Fred Allen Show* sparkled as before.
He was ready for a change, and perhaps he would return to
Broadway. Lou Holtz four years previously had announced a
revue costarring Allen, although the project never materialized. George S. Kaufman and Abe Burrows planned to write
a play for him. Publicist Jack Mulcahy suggested that Charles
Gaynor, who had done the hit revue *Lend an Ear,* compose
a book musical for Allen and Jack Haley. Meetings were

arranged, but came to nothing, and one of the reasons was Allen's unstable health. Fred needed a rest, opportunities to read and write, a different, leisurely pace.

High blood-pressure seemed the outcome of radio's exacting toll. He had inherited his predisposition, however (brother Bob suffered from ulcers and a rare blood disease), and registered dangerously high readings year after year. Even in 1936 he mentioned it. "I went over to Doc Wilson last week and he said that my blood pressure had gone up 25 points since I left for the Coast. He said that if I didn't take a rest this summer I was a cinch for a breakdown and he advised me to forget about either the picture thing or radio."

Medical reports on this order occurred more frequently; in 1942, Fred checked into the Mayo Clinic. He kept hypertension in check only by diligent YMCA exercises. "When I look at Jack Benny with the white hair and a lot of the other fellows who are younger than I am, it seems that the 'Y' has done me a lot of good," he wrote one of his handball partners. "My present blood pressure problem [this was during the hiatus from the airwaves in the latter half of 1943] cannot be traced to the 'Y,' for it is supposed to be an hereditary ailment which might have bothered me sooner if I hadn't kept at the 'Y' all those years."

Among the spectres haunting a comedian, illness is surely the most foreboding. Gallows humor can provoke laughs, but humor curdles if the teller of the joke is manifestly suffering. Some of Fred Allen's funniest scripts appeared during his years of failing health — an act in itself of consummate illusionism. He submitted to the then-standard treatment of bed rest, although his energetic personality did not permit him to stay dormant. Bored by indolence and picture-postcard vistas in 1947, when the Allens summered in Bermuda, he commented, "In the symphony of life, Bermuda is a three-bar rest." Herman Wouk recalls Fred controlling his blood pressure with a derivative of rauwolfia, the dogbane shrub. Despite attentive treatment, the problem became more acute.

"Can Dr. O'Hare see me on November 11th?" he asked his physician's receptionist. "The 11th is a holiday, but I thought the germs might not know it was Armistice Day and keep the doctor on the job." Save for his six-month retirement from radio in 1943 (attributed to "dizzy spells"), the public Allen remained hale and smiling; the private Fred, on the other hand, was keenly conscious of his precarious state. He began to fill in the gaps of his knowledge about his case and became a medical autodidact, a self-taught physician with himself for a patient. The literature of hypertension, professional journals, health-and-fitness studies jostled the lore of comedy on his bookshelves. Miracle cures and the rhetoric of quack doctors engrossed him; while he didn't completely succumb to the blandishments of naturopaths, neither did he dismiss them. A sentence hung over him and he was always willing to experiment with a fresh approach.

Gradually, he developed into a mild health crank, and his eagerness to embrace fad diets and remedies became a byword among his friends. John Steinbeck wrote: "Fred and Porty were up the other day. They look really well. He's on a vegetable diet and very funny about it. Half-starved all the time. He awakened Porty the other night to ask if she had a carrot." Who knows, however, the extent to which exercise, diet, and other nostrums prolonged his life? The relationship of hypertension to exercise and diet was less clearly understood than it is today, and the frequency of his symptoms indicated a worsening condition. Headlines charted the ebb and flow of his health: "FRED ALLEN UP AND ABOUT, DOCTORS REPORT"; "FRED ALLEN QUITS CAPE FOR N.Y. 'FEELING FINE' "; "FRED ALLEN ADVISED TO HALT ALL ACTIVITIES FOR 'INDEFINITE PERIOD.' " In the summer of 1949, at the Belmont Hotel in Harwich, Cape Cod, he suffered the symptoms of a minor stroke; and his 1952 predebut withdrawal from the emcee slot on the television quiz show *Two for the Money* (in favor of Herb Shriner, a comedian whose understated manner and Hoosier storytelling appealed to Allen) was prompted by a heart attack. Only rumors reached print. "Hope you will be able to abandon some of your medication and try the 'Raudixin,' " he told Arnold Rattray in 1954. "I have had a coronary occlusion and a cerebral spasm. Up to now I seem to be holding my own with the Raudixin and even starting to work again. With a minor increase in dosage my pressure level didn't rise too high." At the same time, he confided to Herman Wouk: "I had a rather bad time. On two or three occasions I seemed to have a content of 60 percent ectoplasm. How I ever fended off the poltergeist trend and assumed full dimension again I will never know." The rest of his life he would be plagued by physical ailments, including an appendectomy in his sixty-second year, but as the radio period approached its close, the opportunity to relax must have looked tempting. "Agents get ten percent of everything," he explained, "except my blinding headaches."

No longer would he contend with corporate executives who censored the scripts, making each successful broadcast sound like a message from an occupied country. One interviewer even claimed, "he always includes in his script a couple of dubious jokes that he can trade to the censors to keep the ones he wants." Allen had satirized "the echo men," the makers of mountains out of molehills, the "negative men" who "walked around their offices backwards so they wouldn't have to face an issue," and he was the only comedian of his time to speak out so openly against them. During one executive conference, Allen noticed a vice-president who always kept his head down. "Why can't you look up?" Fred said to him. "Is it because you're ashamed, or did you play quarterback at Yale?" Listeners were kept apprised of radio's bureaucratic structure and its denial of idiosyncrasy. Allen pasted in a scrapbook a Young-and-Rubicam office memo concerning Eddie Cantor, and while Cantor was no personal Allen favorite, the ad agency memo suggested what happened when a comedian transgressed corporate limits. It began: "We are all of the opinion that we should present Cantor to the public strictly as a funny man, and try to avoid any publicity that would indicate that Cantor ever has a serious thought or is guilty of a serious deed."

Seven reasons were advanced for Cantor's decline in popularity.

(1.) In [his last radio show,] if he didn't flop, he didn't ring the bell. (2.) His last picture was a flop. (3.) His appearance at the Capitol Theatre was a flop. (4.) His non-comedy activities have tended to present him as a serious-minded person, making it difficult to appreciate him as a

person to be laughed at. (5.) His attack on Father Coughlin was ill-advised. (6.) The manhandling of two studio
guests left an ugly impression. (7.) His charge that radio
editors lack honesty of purpose received unfavorable attention.

The agreed-upon solution was to keep Cantor pop-eyed and
kinetic and presented to the world as a jumping-jack clown.

Allen's skirmishes with the corporate mentality also took
the form of theatrical parody. At first the censors found his
raillery harmless. He did a "North Dakota" takeoff on *Oklahoma,* with Richard Rodgers and Oscar Hammerstein, and an
Alfred Hitchcock show in which Hitchcock was baffled by a
mystery. The Gilbert-and-Sullivan collaborations with baseball manager Leo "The Lip" Durocher were vintage postwar
programs, especially "The Brooklyn Pinafore" of November
1945, with Shirley Booth as Little Bobby-Socks.

> *I'm called Little Bobby-Socks,*
> *Sweet Little Bobby-Socks,*
> *My heart for you, Lippy, could boist.*
> *Before you make me your mate*
> *Let's get dis fact straight,*
> *Frankie Sinatra comes foist!*

The program also featured the Durocher equivalent of Sir
Joseph Porter, K.C.B.

> *When I was a lad, I could not see*
> *A hand held up in front of me.*
> *In spite of how I'd squint and peer*
> *I couldn't tell my father from my mother dear.*
> *My eyes were oh so very very weak*
> *That now I am an umpire in the National League!*

In October 1946, Allen embarked upon another "apologies
to Gilbert & Sullivan" satire, but his target was commercial
radio itself. He had no reason to suppose he would reap a
whirlwind; previous brushes with authority were received in a
playful spirit. When he alleged, for instance, that hotel rooms
in Philadelphia were so small a moth had to furl its wings and

walk on the floor and even the mice were humpbacked, he was remembering the cubicles at Dad Frazer's Theatrical Boarding House and the hundred rooms at the Hurley House without running water. The Philadelphia newspapers, under pressure from the municipal innkeepers' association, inveighed against him; he replied, the papers replied, and the quips flew back and forth. The argument generated prime publicity sustained by a mea culpa and assurances that the hotel rooms in Philadelphia were so large that herds of elk roamed the closets and the name of the Benjamin Franklin Hotel guaranteed that guests could fly a kite in any room. The reproaches of Nutley, New Jersey, an obvious target, also took place amid cordial circumstances.

"The Radio Mikado," however, was biting, and, like Allen's routines almost from the start of his career, self-reflexive. All the same, he assumed the "Mikado" would be greeted with as much tolerance as his remarks about testy Mayor Frank Hague, the boss of Jersey City. Nicked by a polemic dart during a free-speech ruckus, the mayor had vented his outrage, whereupon Allen paused in the middle of his next program to announce, "This is where we break the program to ask Mayor Hague if the remainder of the broadcast can go to Jersey City." The "Mikado" script gored sacred cows; no more so, however, than the kind of statements the comedian had been making about censorship's sanctimony.

> If by chance any of you folks [the studio audience] are in the wrong place, you still have ten minutes to get the heck out of here. Heck, incidentally, is a place invented by the National Broadcasting System. NBC does not recognize hell or the Columbia Broadcasting System. When a bad person working for NBC dies, he goes to Heck, and when a good person dies, he goes to the Rainbow Room. I'll probably have to wait until Resurrection Day and look into the Rainbow Room as I go by.

Allen refrained from noticing that radio advertising, the subject of "The Radio Mikado," was a different and taboo matter.

During rehearsal, the operetta opened in the advertising agency of Button, Burton, Bitten and Muchinfuss, a pointed

STOP THE MUSIC 287

allusion to Batten, Barton, Durstine and Osborn, a firm that, Allen said, "sounded like a steamer trunk falling downstairs." The head of the company, Philmore Updike Muchinfuss ("known to the trade as 'old P.U.' "), is conferring with his underlings.

> If you want to know who we are,
> We're the hucksters of radio . . .
> We're vice-presidents and clerks,
> Confidentially, we're all jerks . . .

They need a sponsor. Enter soap tycoon Fred Allen. How can he peddle his "soap with the built-in bubble"? Muchinfuss suggests a radio program, but Allen rejects the idea. ("If you mention that again, I'll have your entire agency barred from Toots Shor's!") Then he proceeds to voice his scorn of the medium.

> The day that I take over, I'll clean up radio,
> I've got a little list. I've got a little list
> Of things that upset listeners, I'd see that they all go
> And they never will be missed. They never will be missed.
> There's those fat off-key sopranos who keep singing Rinso
>   White!
> And that fellow Gabriel Whosis, and his "Ah there's news to-
>   night."
> There's those mournful serial programs all unhappiness and
>   grief,
> Where the baby's a delinquent and the grandma is a
>   thief. . . .
> And those honeymoon atrocities, where the bride is always
>   kissed;
> They never will be missed. They never will be missed.

Tycoon Allen proposes a better method of selling soap than a radio program — a "world symphony," including ninety French horns "direct from Marseilles." A frenzy of board-room creativity seizes him until he realizes he has forgotten an essential factor: his recommendation has not taken into account Cesar Petrillo, the president of the Musicians Union then enforcing a boycott of broadcast music. So the curtain falls on the echo-ballad of Petrillo and "Tit-Willow."

"The Radio Mikado" incensed network censors lenient about earlier offenses. Allen had expressed his feelings too explicitly. Deleted between the rehearsal and the performance were references to "hucksters," "jerks," "old P.U." and other transgressions, and just before airtime the author was desperately struggling to make his improvised lyrics rhyme.

The "Mikado" clash dwindled into a prelude to a fiercer skirmish six months later. Early in April, the show ran overtime and the last part of the broadcast was cut. The following week, Allen wrote the incident into the script. Asked why the program didn't finish the previous Sunday, he replied, "Well, there's a little man in the company we work for. He's a vice-president in charge of program ends. When our program runs overtime, he marks down how much time is saved." What did he do with all this time? "He adds it all up," Allen said. "Ten seconds here, twenty seconds there, and when the vice-president has saved up enough seconds, minutes and hours to make two weeks, he uses the two weeks of our time for his vacation."

Just as the show was about to begin, Allen was instructed by censors to delete all comments concerning NBC's bureaucracy. He refused. On the orders of Clarence L. Menser, the network's vice-president in charge of programming, Allen was cut off the air for thirty-five seconds (a costly thirty-five seconds for which the J. Walter Thompson advertising agency submitted a substantial bill) when he began speaking the forbidden lines. The incident rapidly escalated into a First Amendment issue, and Allen took the position that NBC's only rightful role in the program was lending the use of the hall. "You know," he said, "it's like walking into a poolroom and plunking down your sixty-cents for an hour's play, and then you find the owner has hidden the cue on you."

Comedians Bob Hope and Red Skelton, protesting the cut-off, were summarily cut off, too. Newspapers, magazines, and columnists debated the problem. One of the cleverest comments, a cartoon by Francis Dahl on the editorial page of the *Boston Herald,* showed the aghast office staff of "the NBC vice-president in charge of program ends, who realizes he has lost an hour due to Daylight Savings." The network, sensing the tide of public opinion running against it, offered Allen, Hope, and Skelton honorary vice-presidencies. Brushing aside that hollow gesture, Allen planned his next program, a half-hour of songs and fairy tales. "This apparently is the only kind of program I can put on that will meet the approval of all the vice-presidents," he said.

At length a penitent NBC assured comedians they had the right to laugh at the network without reprisals. Fred Allen, troubador of nursery rhymes, never appeared, but he regarded the censorship as a personal affront, and the memory chafed. Three months before the end in 1949, the agency requested him to give up the program so that he could go into television alone. "The only reason that our program is finishing out the season," he wrote an ardent fan, Mable Dawson, "is because I refused to leave my actors and musicians to their own devices without adequate notice." As seventeen seasons on radio drew to a glorious close — a flight, said James Thurber, "for me, more interesting than Lindbergh's" — Allen looked back on bureaucratic interventions that never would be missed; no, they never would be missed.

18 | Fending Off Oblivion

"The reason why television is called a medium is because nothing on it is ever well done," Allen said. His anti-television jokes not only ridiculed pretension but masked a personal disappointment. He never adjusted to television as he had never adjusted to Hollywood, and on the same grounds. He didn't photograph well, he failed to submerge himself in a character, and after years of performing with a script, on a stage before a live audience, he found the technical clatter of TV production distracting. In effect, television meant starting over again.

"It broke my heart to watch him on TV," Pat Weaver says. Weaver still feels that, given the proper format, Allen would have been as successful on television as he was on radio. Had he fashioned a revue similar to the Sid Caesar–Imogene Coca *Show of Shows,* Allen, in Weaver's opinion, might have made a happy transition. Another possibility was the role of conversational talk-show host. Allen's off-the-cuff interviews with the *Town Hall* amateurs had inspired fanciful embellishments, like his memory of an uncle, a tuba player who got so carried away by his solo that he screwed himself into the ground and twenty feet down struck oil.

The same spontaneous invention distinguished less hyperbolic banter. "In the season of '36–'37," Weaver recalls, "I took a week's vacation in Bermuda and started to grow a mustache. When I returned I walked into the studio where Fred and the cast were rehearsing, and Fred lowered his script and drawled, 'Why look, it's Mr. Weaver; he just goes to show that puberty has no sense of direction.' " Appointed head of the NBC television operation in 1949, Weaver hoped producers would appreciate the unorthodoxy of Allen's gifts. Nineteen forty-nine, however, was a year of illness and change; after summering at Cape Cod's Belmont Hotel, where he contributed sketches to the resort's casino stage and endeared himself to manager Allan Schlesinger by returning a wire coathanger with a courtly note inquiring after the missing trousers that went with the hanger, Fred settled into semiretirement. He remained in demand as an after-dinner speaker and guest star, but waited for an opportune role.

That August, he wrote columnist Earl Wilson:

> I am not going to be a guest on the Shirley Booth TV show. I didn't know that Shirley even had a TV show. The only obligation I have between now and oblivion is a date to appear with Portland on Sept. 9th at the christening of James Mason's daughter. As you perhaps know, the Masons named their baby Portland, and Portland is to be the child's godmother. Because of the recent hot weather and drought in California we have had to wait until a small amount of water was available that would permit the holding of the baptismal doings.

Warily, he surveyed the television scene as he had surveyed radio in 1931. He went so far as to purchase a TV set — the only set he would ever own, with a magnifying glass over the miniature screen — although he felt appalled by what he saw: Milton Berle capering in female garb provided as fatuous a standard as the shrieking of Joe Penner. In the early thirties, however, Allen had boldly advanced into radio, bringing along the experience of vaudeville and the Broadway theater and originating a novel mode of comedy; but he was older and ill, and when he tried to translate his radio experience into television, he found himself hesitant and disposed toward false starts. He adopted Norman Krasna's suggestion of a televised "Allen's Alley" with puppets, but the puppets, of course, reduced the original concept to a papier-mâché impossibility. A separate version with members of the original cast fared no better. Intrinsically a radio show, "Allen's Alley" would remain forever situated in every listener's imagination.

Despite the inroads of TV, radio in 1950 retained a facsimile of its prewar energy, and, as if to flaunt its vital signs, NBC fabricated *The Big Show,* a ninety-minute Sunday-evening extravaganza with "mistress of ceremonies" Tallulah Bankhead and "the greatest stars of our time on one big program." Allen emerged from retirement to join her. The premiere, November 5, 1950, featured the regular stars with Jimmy Durante (described memorably by Fred as "the man with the double-breasted nose"), Ethel Merman, Paul Lukas, Jose Ferrer, Frankie Laine, and Danny Thomas. Announced for the following week were Bankhead and Allen with Groucho Marx, Fanny Brice, Jane Powell, and Ezio Pinza.

"Well, now, don't just sit there with your mouths open dahlings," crowed Miss Bankhead. "I know what you're thinking. You think such a radio show every week is impossible . . . but NBC says nothing is impossible. All it takes is courage, vision, and a king-sized bundle of dough."

Notwithstanding her financial candor, *The Big Show* never fulfilled the promise of its budget, reputedly more than $100,000 a program. It can be seen in retrospect as radio's last chuck of the dice, a desperate and futile high-stakes gamble. Allen collaborated on the scripts with Goodman Ace and a platoon of prestigious writers. The program had memorable moments, Durante's warmth, Merman's clarion voice, the sketch replicating the breakfast talk-show of *We're Not Married,* with Bankhead in the Ginger Rogers role and Allen repeating his surly spouse, both of them gushing on the air and squabbling off-mike. (The Lunts had done it in *The Guardsman,* illustrating Fred's thesis that no joke is wholly original.) Talent, though, was not at stake on *The Big Show.* No matter how much money the network poured into the program (for the opening of the second season, the cast and crew was flown to London and Paris to perform with foreign stars such as Beatrice Lillie), *The Big Show* confronted the reality of a cultural revolution. The year *The Big Show* departed, leaving a million-dollar loss in its wake, there were some seventy-two million television sets. Advertisers, as in the radio decades, responded accordingly.

"THE DOCTOR HERE told me to give up the Colgate show," Fred wrote Herman Wouk.

If I had seen the kinescopes first I could have told him that I should give up the show. I have several half-hour formats, but it doesn't look as if I will be able to do much with them. Outside of a panel deal or some easy show that I could ad lib, I don't think I can cope with the furore most of these musical revues stir up. I have only done the TV guest dates to keep occupied. It has been a new experience doing what the other comedians have wanted. For almost 18 years I was telling them what to do on my show. Most of the revues are assembled to the accompaniment of the bloodiest bedlam you can imagine. It is almost impossible to be relaxed working with comedy material you barely know. At least, that is the way I feel about it.

Introduced as a big-budget NBC competitor to the enormously successful Ed Sullivan program, *The Colgate Comedy Hour* overlapped *The Big Show* in Allen's career. Like the radio mélange, it lacked the impress of Allen's sensibilities, and his association with it was ephemeral. The intention was to rotate three shows and casts, with each weekly program complete in itself, starring, respectively, Eddie Cantor, the comedy team of Dean Martin and Jerry Lewis, and Fred Allen. Allen went on the show in September 1950; he withdrew when his standard thirteen-week contract expired in December. *Chesterfield Sound Off Time,* a half-hour program in the fall of 1951, was another fiasco. The same rotating pattern presented Bob Hope, Jerry Lester, and Allen, and Fred doubtless preferred the rotation since his doctor had prohibited a weekly show. The program went dark in January 1952 after previewing the first *Dragnet* episode, starring Jack Webb and Raymond Burr, a show destined to become a popular police-procedural series.

Judge for Yourself, an audience-participation quiz show, from August 1953 to May 1954, held more potential. "Our premise is that since television arrived everyone has become a critic," Fred told newsman Jack Gaver. "It doesn't take long for the fellow who sits at home in front of his TV set to get the idea that he can judge talent as well as the people who make a business of it." Three professional acts appeared on the show, and were judged by two panels of judges — three persons prominent in entertainment and three persons selected from the audience. The amateur judge who rated the acts in the same order as the show-business panel received a thousand dollars (the money was divided in case of a tie). Allen's powers of repartee should have shone here when he interviewed the amateurs; moreover, he was associated with a close friend, Arnold Peyser; but owing either to the complicated mechanisms of the game or the uncertainty of Allen's health, the program never established the daffy mood of a similar interview-quiz, Groucho Marx's *You Bet Your Life*. After the debut of *Judge for Yourself*, Groucho wrote, "to get right to the point, I would say that the chief trouble with it is the fact that there isn't enough of Fred Allen. Some way should be found to eliminate those three professional judges who have big reputations and do nothing. Besides, they look terrible." (The sponsors complied by removing the panel and asking the amateurs to judge potential song hits.)

During the early fifties, Allen's career seemed to him to have lost impetus. Sustained as always by religious faith, he held depression at bay. "Since I gave up my program," he wrote Wouk, "it seems my days have no pattern." After so many years on a rigorous schedule, he had fallen into a vacuum. "The other day I wrote a preface for a cookbook," he said. "I've spoken at dinners. It's all very nice. Very stimulating. But don't think for a minute I'm doing all this to be popular. I'm just trying to keep from being unpopular. I'm fending off oblivion."

Strenuous assignments no longer attracted him, and though his financial status was secure, the scrambling fun of his vaudeville days had diminished and he was a celebrity, famous for being famous. Allen said of George Jessel, "Georgie loves after-dinner speaking so much he starts a speech at the mere sight of bread crumbs," but Fred himself was fast becoming a fixture on the banquet circuit, a role requiring agile forensic talents, strong digestion, and a capacity to absorb postprandial oratory. Two such occasions, however, were sentimental journeys, the first a dinner honoring his old headmaster of the

Boston High School of Commerce ("at Commerce they si-phoned the dew off your ignorance"), and the other a dinner for Jack Benny in January 1952 sponsored by the Friars Club of New York. Governor Adlai Stevenson of Illinois, then a comparatively unknown national figure, attended because he was the chief executive of Benny's home state and he and Jack had taken a liking to each other when they met the previous summer. Irving Fein relates:

> With all the comedians at the dinner, there were many funny speeches, but one of the most gratifying spots of the evening was Fred Allen's speech. Fred, an outstanding wit, had been on a decline for a number of years, ever since his radio program had been badly outrated by a game show called *Stop the Music.* . . . Since he was to make a speech about his friend Jack Benny, the entire audience was rooting for him to be good. He wasn't good; he was brilliant. Fred made one of the funniest speeches of his life and when he finished, the whole audience rose and gave him a cheering, standing ovation.
>
> Then Jessel introduced the next speaker, who was sitting beside Fred Allen.
>
> "And now the next speaker, a man with a spot I wouldn't give to a leopard, the governor of Illinois — Adlai Stevenson."
>
> Stevenson rose and received a smattering of polite applause since just a handful of the 1200 in attendance had ever heard of him. It was just six months later that he was nominated for President on the Democratic ticket. Stevenson looked at the audience and then said, "Ladies and gentlemen, I was sitting next to Fred Allen and during the dinner I looked at his speech and he looked at mine, and we thought it might be fun if we exchanged speeches. So now I would like to read Fred Allen's speech."

The resultant laugh could have swept Stevenson into the nomination. Except for incidents like these — a mock-heroic battle with Massachusetts tax commissioner Henry Long over whether the comedian was a legal resident of Massachusetts or New York, a television pilot for a new show that was making the rounds of the ad agencies — Allen was steadily slipping into the limbo of superannuated actors. Lunching with John Crosby, Fred returned the wave of a smiling woman across the room. "My public has shrunk to such an extent that I even say hello to people in sewers," he explained. Television ("a device that permits people who haven't anything to do to watch people who can't do anything") had changed beyond recognition the America he celebrated.

> Audiences have to pay to see actors in the theater or in motion picture houses. Television has made it possible for audiences to see actors on the installment plan. . . . Television is here to stay, and so is the Empire State Building. As soon as the novelty wore off, people stopped looking at the Empire State Building. This could be an omen. . . . They ought to get one of those African fellows over here to shrink all the actors. We're all too big for this medium.

Oddly enough, Allen had predicted his frustration about television on April 2, 1944, when Jack Haley was the guest star on Fred's radio show and the two vaudeville veterans discussed their futures.

> JACK: In television everything is sight. You have to use jokes so old they don't even get laughs in radio.
> FRED: There are jokes that old?
> JACK: There must be. Let me see. Do you know that old gag —
> FRED: Which one?
> JACK: I say — Hello, Fred, I'm going to Chicago.
> FRED: Are you going by Buffalo?
> JACK: No, I'm going by train.
> FRED: Radio audiences won't laugh at that. It's too old.
> JACK: Here's how it will be done in television. Let's tell it again. Hello, Fred, I'm going to Chicago.
> FRED: Are you going by Buffalo?
> JACK: No, I think I'll go by train.
> (*Both put on derbies*)
> JACK: See. For television you just tell an old joke and put on a funny hat.

FRED: But you can't keep putting on the same hat after every gag.

JACK: No, I'll show you how it works. Let's try another joke. Do you file your fingernails?

FRED: No, I cut them off and throw them away.

(*Both put on false faces*)

JACK: See! After a joke like that you put on a false face.

FRED: Jack, you go into television. I'll stick to radio.

Mark Twain put it another way:

I was a pilot now, full-fledged. I dropped into casual employments; no misfortunes resulting, intermittent work gave place to steady and protracted engagements. Time drifted smoothly and prosperously on, and I supposed — and hoped — that I was going to follow the river the rest of my days, and die at the wheel when my mission was ended. But by and by the war came, commerce was suspended, my occupation was gone.

Fred Allen's occupation was gone, but at that moment he discovered what he had hoped to discover throughout his life.

HUMORIST IN PRINT

Book: A small lamp hung out in the darkness of our time — to cheer us on the way.
                    — jotted on crumpled scrap-
                      paper containing other
                      Allen definitions

19 | Ink and Enthusiasm

Five authors launched Fred Allen as a man of letters: Herman Wouk, H. Allen Smith, John Steinbeck, Edwin O'Connor, and author-editor Edward Weeks.

Wouk supplied instructive example. "He writes so well, he makes me feel like putting my quill back in my goose," Allen said. Like a surrogate son, Wouk had gone forth on a quest, slain the dragon, and returned triumphant. In the postwar years, he published *Aurora Dawn,* a satirical novel about advertising couched in the diction of Fielding and Smollett, and then *The Caine Mutiny,* winner of the 1952 Pulitzer Prize, a best-seller about the Navy, the Pacific, and the Second World War. When *The Caine Mutiny* appeared, it must have seemed to Allen that Wouk had realized a dream almost sacrificed to popular comedy. "I think your book is excellent. The chapters describing the storm at sea and the court-martial are really wonderful. The Queeg character is a perfect portrait of a weakling rampant and the love story is sustained well. It just occurred to me that since you are no longer in my employ I have a nerve turning critic at this late date." Wryly, he added: "One satisfaction I imagine a writer enjoys is the knowledge that as his talents develop he has something that cannot be taken from him."

H. Allen Smith supplied opportunity. An elfin man described by Fred as "weighing 110 pounds with his bridgework in and the complete works of Dale Carnegie under his arm," he belonged, like Arnold Rattray and Alton Cook, to Allen's circle of journalistic pals. On the *New York World Telegram,* Smith had taken the first legal drink after Prohibition ended, "kidnapped" Albert Einstein from a banquet in his honor, and greeted a morose J. P. Morgan with the phrase, "Hiya, toots." As this suggests, Smith took impish delight in deflating pomposity, and Allen found his point of view highly congenial. They had other common ground, for Smith, a ninth-grade school dropout from Indiana, devoted himself to overcoming his perceived educational disadvantages by reading material recommended by authoritative friends. In 1941 he asked Fred Allen to contribute a preface to a collection of humorous pieces, *Low Man on a Totem Pole.* There was no reason to expect success — Smith's previous two books had not been profitable — but the volume was an overnight sensation, selling more than a thousand copies a week. He began turning out sequels at the rate of one a year, and between 1941 and 1946 his works sold 1.4 million copies. Although Smith's reputation declined until his death in 1976, he produced forty books. The Fred Allen preface attracted widespread and favorable attention; it was his first publishing success since "Don't Trust Midgets," and it unquestionably aroused aspirations dormant during the radio years.

John Steinbeck supplied psychological reinforcement. The Allens, songwriter Frank Loesser and his wife Lynn, and John and Gwynn Steinbeck formed an intimate social circle. They had come to know each other well in wartime Manhattan, and a decade later Steinbeck asked Allen to serve as godfather to his son John, Jr., known as "Catbird." Notwithstanding Fred's many trips to the baptismal font, this was a repeated obligation he took seriously. When Steinbeck wrote, inquiring about the duties of the godfather, Fred spelled out the role as defined by the Catholic church, appending: "You can advise me about John, Jr.'s religious bent, also his artistic hopes. If he wants to be an actor, between Frank Loesser, Abe Burrows and you, he should be able to find a vehicle for Broadway." In the early forties, the three couples, Lynn Loesser recalled, "would start out with cocktails and end up going to God knows what kind of places, tootling around in taxicabs, singing together, telling jokes." Once, with the merriment at its height, the cabbie slowed down and turned around and said, "Can I tell one, please?" During such an evening in the summer of 1944, Steinbeck and Loesser conceived the idea of writing a musical for Allen, "The Wizard of Maine," about a gregarious itinerant snake-oil salesman who performs magic tricks and whose altruism lurks behind a cynical facade. Steinbeck dallied with the project again a year later, mentioning the role to Burl Ives and collaborating on a script briefly with journalist George Frazier, but nothing ever came of it.

To the Steinbecks and Loessers Fred divulged his hankering to write a book, plus his doubts that he wasn't up to the task. This became a "cause" among the couples, Lynn Loesser said, and particularly with John Steinbeck, who insisted that if Fred got something down on paper, he, Steinbeck, would edit, make it publishable, and contribute a preface. The collaboration, however, dissolved among the weekly deadlines of radio.

Edwin O'Connor and Edward Weeks supplied the requisite editorial spark. "The only American fiction writers I always read," said critic Edmund Wilson, "are Salinger, James Baldwin, Edwin O'Connor," but O'Connor's association with Fred Allen antedated *The Last Hurrah* and the 1962 Pulitzer Prize novel *The Edge of Sadness* by nearly twenty years.

A third-generation Irish-American from Woonsocket, Rhode Island, where his father practiced internal medicine, O'Connor was fourteen when *The Linit Bath Club Revue* went on the air. He immediately became an ardent fan, and grew up listening to the program at school and college (Notre Dame, where he pitched on the baseball team, accompanied by chants of "Allah, Allah" because the bleacherites claimed his elaborate windup looked like a Moslem at prayer). Unlike Allen, he had decided while still in his teens to be a writer; but that was virtually the only bond they lacked. After college, seven years as a radio announcer in Rhode Island, Florida, New York, and Connecticut gave O'Connor, a tall, buoyant man with a resonant voice, firsthand encyclopedic instruction in the inanities of the medium. "The first commercial announcement I read over the air," he related in an unpublished memoir, "was a powerful appeal to all women who were in dire need of hosiery. 'Ladies!'

it began, 'How are your legs?' This abrupt question always struck me as overly-familiar, and I could never read it without a feeling of deep embarrassment. My employer, whose duty it was to notice such things, told me that the trick was to strike a happy medium between absolute indifference and lechery."

Broadcasting was O'Connor's livelihood; he also maneuvered the frail bark of his literary career among the cross-rips and reefs of the free-lance writer's chartless seas. While working for station WDRC in Hartford in November 1941, he submitted a sketch titled "Where Do You Hail From?" to his favorite comedian, Fred Allen. The sketch was rejected; nevertheless, it was a creditable pastiche of the *Town Hall* style, dealing with a sleuth named Philo Smythe and commercials for vanishing cream. The twelve-page script even reveals an uncharacteristically ribald pasquinade.

> QUIP: Lissen brother. When I find a quiz show in me own home town, and the dope that's askin' the questions doesn't even know what country he's in —
> PHILO: Yes, Mr. Quip. What do you figure?
> QUIP: I figger . . . He don't know his ask from his answer.

The would-be gagman appended an editorial note: "I know it's not admissible, but it stuck me as irresistible."

"Where Do You Hail From?" was not the first apprentice work he submitted to Allen. A letter dated June 28, 1941, when O'Connor was announcing at WJNO in West Palm Beach, evidently concerns a joke he submitted about the Russian leader V. M. Molotoff. "All I needed at that precise moment was more trouble," replied Allen, turning down the joke. "The surest way I knew of getting it was to tell the Molotoff joke. Then I would have had Russia after me."

Hugh Rank, an O'Connor scholar, points out that

> these years were important for O'Connor's development as a writer because the radio experience trained and disciplined his attention to dialogue and speech patterns. Here, as Edward Weeks has said, O'Connor "learned to write with his ears." In addition, O'Connor's satiric insight

deepened as he was daily saturated with a flood of words, yet kept a critical perspective because he had an insider's view of how radio really worked.

Enlisting in the Coast Guard early in the war, he was posted to Boston and the beaches of Cape Cod. He broke the monotony of patrols with occasional leaves to New York, where he attended the Fred Allen broadcasts — much as Fred, years before, had attended vaudeville shows to study his heroes.

The Oracle (1951), O'Connor's first novel, concerned an unctuous, Gabriel Heatter-like radio commentator; the author did not come into direct contact with Allen until late 1952. With *The Last Hurrah* under way, O'Connor lived in the cramped top floor of a rooming house at 11 Marlborough Street, Boston, across from the office of *The Atlantic Monthly,* and he needed a job to keep him afloat while he wrote his book. Although insolvent, he was well connected. Weeks tells the story of O'Connor and two friends contemplating their futures. "I'm going to run for Congress," said Torbert McDonald, a former Harvard football captain studying at Harvard Law School. O'Connor said that he would like to write a novel about Boston. They turned toward their mutual friend. "I'm going into politics," said John F. Kennedy; "what else can I do?"

Hired as a pioneer television columnist for the *Boston Herald,* O'Connor commented upon the medium three times a week under the pseudonym of "Roger Swift." The managing editor, however, decided to replace his columnist with a cheaper in-house substitute, and fired the nonunion O'Connor (as it happened, on Christmas Eve). Whereupon Edward Weeks, the editor of *The Atlantic,* decided he could help a straitened young writer and inaugurate a special project: editing a book-length collection of Fred Allen's radio scripts.

Weeks had been enthralled by *The Little Show* and *Three's a Crowd.* "I was sure [Allen] could write a book," he said, "and I wanted to publish it." Chairman of the judges of the Peabody Awards in Radio, he conferred a medal on Allen for having presented "the finest comedy of the year" in 1941. Subsequently, Weeks sat next to Portland at a New York dinner party and after he brought up the subject of a book, she informed him that as long as Fred was on the air, he would never have time.

More than ten years later, the comedian's health and enforced idleness placed the situation in a new light. O'Connor and Weeks drove to New York and thus O'Connor met Allen. Portland was baking a cake and its aroma filled the apartment; Fred greeted his visitors and mentioned that he had been typing a letter to Commissioner Long in their perennial bout over Fred's legal residence. The situation reminded O'Connor of what Mayor James Michael Curley (often deemed the prototype of Frank Skeffington in *The Last Hurrah,* an identification O'Connor emphatically denied) would have said about the matter: "Surely, my dear man, you would not begrudge our fair state a small return for the schooling and inspiration which have led to your triumphant career." Venturing such an imitation before a virtuoso who had shared the stage with Charlie Cantor and Minerva Pious might well give pause, but O'Connor was a superb mimic and, as Fred would discover, a masterful wit, too. Weeks recorded: "Fred listened with amazement and suddenly, like a stone through a window, his deadpan was shattered into laughter. 'That is very, very funny!' he exclaimed and their friendship had begun."

Did Allen know the young editor was the Edwin O'Connor, whose sketches the comedian had rejected (though always with a note of encouragement) before the war? That disclosure may or may not have taken place. In any event, Allen on first meeting expressed the same reservations he expressed in a similar vein soon thereafter to Herman Wouk: "I have never done any concentrated writing. As you know, radio meant weekly deadlines and pressure. Ideas were needed in profusion. If you knew the medium, the crude craftsmanship could escape notice with a few passages of music, some loud sound effects. . . . All the things I have written have been in short, staccato sentences."

Weeks then outlined his conception of a book of dialogues that involved a minimal amount of writing on Allen's part; they agreed to commence, and the visitors returned to Boston with thirty bound volumes of the programs. The task at first moved slowly. In January, O'Connor suffered a near-fatal ulcer hemorrhage, and in March went to Ireland for recuperation, taking along a generous selection of the radio scripts. (O'Connor visited Ireland again in 1955, with Fred and Portland.) For his part, Allen had numerous professional commitments. Leonard Bernstein had persuaded S. J. Perelman to participate in a panel titled "The Comic Performer" at Brandeis University, and Perelman talked Allen into serving as the evening's master of ceremonies. "The comic performer is frequently dismissed as a jackanapes and pantaloon and nonentity," Perelman opened, and playwright Arthur Kober and Allen had a chance to object; but the discussion then gave way to the burlesque pedantry of "Professor" Irwin Corey clad in a tailcoat and voluminous collar not unworthy of Emil Jannings in *The Blue Angel*. The programs of *Judge for Yourself* consumed the latter part of 1953, and not until the following June did progress on the book become manifest.

James Mason, performing at the Stratford, Ontario, Shakespeare Festival, invited the Allens to Stratford. Fred, however, was immersed in writing. He had encountered more snags than he anticipated, but found these not disagreeable.

I gave them the scripts with the understanding that I would have no writing problems associated with the venture. After the editor had selected the scripts he wanted to use, he felt the whole thing would look like sort of a documentary as it stood. He came over to New York and asked me if I would write a few paragraphs to explain some of the changes and developments that took place down through the years. I agreed to help if possible and the editor returned to Boston.

The next thing I knew, a knapsack of papers arrived with some instructions. I found that all I am supposed to do is supply some thirty-odd prefaces and stories and have them before June 24th when I have to be in Boston for a conference. I have been in the house since we returned from California, and am only halfway through the task. God knows when I will ever get finished, or what will happen to the book.

By August, when he received the galley proofs, Allen had discarded book title after book title. Among them were *To Me It Was Only a Living, Lend Me Your Ears, One Way to Make a Dollar, Looking Back, The Lost Laugh* (donated by Al Hirschfeld), *Microphones and Memories*. The title he liked best was *Yesterday's Laughter* before he settled on *Treadmill to Oblivion*. It summarized his sense of the fugitive nature of the comedian's estate.

"Little, Brown will publish it in November," he wrote Herman Wouk.

> It really isn't a complete book. It is the story of a radio show. A radio program is not unlike a man. It is conceived. It is born. It lives through the experience that fate allots to it. Finally, the program dies, and like man is forgotten except for a few people who depended on it for sustenance or others whose lives had been brighter because the program had existed. As the story progresses chronologically there are excerpts from some of the better shows and odd routines of Min's, Claghorn's, etc. The Little, Brown people are enthused about it, but I guess ink and enthusiasm are the two commodities a publisher requires. The book could have been better if I could write better or if there had been more time. I will appreciate your opinion of the effort when it shows up in November.

Treadmill to Oblivion became Fred Allen's only completed book, the single volume he would see in his lifetime bearing his name. Radio in his opinion "smelled of yesterday's levity"; nevertheless, the account satisfied a long-felt need. A comedian had the dubious solace of forgotten laughter, but here at last was documentation that such laughter once existed. Responding to a questionnaire from the publisher's publicity department, Allen stated he had begun writing about 1923 when he started his *Variety* column. He also answered an entreaty ("Please do not be modest on this page. Use both sides if necessary") for personal material useful in promotion. His reply was concise: "If I am going to be immodest, I prefer not to be on this page."

The memoir received widespread and enthusiastic attention. But in January 1955, notwithstanding the questionnaire, Allen, the old showman, groaned to Wouk about the deliberate pace of his publisher's commercial endeavors.

> You and James, the Thurber, were responsible for getting it off the ground with your endorsements. The first advertising budget was small, but it was used mostly to plug you and James. When the reviews started coming in, they were all good. I thought that Little, Brown would advertise more to take advantage of them. When they didn't do anything about the notices, with the holidays coming on, I paid for the *Times* and *Tribune* ads all through December. I went on as many radio and TV shows [as] I could get on to plug the book, and I guess the cumulative effect of the assorted elements plus the fact that we sent out almost 3000 Xmas cards, using the Little, Brown mailing list to reach the jobbers and book dealers, and the same number of New Year's cards advertising the book, got things rolling.

In the end, *Treadmill* broke all records for a book on radio, helped by the sedulous campaigning of the author. Literary laurels did not rest easily on Allen's brow, for as Herman Wouk noted, Fred felt diffident about his cult among intellectuals. He received fan letters from unexpected quarters, notably from Manfred B. Lee, one-half the team of Ellery Queen, the pseudononymous writer of detective stories (the other half was Frederick Dannay) and the unwitting inspiration of many a One Long Pan episode. On March 17, a fatidic date for the Irish and for Allen, Fred explained to Lee why the Allen correspondence was faltering.

> On November fifth you wrote me a letter. Here it is March 17th and I am answering. When I was in radio all of my mail received prompt attention. Since I have become a Little, Brown client, I'm appearing on TV and radio shows for nothing, speaking to motley groups of antique ladies and going from door to door with my tome in my hand

trying to stimulate the sale. With all of your books you must be accustomed to this routine, but it has dismantled my entire life and caused me to stray from my cluttered rut of yesteryear.

Am happy to know that you liked *Treadmill*. It has been doing well and I know the publisher cannot understand its success. Do not worry about TV passing me by. It has been vice versa. My doctor reduced me to a work diet and I have to avoid pressure and aggravation which, as you know, are the very foundations of our industries. One Boston critic wrote, "It is a shame that television has no place for Allen. He has been reduced to writing books." Regards . . .

Celebrity retirement continued as before. Boston advertising executive Francis W. Hatch, in charge of public relations for the Boy Scouts, sent Allen a scout knife, hoping for an on-air reference, and received a characteristic reply.

Many thanks for your Christmas card and my Boy Scout knife which I hope to use a lot during the coming year. Since you know that I am a Boy Scout at heart, and Mrs. Allen is an ex–Girl Scout, we try to preserve our Scout standing even here in the city.

We are constantly roughing it, eating on the floors, and setting fire to our bits of furniture to get a camp fire effect in the apartment. So far my knife has come in very handy. I've cut the legs off four chairs, cleaned a halibut we baked in a closet last Friday, and threatened the landlord when he appeared at the door January 1st for his rent.

You have made all this possible, Mr. Hatch, and if I ever commit hari-kiri with my Boy Scout knife, radio listeners far and wide will have you to thank.

Already, however, Allen had decided upon a second book, his autobiography, and early in January he informed Herman Wouk that "I should be entitled to an off year to try to write. If I can't make it come out, I can slink back into TV and for-

get my writing ambitions." Only because of them, paradox-
ically, did he join the cast of *What's My Line?*, the longest
running game show in the history of prime-time network television.

His motives were simple; he was doing what countless writers before him had done — buying time for his book by pur-
suing a profitable sideline. The coproducer of *What's My Line?*
was Mark Goodson, Allen's old nemesis who had brought forth
Stop the Music, but that didn't matter. "I am on *What's My
Line?*" he wrote Robert Welch, "to enable me to have the entire week to write." The game was undemanding and the panel,
chaired by the urbane John Charles Daly, consisted of personalities who had made their reputations elsewhere: newspaper
columnist Dorothy Kilgallen, actress Arlene Francis, publisher
Bennett Cerf, comedian Steve Allen. Initially titled *Occupation
Unknown,* the show consisted of the panel trying through in-
terrogation to determine the original or offbeat calling of the
contestant. A mystery guest appeared, and the panel, blind-
folded, attempted to determine the guest's identity. The size
of the panel and the half-hour time frame encouraged general
heartiness rather than quicksilver jest. All in all, it was a decorous party game most popular among viewers aged fifty and
older, and it is worth noting that *What's My Line?* numbered
among its fans President and Mrs. Eisenhower, who often requested that tapes of the program be flown to them in
Augusta, Georgia, when they missed the live broadcast.

Allen's physical presence was required on the show, but his
thoughts heeded a distant music. In February, he began writing and soon had a chapter finished on his family and childhood days in Cambridge. Gathering material was harder; by
1956 vaudeville performers were vanishing. "I am still dig-
ging, trying to get a few colorful items on you," he wrote
Red Pearson. "Up to now it has been tough. A lot of the
fellows remember practical jokes or drunken stories about
[Jimmy] Duffy and others, but most of that type of matter
won't hold up in print." In March he went to Hollywood: "I
want to talk to some of the older smalltime vaudeville actors
to get some color and strange experiences to embellish some

of the chapters I hope to do on vaudeville when I was rampant in it," he wrote Jack Mulcahey.

The work went slowly, but the memories returned; he spoke to surviving small-timers, and from a distance, as he had once heard close harmony beneath the streetlight outside Hamm's Store in Scollay Square, the music lingered.

20 | Nightfall

Because he wrote that a comedian walks a treadmill to oblivion, his reward spectral applause and laughter, it is sometimes assumed that Fred Allen died an embittered man. In fact he had been making similar remarks since he first went into vaudeville. He was always lamenting his task while he reveled in it. Was there not — as Sidney Skolsky pointed out, decades before — an ironic contrast between Allen's work habits and his protestations? Hard work constituted his life, yet in the nineteenth century, where his values were formed, work was a form of fulfillment as well as drudgery. In the last eight months of his life, he was writing as he had wanted to write for years.

The autobiography recovered images he thought he had forgotten: the gleaming elk's tooth on his father's gold watch-chain, Aunt Lizzie treating a stomachache with a hot flatiron wrapped in heavy cloth. He was back in vaudeville with the musical duo called Sharp and Flat, and the clattering duckpins ruining the punch lines in the small-time house in Lancaster, Pennsylvania, underneath a bowling alley. The memories brought back the broadcast he and Jack Haley had done in which they recalled those days to the soft-shoe refrain of "Moonlight on Dear Old Broadway."

> ALLEN: I can't go back in the theater, Jack. I'm used to high living. Underwear. Fat cigars. Tums after every meal.

HALEY: Ah, but you don't get those laughs we used to get
in vaudeville.
ALLEN: No, that's right . . .

And so the past came back. Upon finishing a chapter, he
outlined his plans for the next one to Ed O'Connor, who supplied helpful notes and commentaries and never changed a word.
Except for an emergency appendectomy over the Fourth of
July and the brief Irish vacation with Ed and Portland in the
fall, the writing proceeded steadily. In order to get away from
the telephone, Fred rented a small office from writers Mort
Green and George Foster, and went to the office every morning between 10:30 and 11:00 and worked methodically until
5:00. The routine didn't interrupt his normal pattern. Scotty
the Wino, jailed on Hart's Island, received ten dollars from
Fred late in July. Somebody stole the money, so Fred mailed
a personal check — a breach of regulations incurring the wrath
of the warden.

SNOW STILL FELL across New York on the morning of Saint
Patrick's Day, 1956. Before noon, Fred left the Alwyn Court
Apartments on Fifty-eighth Street, where he and Portland now
lived, and kept an appointment with his doctor. The doctor
took a cardiogram, tested his patient's blood pressure, and
pronounced Fred "in pretty good shape." The weather cleared
enough to allow marching bands, floats, and Irish fraternal
orders passageway among the hastily cleared drifts on Fifth
Avenue. Fred stayed inside and read and tapped a note to
columnist Earl Wilson.

> Thanx a lot for the copy of Charley Jones' laugh book. I
> had never seen it before. It looks like a cross between
> "Captain Billy's Whiz Bang" and Thomas Jackson's
> "Through Arkansaw on a Mule."
>   I have just finished the 10th chapter and only need five
> more for the book. I have never attempted any sustained
> writing before and going over to my closet every day
> looking at white paper I know what the last member
> marching in the Klu [sic] Klux Klan parade sees when he
> looks up.

After mailing the note to Wilson, Fred slipped a letter from Groucho Marx into his typewriter as a reminder to himself. It was the letter he was going to answer next. He changed his mind, however, and took up other matters. The chill afternoon faded into evening and nightfall, and toward a quarter to twelve he told Portland he was feeling well and would like to take a walk. The footing was icy, the sidewalks treacherous, so she decided not to go with him. Usually they took a walk together at night before bedtime, strolling hand in hand.

He put on his overcoat and strode outside, passing the stonework traceries of Alwyn Court's pseudo-Renaissance facade crusted by snow. At the corner he paused to buy a paper and exchange a few pleasantries with Stanley Truchlinski, the one-armed newsboy in his magazine-festooned kiosk. Then Fred started down the slight incline of Fifty-seventh Street opposite Carnegie Hall, but before he had covered fifty yards, he collapsed on the sidewalk. Death was almost instantaneous.

David P. Siegel and his son-in-law Carl Henry Abraham, a neighbor with whom Fred had a nodding acquaintance at the newsstand, helped carry him into the lobby of the apartment house at 171 West Fifty-seventh Street. They rested Fred on a bench and, while someone tried to force a nitroglycerine pill through his lips, called an ambulance. Just then, the gilt doors of the lobby elevator opened, and out stepped Leonard Lyons, the Broadway columnist, as though lowered in an ironic contrivance of stage machinery. He and his wife, Sylvia, had been attending a dinner party in the apartment of Dr. Milton Berliher upstairs. Amid the confusion and attempts at resuscitation, Lyons assumed that Fred when stricken had been walking a dog. The columnist sent for Portland, but before she arrived, Dr. Henry Holle of Roosevelt Hospital pronounced Allen dead at 12:05 A.M.

The Lyonses met Portland outside; they had known her for twenty years, and attempted words of consolation. Portland entered the lobby, knelt beside Fred, and took his hand. "How old was your husband?" a policeman asked.

"Not *was*," she said. "*Is*."

The body was taken to the Eighteenth Precinct police station to await the medical examiner, and an old friend of Fred's,

the Reverend Thomas F. Tierney of the Paulist Fathers, administered last rites. The police removed the dead man's possessions. First, a worn ruby ring given him by Aunt Lizzie
when he graduated from the High School of Commerce. Then
his wristwatch and rosary beads. Finally, two rolls of bank
notes, the first enclosed in a money clasp, the other loose bills
of lesser denomination for dispersal along the way.

EPILOGUE

All that the comedian has to show for his years of work and aggravation is the echo of forgotten laughter.

— *Treadmill to Oblivion*

The funeral at Saint Malachy's did not take place until Wednesday, March 20, because of a heavy new snowfall, and by then it had been established that the cause of death was a coronary occlusion. Twelve hundred mourners jammed the church, another 700 shivered on the sidewalks of West Forty-ninth Street. Monsignor James B. O'Reilly, the pastor of Saint Malachy's, cleared the snow from the street to accommodate the crowd, many of whom waited three hours in the savage cold. The service was simple and dignified, without a eulogy. Honorary pallbearers included Alton Cook, Al Hirschfeld, orchestra leader Don Voorhees, William Thompson, Uncle Jim Harkins, Martin Begley of NBC, and Arthur Hershkovitz; and in attendance were colleagues from every phase of American popular entertainment during Fred's years — Pat Weaver, John Daly, and Bennett Cerf, from television; Kenny Delmar and Jack Pearl, from radio; Jack Haley, from movies, Broadway, and vaudeville; and Joe Howard, composer of the straw-hat-and-cane favorite "Be My Baby Bumble Bee (On the Eight Forty-Five)." A single limousine followed the hearse to Gate of Heaven Cemetery, Mount Pleasant, and burial services attended by the immediate family, Uncle Jim, and Jack Haley.

Herman Wouk eulogized Fred Allen, however, in an eloquent letter to the *New York Times:*

The death of Fred Allen, America's greatest satiric wit in our time, brings to mind Hazlitt's elegaic paragraph on the Restoration actors:

"Authors after their deaths live in their works; players only in their epitaphs and the breath of common traditions. They die and leave the world no copy. . . . In a few years nothing is known of them but that *they were.*"

Fred Allen was an eminent comic actor. But without a doubt his great contribution to life in America came in the marvelous eighteen-year run of weekly satiric invention which was the Fred Allen show on radio. His was the glory of being an original personality, creating new forms of intelligent entertainment. He was without a peer and without a successful imitator.

His knife-like comment on the passing show of the Thirties and the Forties came from sources no other comedian had access to. He was a self-educated man of wide reading; he was a tremendously talented writer; and he had a deep reticent love of life and of people which is the source of every true satirist's energy. Fred's wit lashed and stung. He could not suffer fools. In this he was like Swift and like Twain. But his generosity to the needy, his extraordinary loyalty to his associates (in a field not noted for long loyalties) showed the warmth of heart that made his satire sound and important.

In Fred Allen, the voice of sanity spoke out for all Americans to hear, during a trying period of our history, in the penetrating tones of comic satire. Because he lived and wrote and acted here, this land will always be a saner place to live in. That fact is his true monument.

Over three decades later, though, Hazlitt's elegy must be acknowledged. Fred Allen today is remembered chiefly by the generation reared on radio. "An actor's popularity is fleeting," he said. "His success has the life expectancy of a small boy who is about to look into a gas tank with a lighted match." Granted, his joyful social histories, particularly the posthumously published autobiography, *Much Ado about Me,* preserve the texture of vanished radio and vaudeville; and his affectionate homage to the players who live only in their epitaphs and the breath of common traditions has given posterity a lasting imprint of an era. Nevertheless, he was, alas, correct about the ephemeral span of comedy: the arc it traces is as temporary as a rainbow. For all that, like the rainbow, the essence of comedy keeps returning undimmed and universal. Take, for instance, Fred's dinner at Jack Benny's.

PORTLAND: Did you ever have dinner at Jack's house, Mr. Allen?

ALLEN: And what a dinner! It looked like something he took away from a Boy Scout. When the flies saw how little was on the table, they started wiping their feet on the plates to help out.

VON ZELL: What did Jack serve, Fred?

ALLEN: The appetizer was filet of anchovy.

VON ZELL: Filet of anchovy. They're pretty small, aren't they, Fred?

ALLEN: Small? They look like damp hyphens. Benny served them with a magnifying glass and tweezers.

PORTLAND: Did Jack have soup?

ALLEN: Clam chowder, but the clam was out on location. It had a stand-in that night. The meat course was roast beef sliced so thin it looked like a wet glow on the plate.

VON ZELL: What was dessert, Fred?

ALLEN: A Good Humor man running through the house if you could catch him.

Fred Allen's books are out of print, his movie and television appearances were negligible, and radio, as he conceived of it, is obsolete. Yet he does not dwindle away and disappear. His comic legacy survives: its narrative influence and shrewd observations of the vagaries of small-town behavior extend directly to Garrison Keillor's mythical and engaging Lake Wobegon. Its attitudes affect the viewpoint and characters (Wally Ballou, Agatha Murchfield, Officer Wishmiller of the Alaska State Highway Patrol) of Bob Elliott and Ray Goulding. A gleam of the Allen style illumines the path where the Mighty Carson Art Players on the Johnny Carson *Tonight Show* follow the route of the Mighty Allen Art Players; another gleam

appears in David Letterman's interviews with people in odd occupations; and if Fred and Woody Allen are contrasting sensibilities, they complement each other. Certainly, the latter's *Radio
Days,* with its nation of listeners hanging upon the fate of a
little girl who has fallen down a well, evokes the power of
thirties and forties radio to inspire community.

And there is another sense in which Fred Allen survives: as
one of the representative Americans of his time. Born into a
world of lamplighters and livery stables, he almost lived to
hear about Sputnik. He polished his programs with the pride
of a handcraftsman only to find himself among the technologies of bureaucrats and careerists for whom the substance of
the show was salesmanship. The dominant force in the lives
of early-twentieth-century Americans was change, and the
struggle to adapt to it became a fundamental aspect of their
experience. *Town Hall Tonight* audiences recognized their
origins, yet they were also participants in the drama of change,
the lure of a novel medium. Earlier times reverberated in the
radio audience's collective memory as these did in the curious
pictorial dissonances of silent movies in which Model-T Fords
honk at horse-drawn delivery wagons beneath the crossbars of
telephone poles sailing like masts across a landscape of dusty
roads. Broadway performers entered homes removed by
geography and time from the sophistication of metropolitan
entertainment. Just as vaudeville expressed the culture of the
modern city, so radio diffused urban forms of comedy across
continental space, and for a brief moment, fewer than thirty
years, past and present intersected. Though his personal history was a virtual lexicon of entertainment in his day, Allen
never left behind the Boston neighborhoods of his boyhood
where he sifted the ashes of a cellar furnace and where the
grocer on the corner always stuck a small potato over the end
of a spout on a can to keep the kerosene from jiggling out.

Of course, Fred Allen's charity and decent instincts were
representative as well. "Comedy is the salt of civilization, its
critical voice," declares Guy Davenport. "The comic spirit is
forgiving, stands up for freedom and elasticity, and counters
the corrosive power of evil by refusing to acknowledge its claims
over the human spirit. Its real enemy is custom drained of

significance; it is the ability of life to assert its claims no matter what social forms dictate." Commenting upon the dog item that reappeared from time to time after Allen's death, Edwin O'Connor pointed out, "Fred Allen did not walk dogs, he did not own dogs, and — sad news to dog-lovers — he did not much like dogs. His field, you might say, was people." Allen's grassroots sense of the integrity and importance of each individual's story (and his treatment of traditional comic types) has more in common with the humor of Mark Twain and James Thurber than with the cool, knowing insurgency of self-aware contemporary comedians. His art reminds us that it originates in the native vigor of the word, the intonations and rhythms of living speech. "Well sir. As I live and sit in vaudeville theaters hoping some adagio dancer will throw a girl at me, it's Portland." In an age of mechanical reproduction, of visual images that distance us from ourselves rather than asserting the claims of life over listless social forms, Fred Allen's voice can still be heard, faint but clear, inviting us to find its wavelength.

Select Bibliography

Manuscript Sources

The Fred Allen Collection at the Boston Public Library, the basic resource, contains the radio scripts complete, tapes of the broadcasts, FA's scrapbooks, jokebooks and references, correspondence, miscellaneous jottings, first drafts of the autobiography, photographs, and memorabilia. Few of the letters are dated, however, and the dates must be determined either by internal evidence or postmark. From time to time, occasional letters or copies of letters turn up elsewhere.

Books and Stories by Fred Allen

Treadmill to Oblivion. Boston: Little, Brown–Atlantic Monthly Press, 1954.

Much Ado about Me. Boston: Little, Brown, 1956.

Fred Allen's Letters. Edited by Joe McCarthy. Garden City, N.J.: Doubleday, 1965.

"A Small-Timer's Diary." *Variety*, 16 Sept. 1923.

"Don't Trust Midgets." *The New Yorker*, 10 Jan. 1931.

"The Great Waldo." *Variety*, 5 Jan. 1944.

Books, Articles, and Transcripts of Related Interest

Allen, Steve. *The Funny Men*. New York: Simon and Schuster, 1956.

"Allen Sure Comics Will Survive." *Boston Globe*, 20 June 1953.

Andrews, Bart, and Ahrgus Juilliard. *Holy Mackerel! The Amos 'n' Andy Story*. New York: Dutton, 1986.

Auerbach, Arnold M. *Funny Men Don't Laugh*. New York: Doubleday, 1965.

Australian Vaudeville magazine ("conducted" by Martin C. Brennan and Harry Kitching, Sydney), 7 Jan. 1914.

"B. F. Keith Memorial Theatre." Special rotogravure section of *Boston Sunday Herald*, 28 Oct. 1928.

Bannerman, R. LeRoy. *Norman Corwin and Radio: The Golden Years*. Tuscaloosa: Univ. of Alabama Press, 1986.

Barnouw, Erik. *The Golden Web*. Vol. 2 of *A History of Broadcasting in the United States*. New York: Oxford Univ. Press, 1966–1970.

Barth, Gunther. *City People: The Rise of Modern City Culture in Nineteenth-Century America*. New York: Oxford Univ. Press, 1980.

Benny, Jack. "Jack Benny Tells of Great Loss, Calls Fred Allen a True Friend." *Boston Sunday Globe,* 18 Mar. 1956.

Benny, Mary Livingstone, and Hilliard Marks, with Marcia Borie. *Jack Benny.* Doubleday, 1978.

Benson, Jackson L. *The True Adventures of John Steinbeck, Writer.* New York: Viking, 1984.

Blythe, Cheryl, and Susan Sackett. *Say Goodnight, Gracie! The Story of Burns and Allen.* New York: Dutton, 1986.

Bordman, Gerald. *Jerome Kern: His Life and Music.* New York: Oxford Univ. Press, 1980.

Bradshaw, Jon. *Dreams That Money Can Buy: The Tragic Life of Libby Holman.* New York: Morrow, 1985.

Bryan, J., III. *Merry Gentlemen (and One Lady).* New York: Atheneum, 1985.

Burns, George, and Cynthia Hobart Lindsay. *I Love Her, That's Why!* New York: Simon and Schuster, 1955.

Buxton, Frank, and Bill Owen. *Radio's Golden Age.* New York: Easton Valley Press, 1968.

Chandler, Charlotte. *Hello, I Must Be Going: Groucho and His Friends.* New York: Doubleday, 1978.

Christmas, Linda. *The Ribbon and the Ragged Square: An Australian Journey.* Viking, 1986.

Clark, C. M. H. *A History of Australia.* Vol. 5. Melbourne: Melbourne Univ. Press, 1951.

Corkery, Paul. *Carson: The Unauthorized Biography.* Ketchum, Idaho: Randt, 1987.

Crosby, John. "Breakfast with Freddie and Tallulah." Radio in Review. *New York Herald-Tribune,* 10 May 1946.

———. "Unemployed Actor." Radio in Review. *New York Herald-Tribune,* 5 Dec. 1949.

———. "He Never Got Away from the Common People." *Boston Globe,* 21 Mar. 1956.

Dame, Lawrence. "Birthplace of U.S. Vaudeville Yields to Expanding Press." *Boston Herald,* 4 Mar. 1951.

Davenport, Guy. *The Geography of the Imagination.* San Francisco: North Point Press, 1981.

Dietz, Howard. *Dancing in the Dark: An Autobiography.* New York: Quadrangle, 1974.

DiMeglio, John E. *Vaudeville U.S.A.* Bowling Green, Ohio: Bowling Green Univ., Popular Press, 1973.

Dineen, Joseph M. "Fred Allen Once Worked as Errand Boy in Hub." *Boston Globe,* 22 Mar. 1940.

Dunning, John. *Tune in Yesterday: The Ultimate Encyclopedia of Old-Time Radio, 1925–1976.* Englewood Cliffs, N.J.: Prentice-Hall, 1976.

Earle, Sylvia. "Allen's Allies at Commerce High." *Boston Globe,* 26 Apr. 1948.

Ewen, David. *The Complete Book of the American Musical Theater.* New York: Holt, 1958.

Fein, Irving A. *Jack Benny: An Intimate Biography.* New York: Putnam, 1976.

Fields, Ronald J., ed. *W. C. Fields by Himself.* Englewood Cliffs, N.J.: Prentice-Hall, 1973.

Fisher, Seymour, and Rhoda Lee Fisher. "Schlemiel Children." *Psychology Today,* Sept. 1980.

Fornatale, Peter, and Joshua E. Mills. *Radio in the Television Age.* Woodstock, N.Y.: Overlook Press, 1980.

"Fred Allen and Company." Review by "E.H." *Billboard,* 10 Dec. 1927.

Freeman, Donald. "NBC Show Airs Fred Allen Tribute." *San Diego Union,* 17 June 1956.

Gaver, Jack. "Fred Allen's New TV Show to Give Critics a Field Day." *Boston Globe,* 17 Aug. 1953.

Gilbert, Douglas. *American Vaudeville: Its Life and Times.* New York: Whittlesey House, 1940.

Gilman, Arthur. *The Cambridge of Eighteen Hundred and Ninety-Six.* Cambridge, Mass.: Riverside Press, 1896.

Goodwin, Doris Kearns. *The Fitzgeralds and the Kennedys: An American Saga.* New York: Simon and Schuster, 1987.

Grauer, Neil A. "Forgotten Laughter: The Fred Allen Story." *American Heritage,* Feb. 1988.

Green, Abel, and Joe Laurie, Jr. *Show Biz, from Vaude to Video.* New York: Holt, 1951.

Greenway, John. *Australia: The Last Frontier.* New York: Dodd, Mead, 1972.

Grunwald, Edgar A. "Program-Product History, 1929–1937." *Variety Radio Directory, 1937.*

Hall, Max. *The Charles: The People's River.* Boston: Godine, 1986.

Harmon, Jim. *The Great Radio Comedians.* New York: Doubleday, 1970.

Harris, Warren G. *Cary Grant: A Touch of Elegance.* New York: Doubleday, 1987.

Hartley, Marsden. "Vaudeville." *Dial,* Mar. 1920.

Harvey, Anthony. *The Melbourne Book.* Richmond, Vic.: Hutchinson of Australia, 1982.

Harvey, James. *Romantic Comedy in Hollywood, from Lubitsch to Sturges.* New York: Knopf, 1987.

Hawes, William. *American Television Drama: The Experimental Years.* Tuscaloosa: Univ. of Alabama Press, 1986.

Herlihy, Elisabeth M., ed. *Fifty Years of Boston.* Boston Tercentenary Committee, 1930.

Horowitz, Joseph. *Understanding Toscanini.* New York: Knopf, 1987.

Howells, William Dean. "The Decline of the Vaudeville." Editor's Easy Chair. *Harper's Monthly,* Apr. 1903.

Johnson, Nunnally. *The Letters of Nunnally Johnson.* Selected and edited by Dorris Johnson and Ellen Leventhal. New York: Knopf, 1981.

Josefsberg, Milt. *The Jack Benny Show.* New Rochelle, N.Y.: Arlington House, 1977.

Kenneally, Katie. *Brighton.* Boston 200 Neighborhood History Series. Boston, 1976.

———. *Dorchester.* Boston 200 Neighborhood History Series. Boston, 1976.

Kilgallen, Dorothy. "Tribute to Fred Allen — The Show Went On." *New York Journal-American,* 19 Mar. 1956.

King, Moses. *King's Handbook of Boston.* Cambridge, Mass., 1883–1885.

Kline, Sidney. "World That Laughed with Allen Mourns." *New York Daily News,* 19 Mar. 1956.

Laurie, Joe, Jr. *Vaudeville: From the Honky-Tonks to the Palace.* New York: Holt, 1953.

Lerner, Alan Jay. *The Musical Theatre: A Celebration.* New York: McGraw-Hill, 1986.

Lynn Farnol Group, eds. *Richard Rodgers Fact Book.* New York: Farnol Group, 1965.

Lyons, Leonard. The Lyons Den. *New York Post,* 19 Mar. 1956.

Marc, David. "Prime Time Comedy." *Boston Review,* Aug. 1987.

Marchione, William P. *The Bull in the Garden: A History of Allston-Brighton.* Boston: Trustees of the Boston Public Library, 1986.

Marquis, Alice Goldfarb. *Hopes and Ashes: The Birth of Modern Times.* New York: Free Press, 1986.

Marx, Groucho. *The Groucho Letters: Letters to and from Groucho Marx.* New York: Simon and Schuster, 1967.

Metcalf, Fred. *The Penguin Dictionary of Modern Humorous Quotations.* New York: Viking, 1987.

Norton, Elliot. "Boston's Fred Allen Successor to Great Will Rogers." *Boston Sunday Post,* 4 Apr. 1948.

O'Connor, Edwin. "Fred Allen's Letters Make Ideal Reading." Review of *Fred Allen's Letters,* edited by Joe McCarthy. *Boston Globe,* 23 Apr. 1966.

O Corrain, Donnchadh, and Fidelina Maguire. "Irish Personal Names." *Bulletin of the Department of Foreign Affairs* (Dublin), May 1982.

O'Donnell, Richard W. "Boyhood Chum Recalls Fred Allen." *Boston Globe,* 17 Aug. 1976.

"Perennial Comic." *Time,* 7 Oct. 1940.

Porter, Peter. *Sydney.* New York: Time-Life Books, 1980.

Rank, Hugh. *Edwin O'Connor.* United States Authors Series 242. New York: Twayne, 1974.

Ryan, George E. "Fred Allen's Best Man Recalls Good Old Days." *Boston Sunday Globe,* 5 May 1957.

Seldes, Gilbert, and Clifton Fadiman. Transcript of the radio program *Conversation,* broadcast 22 Mar. 1956. Edwin O'Connor Collection, Boston Public Library.

Settel, Irving. *A Pictorial History of Radio.* New York: Grossett and Dunlap, 1960.

Shipman, David. *The Story of Cinema.* New York: St. Martin's Press, 1982.

Skolsky, Sidney. Untitled newspaper column, 19 Nov. 1935. Fred Allen Collection, Boston Public Library.

———. "He Took Up Acting as a Substitute." *Boston Globe,* [?] July 1945.

Slide, Anthony. *The Vaudevillians.* Westport, Conn.: Arlington House, 1981.

Smith, Bill. *The Vaudevillians.* New York: Macmillan, 1976.

Sobel, Bernard. *A Pictorial History of Vaudeville.* New York: Citadel Press, 1961.

Spitzer, Marian. *The Palace.* New York: Atheneum, 1969.

Stagg, Jerry. *The Brothers Shubert.* New York: Random House, 1968.

Staples, Shirley. *Male-Female Comedy Teams in American Vaudeville, 1865–1932.* Ann Arbor: UMI Research Press, 1984.

Stein, Charles. *American Vaudeville As Seen by Its Contemporaries.* New York: Knopf, 1984.

Stempel, Tom. *Screenwriter: The Life and Times of Nunnally Johnson.* San Diego: A. S. Barnes, 1980.

Sullivan, Ed. "Like Two Kids in Love." Column. *New York Post,* 20 Mar. 1956.

Sullivan, Elizabeth. "Fred Allen Devoted Husband; Wife Named for Portland, Ore." *Boston Globe,* 22 Mar. 1956.

Terrace, Vincent. *Complete Encyclopedia of Television Productions, 1947–1979*. South Brunswick, N.J., and New York: A. S. Barnes, 1980.

Thurber, James. "To Fred in Heaven," 29 Aug. 1961 (includes "The Crow and the Scarecrow" from *Further Fables for Our Time*). Fred Allen Collection, Boston Public Library.

Tucci, Douglass Shand. *Built in Boston: City and Suburb, 1800–1950*. Boston: New York Graphic Society, 1978.

Tucker, Sophie. *Some of These Days: An Autobiography*. New York: Doubleday, Doran, 1945.

Vallee, Rudy. *Let the Chips Fall . . . .* Harrisburg, Pa.: Stackpole Books, 1975.

Vaudeville magazine, 19 Apr. 1917, letters column.

Wallace, John. "Why It Is Difficult to Be Funny over the Radio." *Radio Broadcast,* 9 June 1926.

Wallstein, Elaine, and Robert Wallstein, eds. *Steinbeck: A Life in Letters*. New York: Viking, 1975.

Ward, Russell. *The History of Australia*. New York: Harper and Row, 1977.

Warner, Sam Bass, Jr. *Streetcar Suburbs: The Process of Growth in Boston, 1870–1900*. Cambridge: Harvard Univ. Press, 1962.

―――. *Province of Reason*. Cambridge: Harvard Univ. Press, Belknap Press, 1984.

Wertheim, Arthur Frank. *Radio Comedy*. New York: Oxford Univ. Press, 1979.

White, Osmar, "Toowoomba," in *Guide to Australia*. New York: McGraw-Hill, 1968.

Wilson, Earl. "Letter from Fred Allen Arrives after His Death." It Happened Last Night. *New York Post,* 21 Mar. 1956.

"World's Worst Juggler." *Time,* 7 Apr. 1947 (cover story).

Wylie, Max. *Best Broadcasts of 1938–39; Best Broadcasts of 1939–40; Best Broadcasts of 1940–41*. New York: Whittlesey House, 1939, 1940, 1941.

Younger, R. M. *Australia and the Australians*. Adelaide: Rigby, 1970.

Zolotow, Maurice. *No People Like Show People*. New York: Random House, 1951.

Index